(2734)

NATIONALISM–

The Last Stage
of Communism

Tran van Dinh

NATIONALISM—

The Last Stage of Communism

BY

EMIL LENGYEL

FUNK & WAGNALLS

NEW YORK

To Gilbert Godfrey,
my friend of many years

Contents

CONTENTS

Introduction

In the beginning there was the belief that the workers of the world—the poor—were ready for the great integration, an international organization to fight for their rights. The Communist Manifesto of Karl Marx and Friedrich Engels proclaimed: "Proletarians of all countries, unite!" It was the birth certificate of an abortion—the First International. It turned out to be the International of Starry Eyes—proletarians seeking unity across the national borders; nationalists in search of nations, particularly Germans and Italians; dreamers of a completely "free" world, without the restraining influence of governments—anarchists. It collapsed quickly under the heavy burden of unfulfilled expectations.

Eventually the nationalists found their nations and the anarchists their anarchy. There remained the industrial workers, who considered themselves the "damned of the earth." On the continent of Europe, and particularly in Germany, this was the age of the Industrial Revolution, the revolution of capitalism. It was united and strong, while the workers were disunited and weak. In the centennial year of the Great French Revolution, a new integration of the "proletariat" was achieved—the Second International. It assumed that the workers could best

assert themselves by disregarding national frontiers.
There were only two "nationalities" in the world, according to its founders—the workers and the bourgeoisie, the
proletariat and the profitariat. Thus the Second International was born. It was in the interest of the proletariat
to ignore national boundaries. To the French worker the
German worker was a co-national, the French capitalist
an alien. The solidarity of the proletariat across the national lines was to stave off wars among the nations. The
Great War—which we now call the first World War—
broke out, and promptly the French workers and capitalists formed a united front. The German workers and
capitalists did likewise. That was the end of the Second
International as an instrument of integration.

On January 24, 1919, the Soviet government, still
under the pressure of counterrevolutionary forces and of
foreign armies, addressed a manifesto to revolutionary
groups throughout the world to dispatch delegates to a
congress in Moscow for the establishment of a new International. It was to be known as the Third International—
also as the Communist International, *Comintern,* the
Moscow International.

The Third International was founded in March 1919
and the Manifesto of its First Congress, drawn up by Leon
Trotsky, summarized its objectives:

Our task is to generalize the revolutionary experience of
the working class. . . . The proletariat must create its own
apparatus, designed first and foremost to bind together the
working class and to insure the possibility of its revolutionary
intervention in the further development of mankind. . . .
The task of the International Communist Party consists in
overthrowing the [bourgeois] order and replacing it by the
edifice of the socialist system.

Within weeks the strength of the Third International
was tested. A Soviet Republic was established in Hungary.

It lasted for three months—and the *Comintern* was not able to aid it. Another Soviet regime was established in parts of Bavaria and it lasted for three weeks. Moscow was not able to help it either. During its existence of nearly a quarter of a century the Moscow International was unable to fulfill its task of "overthrowing the [bourgeois] order and replacing it by the edifice of the socialist system." It went out of existence during the second World War.

After the second World War, China went Communist. It did so under its own indigenous leadership. Communism was imposed upon half a dozen countries in eastern and central Europe—the "satellites," as we call them, the "Communist bloc"—from the Baltic to the Aegean: East Germany, Czechoslovakia, Poland, Hungary, Rumania, Yugoslavia, Bulgaria, and Albania. We in the United States came to call this "international communism." It never was that. It was Soviet imperialism. "International communism" would have meant the union of independent countries, ideologically related, which it was not.

Then came the "Reformation" within the presumably ecumenical Communist establishment. The year of 1948 was to communism what 1517 had been to the Catholic Church. The Martin Luther of communism was Josip Brozovich, better known to the world as Marshal Tito of Yugoslavia. This was the beginning of the nationalist "heresy" within the Soviet-controlled Bolshevik Ecumene. Moscow slashed out against Titoism. This was the period of the Reign of Terror within the Communist bloc.

China turned against the Kremlin with a ferocity that characterizes ideological and religious feuds. Within the European "bloc" itself there was for a time a period of quiet and then signs of unrest, first in Poland, then a revolutionary outbreak in Hungary that was brutally smashed by the Kremlin. Another period of quiet ensued —which turned out to be a period of incubation. Two decades after the onset of the reform movement in Yugoslavia the nationalist movement within the bloc was on the march, first in Rumania, then in Czechoslovakia. Signs of it elsewhere were in evidence. . . .

This book will attempt to analyze the predominant national traits of the Communist countries, beginning with the Soviet Union itself. Is its communism an accentuated form of nationalism? Has Russia become truly nationalistic under the aegis of the Soviets?

The other "Communist" countries are veering off from the party line of the "mother church" in the directions prescribed by their national traditions. What are these traditions, and what is the trend of these changes?

The history of each country contains the code signal of its potentialities and the anticipation of its future. Therefore, a short historical analysis precedes the narrative of the recent "nationalist explosion" of the countries under review. The nationalist trend encompasses not only political and social phases but also economic changes, different from the classic Communist model. What are the most significant developments along these lines, too?

. . . The "fraternal solidarity" of the Communist bloc was now largely over. The Millennium—at best an anticipation—of a unified realm within the web of a compelling ideology had not been able to bear the strain of the overriding idea of the age: this was still the Age of Nationalism. Time could not be hurried, not even by Communists, people in a frightful hurry. Fantastic new inventions followed one another in a fantastically short time. Man now held the thunders of Zeus in his hands. He commanded space; he was ready to wrest from the endless universe its secrets. But the social reorganization of man could not be hurried. The sacred code of nature could be cracked but not the secret code of man's ideologies, of his loyalty. Internationalism, no doubt, was superior to nationalism. The one-world-nation could eliminate the most insane drive of man to kill his fellow man for real or imaginary reasons. Such an Ecumene could possibly head off a global suicide. But the time was unripe for that. Even the Communists—the followers of an impatient ideology —had to bow to the mysterious inner forces operating in the darkest cells of man's mind, his accustomed loyalties.

The "nationalization" of communism is thus an ineluctable consequence of something that we can feel more than we can explain. But there it is. It is only now that national communisms have burst into life. The object of this book will be to analyze them.

Each country in the Communist bloc will be analyzed. What are the main national traits of each individual country? These characteristics are not always easy to find. An attempt will be made to look into the "national genes" by picking out the highlights of a nation's history. Each chapter therefore will contain a summary of that portion of the country's history that seems to be most revealing of its basic ways.

Personal observations will be included where they may be helpful in finding what we are looking for. There seems to be no reason to depend upon the observations of others when the author himself has been a witness of revealing developments, an eyewitness of historic actions.

There are three "half-countries" at the present time, partly Communist and partly non-Communist. They will be left out of consideration. First they will have to find their own "souls," or the lack of them. They are victims of split-personality problems, and no purpose would be served by trying to look into each of the split halves.

The title of this book is *Nationalism—The Last Stage of Communism*. Nationalism is not merely a political phe-

nomenon. It is linked to social and economic problems
that are also part of the story and should therefore not be
overlooked. At a time when nationalism in the West
shows signs of yielding to a higher integration, the presumed international East provides evidence of a different
trend. Never has Russia been more nationalistic than
under "international" communism. And what about all the
other countries that call themselves Socialist and Peoples'
Democracies and that we call Communist? The answer
to this question is the content of this book.

E.L.
New York City
February 1969

NATIONALISM–

The Last Stage
of Communism

1

Russia and the Soviets—
Third and Fourth Romes

First it was a trading town and then it became a
religion. That, in turn, became an empire of the Czars.
In a great world conflagration the empire was gutted and
was replaced by the Soviets. It proclaimed itself an international creed, a new beginning, without end, the herald
of the future. The communist creed of the Soviets also
proclaimed itself the redemption. Since it was also the
offspring of the past, let us see what it had been like, so
that we may comprehend the present and, perhaps, foresee the future.

Today one-sixth of the land surface of the globe, Russia
a millennium ago was only a town and its environs, Kiev.
It stood on the top of a hill, the Judaea of the Dnieper, and
all around it there was darkness. But there was light in
the town, the illumination of the true faith.

At first the town was animist, filled with souls—*animi*
—some of them good and others evil. They had to be
propitiated, the good ones, too, so that they would not
turn bad. The propitiation rites required the assistance of
priests, and this resulted in wars without end, each tribal
chieftain's priest claiming supremacy over all the others.
Human sacrifices were exacted, too, and the city on the
hill was filled with fear.

The town was in a strategic location, linking the supply of slaves with the slave markets, the land of raw materials, fur, lumber, and honey, with the rich land of gold-bearing customers. The river linked the raw-material-rich north in what is Russia today with the affluent society of Constantinople, pivot of the Byzantine Empire.

The trading city on the hill was endangered by the quarrels of the grasping priests, the tribal medicine men. To eliminate the cause of wars it was decided that there should be only one prince, shielded by only one set of priests and one God. Which God should it be?

Should it be the Allah of the Moslems whose domains were spreading across the steppes? Should it be the Jehovah of the Jews, also adopted by the steppe Khazars, Kiev's neighbors? Should it be the God of the western Christians, the fame of whose Supreme Pontiffs had reached the people on the Kievan plains? Or should it be the Christian God of the East, whose mystery was in the keeping of the Ecumenical Patriarch, the Pontiff of the Universal realm, in the city of Constantinople, situated on the bay of the southern Straits, so beautiful that people called it the Golden Horn?

The market of the Kievan traders was in the capital of the Byzantine Empire, Eastern Rome, which was to survive the fall of Rome on the Tiber by a thousand years. Prince Vladimir, the son of Svyatoslav, embraced the eastern Christian creed—the Holy Orthodox Catholic Apostolic Eastern Church. It claimed to be the only accepted gate to the Divine Realm, *orthos* (true) *doxa* (opinion)—in one word, orthodox. This decision, made a thousand years ago, prepared the path Kiev was to follow—and beyond Kiev, Muscovy and Russia, its successor states.

Who were the Kievan princes and their people? As to the princes and their retinues, a controversy rages. They were of Scandinavian origin, *Varangians,* blood brothers (some say "kin") to the Vikings, people from the distant north, hungry, brave, adventurous. This view was held by historians in the past, under the Czarist regime. The founders of Kiev were not native Kievans, not Slavs at all, according to this view. What about the rest of the inhabitants of the trading town? They were mainly Slavs, such as the Ukrainians and Russians, speaking Slavic dialects.

(The Varangian origin of the dynasty in the heartland of the steppes, the Rurik family, never questioned under the Czars, is, however, being questioned by the Soviets, who marshal numerous arguments against the prevailing view. They want the world to know that it was not alien Scandinavians who founded the first Russian city-state, Kiev, but native Slavs. Under the presumably internationalist Communists, even the origin of the Kievan dynasty is seen from a Russian nationalist point of view.)

In the West, Christianity was rent then by a monumental schism—the conflict between the Holy Roman Empire and the Holy Roman Church, the first claiming to be the universal will and the latter the universal faith. Throughout the centuries they fought wars for the true interpretation of their views.

In the East, on the Golden Horn, there were no two arms of Christianity—the temporal and the religious—no two rulers—the Supreme Pontiff and the Emperor. The Ecumenical Patriarch there was the executive organ of the Supreme Will, divine and mundane, fused in the person of the Emperor, as the divine and human were merged in the unique nature of Christ. When the Emperor spoke, God spoke, and when God spoke, he did so through the Emperor. This was the heritage of Kiev and, later that of Muscovy and of Russia.

Divine wisdom had been first revealed in Rome, and from there transferred to Constantinople, residing in the

Aya Sofia, sacred wisdom. When the Turks desecrated the House of Wisdom on the Golden Horn its spirit proceeded to Moscow, Kiev's successor in the distant north. This was how Philotheus, abbot of the monastery of Pskov, summed up the substance of the changing residences of divine wisdom:

The first Rome, on the Tiber, fell, because of heresy; the second Rome, in Constantinople, was brought down by the axes of the Ismaelites [Turks]; but this Third Rome [Moscow], the seat of the Holy Apostolic Church, shines throughout the world more brightly than the sun. . . . Two Romes have fallen, but the Third stands, and no fourth can ever be.

That church, first in Kiev, then in Moscow, was the shield of Christianity against the Apocalyptic monsters, the bastion of the faith against the "blood-drinking beasts, carrion eaters," Petchenegs. Fighting for Christ and their Prince against the Polovtsi and the Kumans while the "eagles screech and gather for their feast of bones," the valiant Slavs of the steppes built pyramids with the enemies' skulls. They were blessed because they were knights of the cross. Then came Cheng-Sze.

That was the name under which his contemporaries came to know the Perfect Warrior. When his followers found that no earthly power could resist him they invested him with the name of "Heavenly Ruler"—Genghis Khan, leader of the Gray-Eyed Men, descendants of the Blue Wolf. He had sallied forth from the land of the black sand, Karakorum, and never had man seen a warrior of his stamp. His Mongols—"braves"—encompassed the world, from the dark waters of the Pacific to the azure waters of the Adriatic. What was the secret of the institutionalized horror? The panic they drove into the peoples' hearts; their swift horses, their looting, their determination, and above all, their organization in an unorganized age. Kiev was taken in 1240, razed and its people butchered.

THE SPIRIT OF SOBORNOST

The Mongols lived by the sword. Fortunately for the world, internal difficulties forced them to withdraw their extended lines. A branch of them settled in the Russia of today, along the Volga, the country's "river of sorrow," which became even more sorrowful by this propinquity. The Mongol rulers—"khans"—displayed their emblem of authority, a gilded pavilion, at the town of Saray, and so the Mongol intruders came to be known as the "Golden Horde."

From devastated Kiev the Slavs sought the protection of the forests, and so they settled in Moscow, which thenceforth became the capital of the Russian land. The Muscovite princes were the collectors of the *yar-lik,* tribute, they had to deliver to the khans of the Golden Horde. For generations they did that, and then gradually they stopped doing so, some two centuries after the Mongol invasion.

The Mongols, once "pagan" animists, were now mainly Moslems. To the Russians they were the offspring of Satan, infidels, the enemies of Christ. As the strength of the Golden Horde waned because of their torpid life, that of the Muscovites increased. They were animated by the faith of their fathers, and now they realized the enormity of the fact that the enemy was usurping the best parts of their land. They tested their strength and—lo, and behold—Christ upheld their arms. With the might of the cross, the Slavs—Russians—destroyed the might of the antichrist along their river of sorrow, which now became their river of triumph.

During this fight, which lasted for generations, the Russians became convinced that they were the elect of Christ and that theirs was the holy land. After the coreligionists of the Mongols took Constantinople in the middle of the fifteenth century, Moscow became the holy city of the only true Christianity: in the words of Philotheus, the "Third Rome"; and there was not to be a fourth.

In the Russian princes, too, now, as previously in the Byzantine princes, two natures became fused—man and Christ. Asked about his nationality, the Russian peasant answered: "Christian." He meant "true" Christian, Orthodox. The theologian Aleksai Khomyakov summarized the Russian view when he asked the question and provided the answer:

Where is unity without tyranny, freedom without revolt? Only in the ancient, continuous, unadulterated traditions of the [Orthodox] Church. In our midst unity is based upon mutual love, unadulterated by the despotism of the Vatican. In our midst, too, liberty is found, freer than the license of Protestantism. Ours is the Refuge and the Rock.

Because his Christian faith was constantly endangered, first by the Petchenegs, Kumans, other Asian tribes and, above all, because of his successful fight against the "seeds of Satan," the Mongols, the Russian came to consider himself *the* Christian man. He saw himself a member of a consecrated community, lay and clerical, gathered together in mutual love. His faith, the only true creed, as he saw it, was attributed to the totality of the faithful, standing together, under the protection of the Prince—the Czar—whose authority combined the religious and the temporal. He thus came to consider his breed transported to a level higher than the earth, into a more rarified atmosphere. His country was one vast cathedral. He was a member of a religious congregation, and all Russia formed a consecrated community, *sobornost,* in which the fallible parts of the infallible whole created a Christlike perfection. The site of the consecrated community was on consecrated soil, Holy Russia, the reflection of heaven on earth.

The hut in which the *muzhik*—peasant—lived, the work he performed, the food he consumed, were all consecrated in the celestial dwelling that was his land. The ikon corner in his hut set it aside as a sanctuary under the Holy Trinity. The Russian made the sign of the cross before eating, before the start of his work, at the outset of a voyage, in sickness, in the face of death, when he enjoyed small joys, and when he endured the great trials of his life. He had a consolation: he was never alone. His universe was saturated with the spirit of Christ.

That universe was also saturated with autocracy. There was no *veche* (town assembly) in heaven. God was an autocrat and so was his earthly image, the Czar. The more inscrutable the ruler appeared to be, the greater was his likeness to God. Ivan the Terrible provided an illustration of how the ruler was accepted as an elemental force, a natural calamity. Ivan achieved his terrible reputation because he was autocratic, capricious, and mad. In one of his most insane moments he declared his will to abdicate, and there should have been rejoicing in the land. Instead of that, there was panic. The terrible Czar was a fixed pivot, and his wrath the punishment for his subjects' sins.

THEN THE SCHISM

In the land of the *sobornost* every religious symbol was hallowed, assumed to have existed from the beginning of time, and expected to last to the end, in a world without end. Then along came Patriarch Nikon, a century after Ivan the Terrible, and what he did was awesome. Incredible as this may sound, he changed the spelling of the name of Christ. Also, he changed the making of the sign of the cross from two fingers to three. He also changed the joyous outcry of halleluiah from two to three. Archbishop

Avvakum thundered: "Under our princes the Orthodox faith was undefiled till the time of Nikon, the apostate."

The sign of the cross with three fingers was the sign of Satan, said the old believers, the traditionalists, and the triple halleluiah was the sound of hell. Countless old believers immolated themselves in communal conflagrations, rather than accept the change. Or they set the torch to churches in which the halleluiah was tripled. Archbishop Avvakum and many others perished at the stake for their refusal of the innovations. This was the only "Reformation" in the eastern branch of the Catholic Church. The majority of the Russians accepted the changes, forced upon them by the Czar. The ruler spoke in the name of Christ, who wanted the changes. The greatest issues of Russia were thus linked to religion, and the Czar demanded conformity. This was also part of the spirit of the *sobornost*—the Holy Ghost residing in Russia's consecrated community. In due time came Pyotr Veliki.

It was a revolution Peter the Great brought about. "In fifty years the Russians made more progress," said Voltaire, "than other nations in five centuries." He was also hailed as "Christ's foremost pillar and the Christians' prop, whose powerful work subdues both Mahomet and the ungodly Turk."

Under Peter, the Orthodox church was placed even more directly under the Czar. He set up the Holy Synod, administered by the Ober-Procurator, in turn appointed by the Czar. A nonbeliever Peter himself may have been, but he wanted his subjects to be believers—in Christ and in himself, the delegate of heaven on earth. Under his reign the church and the state became more closely knit. The church and the state were beginning to drift apart in the western world, the world that Pyotr Veliki took as the model. Not in Russia, though. There the two moved closer together. If it had been the content of religion, not merely its form, that Peter's country took to its bosom, Russia could have been described as the "God-intoxicated land."

HOLY RUSSIA'S HOLY ALLIANCE

A world war had been fought early in the nineteenth century, the Napoleonic wars. Russia was winner and she dictated the terms. The other allies were in a mood to listen to the man from the north, Czar Alexander I.

"From the north and from the rising sun" a man was to rise, the Prophet Isaiah had predicted. One of the people who fixed their eyes on the north and the east was Baroness von Kruedener, a Baltic-German woman. Now that the great war was over, mankind was yearning for peace. It was to be a Christian peace among Christian monarchs, led by the ruler from the north—from the land of the rising sun—the Autocrat of Russia, Czar Alexander I. Who but a Russian ruler could lay the foundation of a Christian universe ruled by the laws of Christ? And who but a Russian ruler could think of a new world-order and call it the Holy Alliance?

The allies of the Czar were dumbfounded to hear about his plan. "Nonsense," "insanity," was their reaction. Then they pondered: they had to deal with the ruler of the country that considered itself holy, the capital of which was called the Third Rome. The head of the country was also the head of the church. By sanctifying their alliance, the world was to become the abode of sanctified humanity —a new interpretation of the *sobornost*. So they signed the pact. At worst they were "humoring a madman," and at best the pact was harmless. Only a Russian could be the

author of the document that nearly all the major countries signed.

The document was drawn up "In the name of the Most
Holy and Indivisible Trinity," and this is what its Article I
said:

Conformable to the words of the Holy Scriptures which
command all men to consider each other as brethren, the
three contracting Monarchs will remain united by the bonds
of true and indissoluble fraternity; and considering each
other as fellow countrymen they will, on all occasions and
all places, lend each other aid and assistance; and regarding
themselves toward their subjects and armies as fathers of
families, they will lead them in the same spirit with which
they are animated, to protect Religion, Peace and Justice.

The Second Article of the Pact of the Holy Alliance
soared to even loftier heights:

Therefore, the sole principle of force, whether between the
said governments or their subjects, shall be that of doing
each other reciprocal service . . . to consider themselves all
members of one and the same Christian nation; the three
Allied Princes looking on themselves as merely delegated by
Providence to govern three branches of one family . . .
thus confessing that the Christian World, of which they and
their people form a part, has in reality no other sovereign
than Him, to whom alone power really belongs, because in
Him alone are found all the treasures of love science and
infinite wisdom, that is to say God, the Divine Savior, the
Word of the Most High, the Word of Life. . . .

With paternal solicitude the Princes enjoined their subjects to strengthen themselves every day more and more
in the exercise of duties that the Divine Savior taught to
mankind.

The Three Princes were joined by the others. The Holy
Alliance became the instrument by which incipient de-

mocracy and nationalism were repressed. Democracy was regarded as blasphemous because it attempted to replace the rule of the monarch—the delegate of God—by the rule of the people, born to serve. Nationalism was an abomination, too, because it deified the nation in the place of the divinely anointed King.

Wherever democracy and nationalism bestirred themselves—and the two of them were linked—the Holy Alliance intervened. It did so, particularly, in Italy, under foreign rule, and in the German lands. Its two members Austria and Russia repressed the Hungarians' fight for freedom. The Alliance crushed the Spaniards' attempts to vault across time into the modern age. It made preparations to suppress the "independence explosion" in Latin America, too, but there it failed because of the policy of the United States—the Doctrine of President Monroe.

As nationalism insinuated itself into Europe, quietly, members of the Holy Alliance sneaked out of their "club." Only Russia stood apart with its *sobornost,* consecrated community, in which every day was infused with religion. So it continued to stand apart, from democracy and from the peoples' nationalism. "Orthodoxy, autocracy, fatherland," were its lodestars, stated a minister of Czar Nicholas I, Count Sergey Semenovich Uvarov, in mid-nineteenth century. Popular education was not one of the lodestars. The Count was the Czar's Minister of Education.

THEN THE OBER-PROCURATOR

Was it possible for a nation with a capital in Europe to look the way the Ober-Procurator described it? He was Constantine Petrovich Pobedonostsev, member of the

Council of the Empire, Ober-Procurator of the Holy
Synod, one of the most representative of all the Russians
at the turn of our twentieth century. He knew his Russian
history, and was a professor at Moscow University, the
author of respected books.

The role of religion in Russian history was known to
him. Russia was not just any other country, because its
soil was consecrated, its spirit was God's, and its ruler
carried out the Savior's will. Religion, he said, held the
country together. To him the Russian Orthodox Church
was *the* unique divine institution. The Russians were
Orthodox, true believers, children of God acting through
the Czar. No healthy state could have, or should have,
more than one religion, the official creed, its way of life,
the Ober-Procurator said. The Roman Empire collapsed,
he held, because it had accepted several creeds. Religious
tolerance would destroy continental Europe. Such tolerance caused fragmentation, lack of unity, and final decay.
Surveying the world scene, he saw such a dire fate for the
United States, too, since a religious conflict was brewing
there. America then, as he saw it, was a Protestant country, guarantor of its unity. But he saw the power of the
Catholic Church across the Atlantic on the increase, the
cause of an irreppressible conflict. Should America's historical Protestantism lose, the Ober-Procurator felt, the
existence of the country would be imperiled.

Since there were many members of other religions in
Russia too, what should be their fate? The Ober-Procurator had the answer. To him, the Catholics had di-
verged from the Savior's ways and should be converted to
orthodoxy. Not all Catholics, though. Pobedonostsev held
that the Poles were "unassimilable." A resurrected Poland,
he held, would mean Russia's end. There were several
millions of Jews in Russia, too. What should be their lot?
They should be shown the "light"—conversion to the

Greek Orthodox faith. Those who continued to live in "darkness" should be encouraged to "drift away," to emigrate.

"Every country is the captive of its past," the Ober-Procurator said. Russia's past was community-oriented, under the "patriarch" of the family, head of the government, the Czar. Russia was at the opposite extreme from the Anglo-Saxon and Scandinavian countries, in which the accent was on individualism. They were ready for democratic institutions, but Russia was not.

Education, freedom of the press, trial by jury, Pobedonostsev held, were both evil and unapplicable in Russia, because the Slavs were lazy, and ferocious passions lay dormant in their breasts. In other countries human nature was overlaid with hypocrisy. "Every man is a lie, and every word he utters is self-delusion." The Grand Inquisitor in Dostoevski's *Brothers Karamazov* was right in describing man "as vicious, weak, worthless and rebellious." Therefore the creed for iron-handed authority.

Why was the Ober-Procurator so vehemently against education? Would it not quiet the ferocious passions of the human beast? He elaborated on this theme: Three forces formed the peoples' minds: the unconscious, the natural environment, and history. Most important of these was the unconscious, partly the generator, and partly a product, of the two other influences. Ideas and ideals generated by intellectuals were pernicious, because they questioned the divine quality of authority and fostered insecurity. Trusting and believing was for the masses, and keeping political thoughts for them was the censor's task. Basic truths were intuitive and above cognition. The education of the majority must be limited to official versions of censored history and sacred books.

The ideal of this spokesman of nineteenth-century Russia was Saint Louis, King of France, under whose reign the church was the state and the state was the church. He was the fountainhead of justice and its administrator. Under his rule the estates knew their places, were content, and made no attempt at change. The sainted ideal of the Ober-Procurator lived in the thirteenth century. Pobedonostsev expressed these views under the rule of Czar Nicholas II, the last and the least competent of latter-day Czars.

The Ober-Procurator stood at the apex of the power structure, and uttered policy statements, not mere personal views. Also, he expressed himself well, with the urbanity of the scholar he was.

WAS IT RELIGION?

The "religious" coloring of Russia is an historical fact. Was it really religion, affecting the lives of high and low, introducing ethical standards? Or was it merely ecclesiasticism, unrelated to moral conduct? Were the Russians basically a consecrated community? How did the world see them?

"It would seem," noted the Earl of Carlisle, the envoy of Charles II of England to Russia, Sweden, and Denmark, who must have done a lot of traveling to cover his beat, "that the mother of all vices, laziness, is a Russian heritage. They perform their work only under duress, and frequently prefer to be flogged to being honestly occupied." The noble lord continued: "Hence drunkenness is most common among them, and the clergy is as much addicted as the laity. Vodka, which resembles Circe's drink, makes them act like pigs."

The Czar offered a state dinner in honor of the envoy during the Lenten season, when no meat was consumed.

The carousal lasted from two in the afternoon until eleven at night, during which time, Lord Carlisle recorded, some five hundred dishes were served.

Low ethical standards on high levels were noted also by Councilor Baron von Meyerberg, the ambassador of Emperor Leopold of Austria:

The Moscovites are so addicted to duplicity that sincerity should not be sought for in their words. They exhibit so much impudence in buttressing their lies with additional ones that no matter how sure you are of their falsity, you begin to doubt. When faced with incontrovertible evidence, they smile without a blush, as if surprised in the performance of a laudable deed.

This about the clergy and their deeds:

Before burying the dead, the priest places a certificate in the corpse's hand, composed by the notary, signed and paid in gold, to the effect that the deceased had lived in communion with the Orthodox Church, had observed the fasts, kept awake at prayers, honored God and all His Saints, gained absolution and partaken of the sacraments of the Holy Eucharist by confessing his sins, and that the certificate had been handed to him to be shown to St. Peter, so that he may enter through the heavenly gate.

So it was throughout the generations. A member of the French Academy af Sciences who visited Russia at the end of the eighteenth century, Chappe d'Anteroche, noted: "Fear is the force animating the nation. . . . Everybody distrusts everybody else." The Holy Alliance was in the making when the English traveler Robert Johnson noted in 1815: "The Russian is perfidious and malevolent, leaning to theft, mendacity and deceit. One encounters many of them in a revolting state of inebriation, although some of them avoid hard drinks."

Where was the consecrated community, the *sobornost?*

The classic of nineteenth-century travel books about Russia was *La Russie en 1839,* by the Marquis Adolphe de Custine, grandson of a general guillotined during the French Revolution. This is his famous characterization of Russia:

Without medieval and ancient memories, without Catholicism and knighthood in their past, without respect for their word . . . they are as meaninglessly polished as the Chinese, as coarse as the Kalmuks, as filthy as the Laps, as beautiful as the angels, as ignorant as the savages, as subtle as the Jews, as intriguing as liberated slaves, as cloying as the Orientals, and as cruel as the barbarians. These are the Russians.

Then, this, too:

In Russian bureaucracy application to trivial details does not exclude disorder. They go to great pains to achieve small aims. . . . They are devoid of genius, but are endowed with grace. Their *esprit* is imitative, more ironic than fecund. . . . The new imperial palace, rebuilt after the fire at a high cost in money and life, is already overrun with vermin. One could say that the ill-starred workers who killed themselves in ornamenting their imperial master's house at such speed, took their revenge in advance by infesting those homicidal walls with their parasites. . . .

A friend of Russia before the Great War, Sorbonne professor Jules Legras, summarized the findings of many in his book *L'âme Russe*. What was that much talked about "Russian soul?" The Russian awaited tomorrow, instead of going to meet it. There was a community-mindedness in the land of the Czars. The concept of life in Russia was negative and passive, compared with the positive and active mentality of the West. The Russian was always kicked about, treated as a slave. That produced the mentality of the slave—mendacity and slothfulness. It also produced the desire to forget, at any price, even if one faced starvation after paying for the drinks. Then there was corruption, aggravated by enormous distances. In Gogol's famous play *The Revisor* a higher official rebukes a minor bureaucrat: "You steal more than your rank permits."

Anarchy was also in the nature of the "Russian Everyman," Jules Legras found. In Tchernigoff province he visited a sugar-refining factory the people pillaged and partly destroyed during the 1905 revolution. "We don't need the factory," they said. "We need the land on which it stands." To them, land was livelihood and life.

Not only foreign observers but also Russia's own sons were critical of the community-mindedness of their country. One of these was the noted author Alexander Herzen: "The history of other nations is the story of their emancipation. Russian history is the development of serfdom and autocracy."

There was "religion" in Russia, too, the self-sacrificing creed of the martyrs. There were the countless men and women who ended their dedicated existence in the frozen wastes of Siberia—banished there because they were truly religious, trying to help their unfortunate countrymen. Then there was the type of people known as the "cholera doctors," who went among the people during the great epidemics that decimated the countryside from time to time. Many of them were clubbed to death by enraged primitives who resented their interference with age-old superstitions and "God's ways." Then there were the sainted young women who went to foreign colleges for medical training so that back home they could place their knowledge—and sometimes their lives—at the people's disposal. There were also the gigantic figures like Leo Tolstoy, who forsook a life of wealth and ease in an attempt to realize his ideals among the common people. In his advanced age, standing at the gate of death, he showed the people of the world, not only of his country, the gate of life—a world in which tolerance and true religion prevailed.

There were the *narodniki*, whose story will be told through the author's own experience with Tovarishch Malakov.

SOROR DOLOROSA

Tovarishch Malakov was the youthful commander of the prisoner of war camp on the left bank of the Volga, across the city then known as Simbirsk. We were the prisoners. Tovarishch Malakov knew of *soror dolorosa* from his father, who had heard of her from his uncle, so that the story, told in the last year of the Great War, which we today honor with the designation of World War I, goes back to the seventies of the nineteenth century.

Malakov did not know the name of the young woman. He just knew that she had been very beautiful, with a sweet smile, and that she was a lady. He did not know Latin and so he did not call her *soror dolorosa*. We young people, just out of our secondary schools in the Austro-Hungarian monarchy, thought of that name. She was a *narodnik*, one who went among the people, out of a secularly religious urge. She never went to church, though, and that aroused instant suspicion.

Suddenly she was there, in the village of the province of Saratov, the birthplace of Malakov. Because of her sudden appearance, the villagers were suspicious. Indeed, they were always suspicious. Perhaps she was a whore, and so they watched her, talking about her constantly, but not denouncing her to the authorities. They wanted to see; they were curious.

She had come, it seems, from the provincial capital. There was no school in the village, nor for many miles around it. Yet, there were children who would have liked to learn, so that they could read the picture books about the saints, and perhaps also because they were intelligent children, curious, who had heard about villagers who had made their way to the big town. The more enterprising children formed a small gang and went from place to place looking for a school that would admit them. They returned home, unhappy, because there were no schools for them.

The young woman had come to teach children to read and write, to teach them the history of their country. She was not paid by anyone, and she was not a whore. She went to the village because she was a *narodnik*.

Although there was no school in the village, there was a Greek Orthodox priest who learned about the "underground classroom," and through him the authorities in the provincial capital learned about it too. It was the official policy that peasant children should not even learn the three Rs. A few years before, the province had been hit by famine that the priest attributed to the *narodnik*'s nefarious work. The peasants should have stuck to the land, instead of streaming into the towns. Instructions had been dispatched to the village to ferret out the young woman.

She was found holding her class in the house of Piotr, the grandfather of our camp commander, Malakov. After being found out, both Piotr and the young woman promptly faded out of sight. He was shipped to Siberia, and nothing more was heard about him. As to the young woman, *soror dolorosa*, the information was contradictory. Some people said that she had been put in jail. Others said that her father, an important man in the province, was on good terms with the governor and she had got away with a rebuke.

For years the villagers kept on talking about the young woman. There was little of exceptional interest in their lives. She could not have known that her work was not limited to her pupils. The family of Malakov remembered her as a saint, the founder of a new religion, concerned with people, not with rites. That is how the commander of our camp had been conditioned to listen to the Communists when they came. His was a revolutionary village.

RUSSIAN NATIONALISM — A RELIGION

Nationalism, like religion, says Carlton Hayes in *Nationalism—A Religion,* calls into play not simply the will, but the intellect, the imagination, the emotions. The intellect constructs a speculative theology, a mythology of nationalism. The imagination builds an invisible world around the eternal past and everlasting future. The emotions stimulate an ecstasy in the contemplation of the national God, all-good and all-protecting. They stimulate a craving for his favors, gratitude for his benefits, and a fear of offending him. They stir unfathomable feelings of reverence and awe at the immensity of his might and wisdom which express themselves in worship—the finite meeting the infinite and partaking of its nature. The nation also protects the individual against unknown dangers—people across the border, the foreign devils, filled with evil designs. God and devils are thus confronted—as in the mysticism of religion. Modern nationalism arose among the Christians—heirs to the Hebrew culture—and it has borrowed Christian customs. In this respect, the non-Christian nations too—the Moslems,

Buddhists, Hindus, Shintoists, and all the others—have
succumbed to the Nazarene. At the knees of their children, the nations of the West, they have learned to worship God the Invincible, the Nation.

The modern Nation—God—is stronger than the
Heavenly Father had ever been, says Reinhold Niebuhr, in
Moral Man and Immoral Society. Stronger because it is
God and Caesar at the same time, its power is undivided,
eternal, absolute, exercised in a world without beginning
and without end. It calls for blood sacrifice too, and
millions of young people, whose training for life had
barely been completed, prepare themselves joyously for
death. Mothers who had toiled for endless nights to shield
their offspring from life's hazards send them off to die.

Nationalism in Russia under the Czars was different
from nationalism in the West. In the Occident, the nation
was the religion; in Russia, the religion was the nation. In
the West, religion, in the dictionary sense of the word,
was separated from the church. The citizens of all de-
nominations—or no denomination at all—were nationals
of the country. In Russia, only the true believers of the
Orthodox Church—the only authentic Christian Church
—could be the children of the Czar, whose Godlike person
represented the mystic unity of the state and faith. Only
the Orthodox was true Russian, not the Catholic, nor the
Moslem, nor the Jew. The consecrated community,
sobornost, was Orthodox Christianity. The capital of the
country was the Third Rome and the only Rome now
standing was the Orthodox Vatican, Moscow. St. Petersburg, the new capital on the river Neva, built at the orders
of Peter the Great, was only the administrative capital of
the country. Moscow remained the spiritual center, the
Eternal Rome of the Eternal Church. Russia was holy for
the true believers, the Orthodox; the others were tolerated.
"L'état c'est moi," Louis XIV said. *"L'état et l'église sont*

moi," the Russian Caesar said. In olden times the Archbishop of Novgorod, one of the ancient city-states in the north, set forth the Russian's relations to his sovereign. All-powerful was God, sovereign, and so was his Vicar, the Prince. "Chief Judge of the Divine College," the clergy came to call the Czar.

> *Thy splendor fills all space with rays divine.*
> *Thou art and wert, and shalt be Glorious, Great.*
> *Light-giving, light-sustaining Potentate.*

Thus the poet laureate, Gavrilo Derzhavin, in his "Ode to God." The mysticism could not have been carried further: the "God" was Catherine the Great. Celestial miracles had no end.

The blood of Christ was the great mystery that transformed a mankind doomed to perdition to one to be saved, Christians hold. The blood of the consecrated community of Russia has purified the land of earthly dross, mystic Moscow held. The blood that fertilized the roots of the celestial flowers was both pure and impure. Pure was the blood of the Muscovite; impure was that of his foe—Tatar and Turk, Swede and Pole, even that of the crusading Teutonic knight, the devil's seed of the polluted West.

Russia was holy, Moscow was holy, the hut of the *muzhik,* peasant, was holy. Particularly holy was the *kivot,* the glass-encased shrine in the ikon corner, with the Holy Trinity, embroidered with red silk, decorated with homespun linen, immaculately clean, as pure as the Russian soul wanted to be. The color of red was beautiful, and so the shrine was also known as the "red corner." It represented the emanation of the Holy Spirit, an immanent spiritual force. In that corner, God, Christ, and the Holy Ghost were present watching over the sanctity of the hut. No evil thoughts or evil deeds were conceivable in the sanctified presence. But man was a sinful creature, and

when the urging of the blood overwhelmed the will, the
ikons were removed. "Carrying out the saints" is a Russian
expression to indicate preparation for an un-Christian
deed.

Did the Russians have a feeling of nationalism under
the old regime? They certainly did. But it was different
from the national feelings of less consecrated lands. The
Russian, it has been observed, is best in war, when protecting his country. The weather and space helped to
destroy Napoleon, but his real nemesis was the Russian
peasant, ignorant, superstitious, and yet possessed of a
clear concept of Mother Russia, a divine creature, the
consecrated land of which he was a part. Only the Moslem idea of the holy war, *jihad,* can be compared with the
Russian idea of his personal involvement.

It was with religious chants on their lips and religious
banners in their hands that thousands of Russians staged
a patriotic demonstration on that fateful Sunday in January 1905 that ended with a holocaust.

Not all Russians saw their nation in this mystic light.
There were the higher social classes, Westernized, with an
Occidental point of view; Russia to them was a historic
fact blended into administrative convenience, fading into
the shadowy field of semireligious loyalty overhanging
collective attachments. Much traveled and mastering foreign languages, they often identified their nationalism
with an unspecified Westernism.

Then there was the intelligentsia, many members of
which saw Russia as a vast territory in search of its
identity, with a national will, transcending the dynastic
power of the ruling circles in the shadow of the throne. As
long as the rank and file of the Russians had little to say
in the affairs of their country, their idea of the community
did not conform to the Western standard of a collectivity
of all the citizens seeking to express a common will.

Then came the Communists, to whom "religion is the opium of the people," a conspiracy of the bourgeois to keep simple-minded people under divine control. The "consecrated community" was to be dedicated to "unconsecration." And what was to happen to the nation, the combination of Holy Russia and unholy individual selfishness and greed?

2

Down with Nationalism— Up with Internationalism

It was mid-March 1917, still deep winter in the Siberian town of Irbit. The news of happenings in St. Petersburg—renamed Petrograd during the Great War— had not yet reached the Hungarian prisoners of war in the Sibirskaya Hotel, once a flourishing meeting place of fur-traders, now a prison camp.

In front of the hotel there was a large space, a military training ground. Across the square was the church, built to the specifications of an internationally known trading town, such as Irbit had been. It was too large now for its shrunken population. All was quiet around the hotel. The town was a quiet place, and we Austrian and Hungarian prisoners of war in this year of 1917 had learned that Russia was a quiet land. People did not talk loudly, and certainly they did not want to be overheard. The Czarist authorities had enormous ears.

Suddenly we, the prisoners, heard the blare of the military band. . . . No, it could not be. Perhaps it was hallucination. War prisoners were subject to the "barbed-wire disease," bad nerves, hallucinations, fear of being away from home forever (and so they thought), during a war when time stood still. This time they heard a march with the strains of which they were familiar. But not in

Russia. There it was a revolutionary chant, and to play it in public might have meant Siberia—not our part of civilized Siberia, but deep down in the *taiga,* or even the treeless *tundra,* with its endless months of numbing cold.

Le jour de gloire est arrivé, the brass band blared, off-key. The military band was not used to this march. Were our senses playing tricks with us? This could not happen in the land of the Little Father, in the city of the Silver Fox.

Colonel Menzelinsov was his real name, and he was the military commander of Irbit and of our camp. "Silver Fox" was the name we gave to him, gray-haired and cunning, very patriotic, too, and religious. Naturally, he was loyal to the imperial family. The name days of the important members of the dynasty were official holidays in our town.

We thronged to the windows facing the street leading to the big square. There was the band playing—and this was not hallucination—the revolutionary song "La Marseillaise"—a revolutionary chant in Russia. And there were the soldiers in their long kaftan-like military overcoats, marching to the stirring strains of the band. At the head of the column, on horseback, was the Silver Fox himself, and next to him, two banners. Where did he get that red banner of the revolution? Possession of that, we always thought, had meant banishment to the *taiga* and *tundra.* But now the Red Flag was carried proudly by the Silver Fox's side. The other banner was a religious flag, to his left.

At the end of the street the column debouched into the square. They were going straight ahead, Silver Fox, banners, music, and all, to that big church, so typical of Russia, with its onion-like, bulbous Byzantine domes. The Silver Fox dismounted at the entrance and was met by a knot of dark-clad, greasy looking "popes," their hair knotted into tassels. Soon we heard the ecstatic *Christos*

Voskresse—"Christ has risen"—filtered through space across the square. In the land of the consecrated community it was an Orthodox religious ceremony that greeted the revolution. History was to know it as the First Revolution of 1917, precursor and antagonist of the Second Revolution, which was to stay, that of the Communists.

How easy it was for the revolution to take over power—the semblance of it, in this instance—in the land of the Czars. A telegram from headquarters had arrived, and the Silver Fox vaulted across a chasm of ideologies from dynasticism to revolutionary nationalism. All over Russia similar ceremonies were taking place—the red flags, religious banners, the *Marseillaise,* and the Orthodox *Te Deum*. The country—one sixth of the earth's land surface—had been trained in this conditioned reflex: orders were obeyed, promptly.

"LITTLE FATHER"—LENIN

"Kerensky Revolution" is the name under which history knows this interregnum of a few months' duration. It offered Russia modern nationalism, without the church, and democracy—the ideology of the West. Russia was to cease to be the consecrated community, *sobornost*, the essence of its past. What was a country without its mystique? A nation must have an attachment to some transcendent force. What was it in this case?

Time was to show that this was a mere temporary transfer of power, not a revolution. The new power structure was presumed to be based on the middle class, which was nonexistent in Russia. Then came the real revolution, sacrificial investments in lives and pain. It created a new mystique, a new ruling class, the involvement of millions.

It recreated Russia as the land of the *sobornost,* an atheistic "consecration" this time.

The Kerensky regime was over, and the Communists were at the helm by the time I reached Petrograd, soon to be known as Leningrad. The war was still on, but for me it was to be over—if I ever got home. I had been selected as an "exchange invalid" to be sent home, with afflicted health, to die in the midst of my grieving family. That was more than half a century ago. The Scandinavian physicians who had chosen me for the exchange (if they are still alive) would be surprised to hear it.

The Communist take-over had left few marks on the showcase city of Peter the Great. The Czars' Winter Palace on the Neva river embankment and the walls of some military barracks exhibited signs of rifle shots. This was not yet the age of mass slaughter and genocide. Many people we encountered in the hospital in which we were lodged and on our walks were extremely critical of the Communist regime, predicting its early end. As one critic put it: "They are an atheistic gang of cutthroats. How can they last in a religious country?" Some of us were intrigued enough to want to see the "cutthroats" and to learn if they were going to last. So we went into their den, the Smolny Institute.

Noisy and chaotic—these were our spot impressions. People were talking at the top of their voices, as if they wanted all the world to hear. The long, bare halls of the erstwhile school of well-bred girls reverberated the cacophony of voices, the tramping of heavy-booted feet. The chunks of ice brought into the corridors, adhering to countless boots, turned into dirty mush, providing a jarring counterpoint of splashing sound. Crowds were pouring up and down the spacious stairways, Red Guards, workers in black blouses and round fur hats, members of peasant delegations, with their long beards resting on heavily padded coats. Orientation was hard in the midst of all this chaos.

Occasionally there were inscriptions on the doors, former classrooms, and teachers' rooms. Several of the girls' lavatories had been transformed into meeting halls. Names were scribbled on scraps of papers: "Lunacharsky," "Kamenev." We were looking for the one marked "Lenin." To us he was the "Communist Revolution" and the man to see. Perhaps we could talk to him, asking for explanations. There were too many contradictions in his movement, and events did not turn out as he had anticipated.

He had been in Switzerland at the time our Silver Fox in Irbit had led his column of soldiers to church, thanking the Holy Trinity for the revolution exemplified by his two banners, the red flag, and the ikons. We had known that the Germans had let him, the enemy alien, go through their country, to Russia. The government in Berlin had facilitated his journey because it believed that the Communist could bring down the bourgeois government in Petrograd, thereby causing chaos. Berlin had not thought that the Communists were strong enough to stay. The Kaiser's government had underestimated Lenin's strength.

The Communist collectivists had beaten the bourgeois capitalists, but could the Communists really establish their regime after the failure of Czarist semifeudalism? Pre-war Russia had industries, to be sure, and some of them were large, but it had not been a capitalist country. The year before the two revolutions in Russia, Lenin still held on to the view that to fulfill the sequence of "historical dialectics," between the semifeudalism of the Czars and the collectivism of the commissars the missing link would have to be capitalism, and capitalism would be installed by the bourgeoisie. The year before, Lenin had had an acrid debate with Rosa Luxemburg, an impatiently radical Polish-German Socialist, who believed that in the wake of war the time was ripe for the proletarians of all countries to rise. In Lenin's opinion only the European West—Britain, France, Germany, and North America—were ready for the change. He had not thought that the proletariat of all countries were ready to act. "The majority of the world's people do not stand even at the beginning of the capitalistic level of development," he had said.

These were some of the problems we wished Lenin to address himself to; but where was he? After much searching we found him. He was in one of the classrooms on an upper floor. We found it by heading in the direction of the greatest noise. His name, scribbled on a torn-off piece of paper, was dangling lopsidedly on a badly battered door. It was hard to get into the room and to stay there, not merely because of the oversized crowd but also because of the odor of countless perspiring bodies in heavy furs. Besides, people were smoking *mahorka,* the foul-smelling tobacco substitute.

Eventually, we were heaved into the room by the sheer weight of the muscle power of people bent on getting into it. We were now in the presence of the man who had stood Russia on her head, the man whom all the world was watching. There he was, a short, stocky man, with his big head, bald and bulging. He had an uncommonly wide mouth, an upturned nose, and small eyes, wide apart. We thought of the proverb: "Scratch a Russian and you find a Tatar." Lenin's skin of nondescript color was tautly stretched over his prominent cheekbones, so that his face looked unusually smooth. When we had penetrated deeper into the room, we noticed that he was sloppily dressed, and that his trousers were too long for his stumpy legs. While he was obviously no matinee idol, he was the idol of the crowd. "A strange popular leader," we were to read later in John Reed, the American upper-class admirer, "a leader purely by virtue of intellect; colorless, humorless, uncompromising and detached, without picturesque idiosyncrasies—but with the power of explaining profound ideas in simple terms, of analyzing a concrete situation."

Surrounded by the perspiring, jostling crowd, Lenin spoke incessantly in a hoarse high-pitched voice—high-pitched, perhaps, because of his weariness. From near the door we saw his bald pate floating, from one wall to the other, cutting a swath in the fur-wearing crowd. At the request of a delegation, he was explaining the basic first act of his regime, the Decree on the Land. He stopped a while for emphasis, then continued his gliding walk, his bald skull floating. Another delegation wanted specific instructions, and asked for an official paper, *bumaga.*

Lenin glided to the desk in a corner of the room, tore off a piece of paper, and scribbled the authorization. This pleased the delegation, the members of which bowed to him and with rapid gestures made the sign of the cross,   ✗ an old habit. Then the peasants of that group shuffled out of the room.

The authorization Lenin had signed was not registered anywhere. But, then, we noticed during our stay under the regime that the Communists had a routine to which they always adhered, doing the reverse of what had been done in the past. Czarist Russia had been a nightmare of addlepated bureaucracy, where an official paper substituted for an official deed. Antibureaucracy was the way of the new regime—at the outset.

This was not the time to ask questions about theoretical points, and eventually we were pushed out the same way we had been pushed in. Meanwhile, the floor of the corridors had become even soupier with the thawed ice. More people came in, and the Smolny Institute seemed to be shaking with the reverberation of the loud voices. On our way back to our hospital we turned over in our minds what we had seen.

We were young, teen-agers, and we jumped to conclusions. We had just seen the Red Czar of all the Russias, and he looked unimpressive to us. The Russians, used to having demigods rule them, might not want the Tatar-looking little man from Simbirsk to hold the helm. Could one rule a country—even a city—by issuing orders on small pieces of paper, keeping no record whatever, as we had seen him do? These Communists impressed us as rank amateurs.

Lenin's writings gave us the answers to our intended questions. He disagreed with "Red Rosa" that only the concerted effort of all the proletariats of all the countries could shake off the capitalist rule. Lenin became impatient with those who maintained that the Russians, being backward, should merely await action by more advanced countries. Russia, he held, together with other under-developed areas, including the colonies, could assist more advanced revolutionary nations by undermining the old order.

The Russian bourgeoisie did not fill the gap left by the end of the old regime, since it had no roots among the masses. Foreign powers, headed by Britain, the pivot of conservatism then, were lining up their forces behind the champions of the *ancien régime,* which had no roots in the masses either. It had tradition, however, and the "sanction of heaven" that had selected Russia to be Holy and granted her the most sanctified of all places, Moscow, the Rome of the Christian faith, which the majority of the Russians believed was the only sanctuary pleasing to the Holy Trinity.

The seemingly endless war was over in a few months, but not for Russia, beset by foes on all sides—counter-revolutionary armies and foreign invaders. A global crusade was on against the "antichrist," the "Abomination of Abominations," the Communists, "the ecumenical plague," to be fought with all the means at the disposal of the civilized world.

The country was devastated, its transportation system in shambles, old values uprooted, and new values still unplanted. Most of the top leaders of Communism were not Russians, but members of minorities, including a brilliant and vociferous Jew from the Ukraine, Leon Trotsky, and a tight-lipped, secretive Georgian, with a name which was difficult even for Russians, Iosif Vissarionovich Dzughashvili, a former theological seminarian, whom the world was to know by his Russian pseudonym, Stalin, "Steel."

3

An Age of Despair
and an Age of Change

There are moments when suddenly one is engulfed by a void, and there is only despair. Former friends look as distant as if they had been blown into outer space. And there is no hope, and no self-confidence. The defeat is inflexible and final. Then, suddenly, there is a dramatic change. The Danish philosopher-theologian Søren Kierkegaard called it the "existentialist moment," when the razor-edge decision of man's will determines his relation with divinity. Kierkegaard called it *Enten-Eller*—Either-Or. Man is no longer alone, because he is in partnership.

The Russian Communist leaders, atheists, saw the world in this light, a secularized version of *Enten-Eller*. This was their "existentialist moment," the age of despair. But there was the choice—a new faith. The new masters in Petrograd, soon to become Leningrad, were trusting in the influence of the "existentialist moment," the comfort of the "religion" of the postwar age, the revolution, destroyer of old shibboleths, creator of new values.

> *Arise, ye prisoners of starvation!*
> *Arise, ye wretched of the earth!*

These were the words of their revolutionary chant "L'Internationale."

For justice thunders condemnation
A better world is in birth.

It was to be the world of "existentialist faith."

No more traditions' chain shall bind you.
Arise, ye slaves! No more in thrall.

This would be the moment of *Enten-Eller*, Either-Or. The choice was up to man.

The world shall rise on new foundations,
You have been naught, you shall be all!

The horror of the "existentialist moment" had overwhelmed the once-proud race of Germans, too. Theirs had been an endless chain of victories during the Great War, from one end of Europe to the other. They had displayed qualities that commanded the admiration even of their foe. They had expected final victory, and got humiliating defeat.

The defeated Germans were not participants in the drawing up of the treaty under which they were to live. It was imposed upon them, and theirs was only one answer: "We submit." They had to submit because they, the great producers, the matchless managers, the fabulously successful inventors, were now hungry. Starvation stalked the land in the wake of the dismal defeat. Forsaken by fortune, crushed into the dust by the wheel of chance, they were facing the great question—Either-Or!

The moment of despair overwhelmed the people of other once-proud dynastic countries—the Austro-Hungarian monarchy, the Ottoman Empire—defeated, crushed, humiliated, overwhelmed by despair. In this strangest of all ages, despondency reigned even in some of the victorious countries, especially Italy.

In the eyes of the Communist leaders, whom an historic freak had hurled into power unprepared, hope would follow in the wake of despair. Most Russians expected little of Russians. They knew themselves and the positive genius of their countrymen to organize disorganization. Communism in Russia could not remain, in their view, because of that national trait. While many of the Bolsheviks thought so, others disagreed. Although they may have never heard of Kierkegaard's existentialist moment, they felt the warming breath of history in the challenge of the critical moment.

Still, they were looking abroad, especially to Germany. In Czarist Russia "efficiency" and "German" were considered synonyms. The most successful business people in Russia had been Germans. The most effective Russian government administrators had been Germans, too. After its stunning defeat, this was the moment for the Reich to turn to the new divinity, revolution. Germany did turn to it with a mighty roar reverberating in the Russian Communist press.

German workers and soldiers set up *Raete*, Councils, corresponding to the Soviets' Workers' and Soldiers' Councils, which roared:

Arise ye slaves! No more in thrall!

The organization of the German comrades adopted the name of the most famous leader of classical Rome's slaves, "Spartacus." Karl Liebknecht, the German who had dared to oppose the war, was a leader of the Spartacists. His fellow leader was "Red Rosa," Rosa Luxemburg. They and their fellow workers were going to launch the New Age, the Russian Communists believed. Quickly, liaison was established between Petrograd and Berlin. This was the "existentialist moment."

Leon Trotsky, the number-two man in Russia, was not only a brilliant theoretician, but also a matchless organizer—one of the few in that country of continental size.

People listened when he spoke because the word of the times was on his lips. He was possessed of both knowledge and intuition, seeing the situation clearly, and expressing his view in his outspoken way: "The war has transformed the whole of Europe into a powder keg of social revolution," he said. "To suppose that this will cause no explosion is to think against the laws of historical logic and psychology." He thought he knew because he was a master of the science of dialectical materialism. The practitioners of that science could gaze into the stars. "To say that the German working class will not rise against the ruling classes in the nearest future is improbable in the extreme," he prophesied.

It did, indeed, but not in Berlin, the Spartacus stronghold, where it was expected. It was in Munich, the capital of Bavaria, that a Soviet regime arose—in Catholic Bavaria, a conservative stronghold. Stranger still, its leaders were intellectual idealists, such as the playwright Ernst Toller. He knew the mass man (*Massenmensch* had, in fact, been the title of one of his famous plays). Could he also manage him?

Then Hungary went Communist, reacting to a crippling treaty of peace, which amputated its arms and legs. It was a regime of wounded pride and resentment. The leaders in Russia were encouraged. Was this the response to the call:

Arise, ye wretched of the earth!

There were deep stirrings in the other defeated countries too. In the depths of the Balkans, the peasant country of Bulgaria veered violently left, with a Peasant Party regime, headed by Aleksandr Stamboliski. Not a Communist, to be sure, but would he not become one with some Soviet help?

The Ottoman Empire—the "sick man" of Europe—was

now a "dead man," and its heir, Republican Turkey, was
facing its own "existentialist moment." Trotsky believed
that to suppose that there would be no explosion in
Turkey was against the laws of logic and psychology.
Turkey was to be amputated, and only its torso was to
remain. A revolutionary leader arose there too—Mustapha Kemal.

It was a strange fact that a victor, too—Italy—should
be facing its existentialist moment. Victor, in the end,
because it had held out on the side of its allies, although
defeated in many battles during the war, and, still worse,
defeated by debilitated Austria. At the peace conference,
the wartime record considered, Italy received far less than
her expected share. Wrought up by the slight, she reacted
strongly. The red flags on factory chimneys hoisted by her
Communists expressed a mood and may have adumbrated
the future—a Soviet government in Italy.

The Russians' attention was glued on Europe, where
the anticipated great transformation was to occur. Europe
was the only continent that counted. Asia and Africa were
fettered giants, held by a few European powers, the
strength of which consisted of their colonies' inability to
act.

THE GREAT "BETRAYAL"

It may have been against the "laws of historical logic
and psychology," to use Trotsky's terminology, but the
explosion of the powder magazines did not occur. What
happened?

The Communist regime of Russia had moved to Moscow. Petrograd—renamed Leningrad—had been too close
to the frontiers, and exposed to foreign invasions. Moscow

was more grassroots Russian to the "internationalist" Communists. It was Moscow that saw Europe's "existentialist moment" of despair vanish, and hope for the world revolution fade.

The Kremlin called this the "Great Betrayal." The Spartacists, in west Germany, in the industrial Ruhr area, and in Berlin, were defeated by the armed forces, under the control of Socialists, fellow Marxists, worshippers at the shrines of the same Marx and Engels who were the Communist's prophets too. Karl Liebknecht and "Red Rosa" were killed by super-nationalists. The republic the Germans established followed in the footsteps of the imperial regime—a bourgeois state, with Socialists in key posts.

The Soviet republic in Munich and its environs lasted a mere three weeks. After its fall, the reaction to it was extreme conservatism, the mushrooming of ultra-patriotism. One of its products, calling itself the National-Socialist Labor Party, had a former Viennese drifter at its head, about whom the world was to hear much—Adolf Hitler. His movement grew out of the Bavarian Soviet fiasco.

The Hungarian Soviet regime lasted three months. It was a grotesque regime run by amateurs whose only skill consisted of doing the wrong things. Its leaders seemed to think that the world was a stage on which history performed a shadow play. Quickly, they vanished from sight, leaving only memories of incompetence. The reaction was "reaction" there, too, an anticipation of facist rules that were to cover most of Europe—the glorification of a godlike nation, authority for the few, subservience for the many, half-hearted attempts to right deeply rooted wrongs.

In the third vanquished empire, Turkey, there had not even been an attempt at the establishment of a left-wing regime. Occidentalization was the keynote of the government of Mustapha Kemal, an attempt to turn a backward Oriental despotism into an autocracy with a Western slant. While the Communist experiments in Western Europe produced bad feelings between those countries and the Kremlin, Turkey and the Soviets formed the nucleus of the "League of International Pariahs."

Reaction followed in the footsteps of the pro-little-people regime in Bulgaria, a return to the traditional ways of the Balkans, enmity toward the neighbor, nationalist isolation, a rural-type economy, with little thought of introducing a more effective system.

THE TIME OF TROUBLES IN RUSSIA

How could the country of the Communists—the new Promised Land—survive? Since Germany had not gone Communist, as the Soviets had hoped, would the Russians have the competence to set up a regime pivoted on effective organization? The Soviets had their doubts. These were reinforced by the cumulative effect of social and natural catastrophes.

The war had corroded the productive capacity of the land, and work in the industrial plants all but came to a halt. There was a shortage of the basic raw materials— only 10 percent, for instance, of the pre-war output of steel was produced. And how tragic was the condition of travel arteries! We prisoners of war had seen some of those blocked arteries; we had seen locomotives resting on their backs, all usable material removed, the skeletons remaining, looking like apocalyptic spiders. The confusion of the "land reform," left to local committees, further enhanced the chaos.

This fantastic inefficiency could not go on. Many foresaw that "Holy Russia" would be forced back to the worship of its historic gods. Out of its tired soil sprouted an
amazing number of counterrevolutionary forces, a free-
for-all of adventure forces led by ex-generals and admirals
of iron will to reconstruct the old regime.

These counterrevolutionary forces received aid from
foreign powers, who dispatched expeditionary armies to
key regions in the Far East, in the ice-free northern port
of Murmansk, across the Caucasus, along the Black Sea
and the Caspian. "Arise, ye prisoners of starvation," *L'Internationale* had roared. What did happen was that, not
the starved, but the well-fed, arose—Britain, France,
Japan, the United States—to crush communism. To the
governments of these countries, the Communist regime
was the Supreme Abomination, the antichrist, denying
the values dear to Western hearts—cultural values (being
atheistic), economic values (being collectivistic), political
values (being autocratic). And, still worse, the Communist regime asserted that, since the future belonged to it,
its duty was to set up an aggressive international organization to propagate the ecumenical antifaith of subversion.

At that point, the most awful event occurred in the
breadbasket of the Soviets, the rich, fat black-soil area,
chernozem, in the southwest—a drought that burned up
soil which madly craved water. There was no water, nor
were there "arteries" of travel to provide food. There was
no use hiding the dread facts; they were there for all the
world to see: the skeletal bodies; the children's bloated
bellies; the desperate attempts to escape grisly death; the
exodus of the strong, smashing their way over limp bodies
to get on the last trains in the monstrous charnel house.
Then came aid from the capitalist countries, mainly from
the United States, too late for the millions, not too late for

thousands. Russia, the Land of Sorrows, had never been so sorrowful. And all this calamity, the faithful thought, because Russia, the Holy, had been desecrated by the Communist fiend.

No other country could have survived all these disasters under the same regime. The Russians had become used to the dreadful trials of life, and so the Communists survived. Unwittingly, they were helped by the counterrevolutionaries and the invaders—helped in reverse. The rulers may have been Communists; the Russians, even the Bolsheviks among them, remained traditionalists. The counterrevolutionaries, helped by the alien invaders, desecrated the sacred soil. The Communist call to resist was answered, and more than answered. Even though the Russians were traditionalists, they did not want their country to return to the past, the goal of the counterrevolutionaries. The time was ripe for change, and it had to be basic. "Holy Russia" had belonged to an unholy age in which God was all and the common man nothing.

Thus the Soviet regime survived the time of troubles. Lenin, in the opinion even of his critics, had risen to the occasion and become an historic figure. He, the dedicated Communist, had broken off the "great experiment," introduced too hastily, and returned to a modified capitalism, the NEP, New Economic Policy. *Réculer pour mieux sauter*, the quick-witted Trotsky said, "to draw back so as to leap farther." It was a temporary move, followed by authentic communism, which, however, Lenin did not live to see.

The counterrevolutionaries had been defeated, and the foreign invaders had withdrawn. They had not been able to defeat the Bolsheviks by physical force. Now they were attempting to do it by isolating it from "decent mankind." Along the western frontiers of Russia a string of countries was organized into the *cordon sanitaire*, separating the house of plague, the Soviets, from the capitalist world, the house of health.

THE GAME OF *NASHI-VASHI*—
"OURS AND YOURS"

After Lenin's death, Trotsky was the presumtive heir. He was a master of dialectics, a brilliant organizer, speaker, writer—a man of authentic genius. His work pivoted on his social philosophy. He held that Russia would be able to remain a Communist country only if the movement spread to other nations, particularly in strategic Europe. Therefore, he saw imperative need for the Moscow International, the Third. It was to be the only and last International. Without it, he believed, the Soviets would be shattered as a glass tube enclosing a vacuum is shattered in pressurized space. Many people subscribed to what he said, although they disliked the impetuous and impatient way he said it.

Trotsky faced the opposition of "the other one"—the Unspeakable One, for him—the Georgian who spoke Russian with the accent of South Caucasus: Stalin. He insisted that the Soviets alone could establish the Communist Commonwealth, and that there was no "glass tube." There was only one way for the Soviets, communism in one country, at first. The other solution—the spreading of the faith abroad—had been tried, and it had failed. Many comrades shied away from the idea of Russia alone embarking upon the great experiment. They remembered the bungling record of their country. But they also remembered what had happened to the leaders of the great Revolution in France after its leaders had run out of solutions. They wanted to live.

They did not believe that North America, which, ac-

cording to the teachings of some of their prophets, was
the most likely place to launch communism, was the
"wave of the future." North America, particularly the
United States, was too prosperous to generate a breed of
discontent. They did not think any more that Germany
was a likely candidate for the change. The "existentialist
moment" of deep despair had already yielded there to
optimism, at least for a time.

Trotsky, the most brilliant leader in Russia, lost the
argument, and was forced into exile, where he had his
tragic end. His adversary Stalin seems to have known
about that end well in advance. The new age in the history
of the U.S.S.R. now began, the age of Stalin. It was the
age of the planned economy, with concentration on essen-
tials, and, presumably, avoidance of the hazards of laissez
faire. And this in a country that had been spawned in the
sign of internationalism—ecumenism.

THE ECUMENICAL SOVIETS

The Union of Soviet Socialist Republics was an ecumenical name, without the designation of any nationality.
It could be applied to all the remaining parts of the former
domains of the Emperors and Autocrats of all the Russias
—Great Russia, Little Russia, White Russia. Also, it could
cover the entire world: the "Soviet Socialist Republics of
all the Continents." The names of the "nations" were
included in the designations of the "component republics."

It was logical, therefore, that the Soviet Union had no
national hymn at the outset. It had an "international
anthem," "The International," also an ecumenical
creation.

One of the most highly revered symbols of nations is

the flag. The Soviet Union had no national flag either. It had an international flag, the red banner of the revolution, the symbol of the proletariat. Under the Communist regime, Russia was to cease to be a nation and became the seed of an Ecumene. Stalin had won the game against Trotsky, to be sure, and the great experiment began to create communism in one country. It was not to remain alone. It was to succeed with its planned economy, against the chaos of capitalist production. It was to solve the problem of full employment, while its opponents were to be buffeted by the gales of business depressions. In the end, the "proletarians of all countries" would force their governments to copy the Soviet pattern. Then the Kremlin Ecumene would proclaim its triumph with the creation of one world, the Communist world.

4

The Nectar
and the Opium

The nation and the "Holy Orthodox Catholic Apostolic Eastern Church" had formed one indissoluble consecrated union under the Emperors and Autocrats of all the Russias, the Czarist Empire. We call it the Russian Orthodox Church, nominally subordinate to the Ecumenical Patriarchate in Constantinople, but in reality, *autocephalous*, independent. The Emperor and the Church represented a divine presence.

The other religions in Russia had been tolerated, at best. Spread across Soviet Central Asia were the Moslems, the largest contingent of whom were Turkic-speaking— Azerbaijani, Kazakhs, Khirgiz, Uzbeks, and, leaning against the mountains of the dorsal column of the world, the Persian-speaking Tadjiks. Scattered over the land were the remaining seeds of the Tatars, on the Volga, in the Crimea, in northern Siberia. Often they too had formed communities in which the temporal and the religious were intertwined: the Supreme Law, the Word of Allah, the Koran; their native ways were sanctified by religious tradition.

The Jews of Russia had been the "Chosen People," chosen for discrimination, ready-made scapegoats, victims of the *chernaya sotnia*, the Black Hand, Czarist adminis-

trative agencies for terror. They were forced into the
limited area of the "Pale," the former territories of Poland,
Lithuania, sections of the Ukraine; in the company of
other nationalities, they were victims of the policy of
"divide and persecute."

One of the religious groups in the Soviets received
special treatment—the Armenians, claiming to be members of the oldest organized Christian body in the world.
The bulk of them had lived in the Ottoman Empire, where
they became victims of genocide. Hundreds of thousands
of them perished. The Soviet Union encouraged the sur-
vivors to cross the frontier into its territory. The Universal
Pontiff of the church, Katholikos, had his seat in Ech-
miadzin, in the Armenian Soviet Socialist Republic of the
Soviet Union.

"Opium of the people" was Karl Marx's term for the
religions. Atheist and Communist were considered synonymous terms. The Kremlin launched a campaign against
religion, mainly the Orthodox Church, with the object of
wiping it out. In Moscow alone there had been some four
hundred churches under the Czarist regime, and nine
tenths of them were transformed under the Communists
into secular buildings—warehouses, manufacturing
plants, community halls, cultural centers, and schools.

The Godless had their publicly supported organization.
Its aim was to show that priestcraft had been employed by
the authorities to make the people complacent, accepting
their fate as the will of the Almighty God. It was obedience
that the churches had preached, extolling the meek, preventing them from gaining their meed. God was represented as a Super Policeman, helping the temporal
authorities to keep the people in subjection.

In the social hierarchy of the Communists the priests
were to occupy the lowermost rank. Misdeeds of some
priests were woven into legends to scare the people.

Rasputin, the "Holy Devil" whose power had been immense in the dying days of the imperial regime, was represented as the archetype of maleficence.

"Parasite" was the most common designation for the priest; another was "bloodsucker." Members of the priesthood were stripped of the rights of their office. They became "unpeople," without rights, denounced as burdens on society. Many of them were transported into forced labor camps to perform arduous and dangerous work in sub-Arctic regions, building the Baltic-White Sea Canal, one of the first Soviet projects to use "slave labor," while others were hauled off into Siberia to fell trees. Unused to the work, they perished.

Since members of the lower levels of the Orthodox clergy can marry, their families, too, felt the heavy hand of the law. Children of clergymen were victims of discrimination. Members of the surviving congregations ran into all kinds of roadblocks. Participation in divine services created an occupational hazard.

The former "consecrated community" thus became the unconsecrated community under the Bolsheviks. But Russia had been the land of the *sobornost* for too long, and its dedication to the creed assumed a strange shape. Within a short time, the greatest enemy of the church, communism, became a quasi-church itself. The national tradition of Russia, the Holy Land with its Holy Town, under the special dispensation of its special divinity, brought forth a re-interpretation. The crusading country that had destroyed the Satan's seed, the infidels of the East, that had waged its crusades against the defamers of Christ, the followers of Mohammed, went on a new crusade against the powers it considered those of darkness, offering its own illumination to a benighted world.

This was an upside-down world in which the anti-religion became the Religion, the antichurch became the

Church, and the antipriesthood became the official corps of Priests. It was in the spirit of the national traditions of Russia that the country again became the dwelling of the consecrated community, this time the Communist *sobornost.*

"The spirit of the people [Russians] could very easily pass from one integrated faith to the other integrated faith, from one orthodoxy to another orthodoxy which embraced the whole life. . . ." This is what happened in the Soviets, wrote Nicholai Berdyaev, existentialist philosopher, and anti-Communist. "And there always remains, as the chief thing, the profession of some orthodox faith. This is always the criterion by which the membership of the Russian people is judged."

Sir John Maynard, in his psychoanalysis of the Russians, *Russia in Flux,* showed that Soviet communism was the progeny. of the Russian Eastern Orthodox faith, a logical sequel. Orthodox Christianity, he concluded, prepared the way for communism, and "nowhere more than in its vision of a Kingdom of God upon earth, of a transfigured universe made perfect for the Second Coming. The period of wars and revolution which precedes it is the period of apocalyptic preparation."

The new consecrated community of historic Russia proclaimed its own *sobornost,* the revelation that the Soviets were in communion with the deep mysteries of human existence, had "broken open" the secret code of communal life, had found the way to *Gloria in Excelsis*— heaven, not as a promise in endless space, but as realization on earth. And thus Sir John Maynard: "The survival of religious habits in thought and action does not mean that the Bolsheviks are likely to become Christians, but merely shows what persistent 'residues' these habits are."

"On the other hand," he continues, "the notion that there is a pattern somewhere stored up, to which it is

desirable to make the life of man conform (such, for
instance, as the pattern of classless society), carries with
it the conception of theology which is in essence religious,
and is hardly reconcilable with the materialistic doctrine
that the deed comes first and the thought comes after."

It is vain to discuss, Maynard continues, whether communism is itself a religion. What is more important is to
notice that it possesses certain of the qualities that have
caused religious creeds to spread. Chief of these, in the
case of communism, is the service of man (who thus
becomes a substitute for God), a duty inspiring devotion
and creating unity, linking together generations in a communion—"we must not say of saints."

In his monumental study of the history of civilizations,
A Study of History, Arnold J. Toynbee called attention to
the same phenomenon: that latter-day Marxian communism could neither be classified correctly "nor understood
aright as anything but a religion." Though its exponents
vehemently denounced and repudiated religion in general
and Christianity in particular, "the Marxian myth, faith
and hope all betrayed their Christian origins, and the
Marxian mission to preach the gospel to every creature
ran true to type by stultifying itself, as other once ecu-
menical-minded religious movements had stultified themselves in their day, when enlisted in the service of a
secular state."

Then, Toynbee's summing up of the case:

Communism called upon post-Christian man to cure himself of a childish nostalgia for a justly discredited other-
wordly utopia by transferring his allegiance from a nonexistent God to a very present Human Race to whose service
he could devote all his adult powers for the attainment of an
Earthly Paradise. In an ecumenical struggle between a Communist Russia and a secularized Modern Western Society for
the allegiance of the rest of mankind the apologists for a

damningly prosaic secular modern western way of life might find themselves hard put to it to "sell" their unconvincing apotheosis of the self-interested human being in competition with the captivating communist cult of the colossal idol of Collective Humanity.

As in the Czarist past, adhering to the basic national character, Russia, renamed the Soviet Union, has again combined the "spiritual" with the temporal in an inextricable whole. This was a signal victory of nationalism over more internationalism.

THE "SACRED BOOKS" TOO

Following the same line of thought, the theologian Martin Wight expounded:

As Marxian communism has developed into a "religion" the writings of Marx and Engels have come to occupy the place of the Old Testament in Christian holy writ, the writings of Lenin (in whose life the Marxian meaning of history became incarnate, as the Christian meaning of history became incarnate in the Life and Passion of Christ) have become the counterparts of the Gospels, and the writings of Stalin have become to resemble the Pauline Epistles—the principal authorized interpretation of the historical revelation. . .

And a footnote by the same author in recognition of changed times:

At the moment Stalin's writings are thrust out of the body of the accepted interpretation. The future may change their role. After all, Stalin was part of Russian history and Russia is Holy (the commentaries by the highest authorities make it abundantly clear) even if it has been renamed the Soviet Union.

The Communist Party itself had been created as a crusading order, to protect the true faith, to convert the hesitant, and to smite the recalcitrant. It required self-sacrifice in the early days when communism was still fighting for its very life *in partibus infidelium* of Russia that was to be sanctified. Virtue was to be the guideline of the party member. In return, he received high priority in reaching more exalted government posts.

Toynbee says:

The instrument of propaganda which communism brought into action as a new weapon in the arena of mundane power politics has first been fashioned by the missionaries of the higher religions for the more ethereal purpose of converting souls. . . . While the communist propaganda could hardly improve on the practice of contemporary commercial advertising in the lavishness of its outlay or in the painstakingness of its "market research", it did show itself capable of re-awakening a long-dormant enthusiasm in spiritually starved post-Christian western souls that were so hungry for the bread without which man shall not live that they recklessly swallowed the word which communism gave them, without pausing to ask whether this was God's word or Antichrist's.

Only the pure could join the ranks, and only the unbesmirched could stay. The final decision about one's state of purity was in the hands of members of the "priesthood" of the consecrated community, fellow party members. In the crusading period of the faith the process of purification was effected in periodic *chistkas*—purges—in the presence of one's peers. Constantly party members had to subject themselves to *samokritika*—self-criticism. Virtue was, of course, expected to be inherent in the party member, but even he could fall from grace. He had to confess, not to one person, but to the community. This was an act of "religion" and also a very Russian deed. The "Russian soul"—Czarist or Communist—craves self-revelation, sympathy, forgiveness. Thence, the verbal self-flagellation, the public confessions, about which the West also knows because of their conspicuous place in the classic novels of Russian writers.

With the wreckage of the Christian churches, under the Communists, the ikons vanished from their walls. But the ikons reappeared in another shape, likenesses of the "saints" of the new *sobornost,* the Communist "consecrated community." There was a new Trinity—Marx, Engels, and Lenin. After Lenin's death, his final resting place on the Red Square of Moscow became a place of pilgrimage. Stalin joined him there for a spell, but his canonization was revoked. The trinity of the godless joined the Trinity of Divinity in peasant houses—Marx, Engels, Lenin, in the company of the Father, the Son, and the Holy Ghost, in two ikon corners. There was nothing unusual in this to the people of the Soviets, where the state is the religion, the religion is the state, as it has always been, a national trait under Muscovy, and also under the Communists.

THE *GOLOS* AND SATAN

"From the beginning to the end there was the *Golos,* the Word." But in Russia, there was to be no end, because this was a universe without end, communism. It was the Word of Marx, of his faithful companion, Friedrich Engels, of Lenin, and for a time of Stalin. After that it was the Collective Word of the Party, represented by the Elect, members of the Central Committee of the Communist Party, and even more so of its apex, the Politbureau, renamed Presidium for a time. The latter was the supreme authority, and its word was the *Golos,* passed on to

the government, which carried it into effect. Top government officials and members of the apex of the party
pyramid performed overlapping functions as in Czarist
Russia. This too was a reincarnation of national history,
the mingling of the spiritual and temporal, the fusion of
the sacred and mundane.

Then there was the "party line." Before it was drawn
there may have been public discussion. The will of the
people could not be ignored, because the Communists
knew from their reading of history what happened to
autocracies that had overlooked the *Zeitgeist,* the whimsi-
cal, capricious, unpredictable spirit of the times, the trend
that starts slowly and then begins to race. People on the
top had to have keen eyes.

After the party line had been established came the
dogma, and it could not be questioned, because it had been
entered into the book of *Golos*—a sacred book. Anathema
was hurled at the heads of the miscreants that tried to
question the transcendent origin of the Word.

A religion faces not only the absolute good but also the
absolute evil—the Devil's breed, embodied by the capitalist, the money-minded evil, the oppressor who had
built his fortune with other peoples' blood and tears. Marx
demonstrated this in *Das Kapital.* In the end, the capitalist turned to the exploitation of the underdeveloped
world. Lenin described this phase in his *Imperialism—the
Highest Stage of Capitalism.* The demonology was useful,
as it kept people stimulated. Psychology teaches that you
love one ideology better if you hate its opposite. The
errors, inefficiencies, and crudities of the new order had to
be attributed to malicious forces too. One needed a
monster one could really hate.

Every religion has a glimpse of the "beyond," its *teleol-
ogy.* The promise of communism to its followers is heaven
here and today, not in the blue yonder and tomorrow. To

everybody according to his needs in the form of the
communal distribution of man's rich storehouse, accumulated through communal effort. How could that be done?
Could human nature be changed, so that the need should
not be overstated, its fulfillment not represented as an act
of charity? The Communist "fathers" seem to have paid
little attention to this feature of the problem. Russia at the
present time is still Socialist. It is not the Union of Soviet
Communist Republics. This is, then, the probationary
period—training for social thinking, action, the replace-
ment of man's concern for the eternal "number one"
by concern for the totality—one is all and all is one. Thus
the lion and the lamb will live in amity. Or perhaps there
will be no lions and lambs in the golden age.

The upshot is this: the Church and State represented
one consecrated community in Russia, a nation of saints.
The Communists wrecked the form but retained the substance through the substitution of communism for the
Orthodox Church. Communism follows the Russian
national tradition in considering itself the only true faith,
which, it believes, all mankind will eventually embrace.
Through its missionaries in non-Communist lands, *in
partibus infidelium,* the Kremlin has been seeking to
thrust its light upon the benighted nonbelievers of the
entire length and breadth of the globe.

5

Then Nationalism

Its coming was not announced by fanfare; and it came like a thief in the night. Suddenly it was there. The Soviet's neutral "International," the hymn, was replaced by a national anthem, extolling the beauties of the fatherland. Each republic acquired a flag of its own, even though the color of red predominated in each. While in the early Communist past there had been only devils in the history of Czarism, except for the rebels, now textbooks began to extoll even Ivan the Terrible's deeds.

First, the concept of nation in communist terminology must be clarified. A difficult concept it is, it seems, studded with contradictions. Internationalism is the official creed of the Soviets, and for a generation there was the Communist International, Comintern—"Moscow International"— to embrace the world in its bear hug. The Comintern was disbanded during the second World War. Its kin, the less ambitious Communist Information Bureau, Cominform, had a short shrift, too. Since then there has been no International in Moscow.

Today the very word "internationalism" and its synonyms are flouted in Moscow, and "cosmopolitanism" has become an outright damning concept. People who fall into disfavor, writers and other artists, are denounced as "cosmopolites," meaning people without grass-roots.

Has "nationalist" become the proper word, then? Although nationalism has become the dominant *sentiment* in the Soviet Union, in China, and in the Eastern European Communist bloc, it is not the popular *word* in that world. The explanation of this incongruity may be this: fascism, *la bête noire,* the black beast, had deified nationalism, making it the center of its idol worship. It had created, as the communists see it, a tribal nation, claiming superiority of "blood," culture, and historic heritage over all others. The fascists' nationalism was to reveal its transcendent nature through national devotees who volunteered the supreme sacrifice in wars. The supreme sacrifice, of course, would have been for all the nationals to sacrifice themselves in a collective self-immolation on the altar of the national idol, the national god. The word "nationalism" may have thus acquired a tainted connotation in the Communist world, but not the concept itself. Therefore, another word had to be adopted. The word that contemporary communism has adopted is "patriotism."

The word has a curious history in the Communist world. At first, it was a word of derogation, describing the attributes of hostile forces. Because the socialists of the West were no longer considered internationalists, the Communists had denounced them as "social patriots." The words "patriot" and "patriotism" had denoted vacuous, high-sounding, breast-thumping identification with parochial values. At the same time, the extreme right, also, extolled patriotism, which came to mean a higher degree of nationalism, in which the nation took the place of *pater*—fatherland—the ultimate refuge and full identification. A patriot is "one who loves his country and zealously supports its authority and interests," the dictionary says. This is in contradiction to the concept of global collectivism of the devout Communist. In spite of this, patriotism is the word the communists have adopted as the description of their politico-social attitude. To distinguish it from the common variety, however, they call it "socialist patriotism," a juxtaposition that is a contradiction too.

NATIONALISM IN DIPLOMACY

Although these events occurred in broad daylight, the Soviets' about-face was overlooked for a long time. It was so, perhaps, because the strong daylight had washed out its features. During the internationalist period of the Soviets, as was shown, Moscow believed that Berlin represented the pivot of the world and that communism was doomed unless the Germans joined the Third International. That, of course, did not happen, and, subsequently, the "communism-in-one-country" concept won. One country, and then the domino effect, as others were to fall into line, as communism demonstrated its presumed superiority.

The year was 1922 and the place a delightful small town on the Italian Riviera, Rapallo. The Soviet Union and Germany signed a treaty there containing several clauses that made history. Its most important clause was this: the Kremlin was to help the Reich to become stronger, more heavily armed than the post-Great-War peace treaty had permitted. This clause appeared to be in the national interest of Moscow, and not in the interest of the Comintern. The strengthened Reich's army could deal more effectively with subversive people, such as its Communists. But making the Weimar Republic stronger would mean that the main enemies of communism, the former Allies, would be counterbalanced. This appeared to be in the interest of both Berlin and Moscow. Thus Russia's national interest prevailed over that of her ideology.

The Soviets had another neighbor, Turkey, which has always been the proverbial "hereditary enemy," because Turkey was the "keeper of the Straits," which the Russians considered of vital interest to themselves. After the Great War, Turkey was prostrate. There too despair had spawned a Communist Party. That country also had a most effective head of state, Mustapha Kemal, whose dynamism often assumed brutal forms. For example, in one instance, he drove a band of suspected Communists on board a ferryboat and had them dumped into the Sea of Marmara, which, with tragic irony, was the very center of the chain of the Straits the Russians have always craved. This done, Kemal signed a treaty of friendship with the Soviets for twenty years. More than that, the U.S.S.R. was the first country to help the Turks start their modest program of industrialization, to help them get strong. Again, while these moves strengthened the diplomacy of the Soviet empire and made the Russians feel more secure on that flank, they weakened communism's missionary zeal. In subsequent moves, never did Soviet policy sacrifice national interests to ideology.

NATIONALIST HISTORY

The assumption until recently was, as indicated briefly in the historical narrative, that the foundation of the Kievan city-state, out of which mighty Russia grew, had been the work of the Scandinavian Varangians. The event was clearly recorded in the ninth century *Primary Chronicle* of the eastern Slavs, a basic source. "Our land is great and rich," the local chieftains are reported to have said, "but it lacks order. Come to rule and reign over us!" The

Scandinavians went and ruled under their native chief, Rurik. They took along their rudimentary jurisprudence, their arts and letters, their ways of life. They were a minority, and in the course of time the "blood brothers" were absorbed by the Slavic majority.

This version of history, which had been good enough for the Czars, was not good enough for the Commissars. Since it seemed to assume that the Slavs were inferior to the Scandinavians, it was not nationalistic enough for the "internationalists." Today there is a compelling collection of Soviet literature to prove that Kiev's founders were indigenous Slavs. This literature seeks to show that authentic Scandinavian words are very few in Russian, that old Russian terms pertaining to navigation were Greek, that those dealing with trade were Oriental and native Slavic, not Scandinavian, and that written literature in Kiev preceded written literature in Scandinavia. Soviet historians have taken great pains to show the scantiness of Scandinavian contributions to Russian law. They also have sought to prove that there is no evidence of the Northlanders' influence on Kievan pre-Christian "animism." Their linguistic analysis of the names of the East Slavic gods seeks to reveal a variety of cultural links, none of them with Scandinavia. Significant is the fact that this form of cultural nationalism has been introduced into historical research by the Soviets, and not by the preceding regimes.

Today the national heroes of the Czarist regime have become those of the Soviets also. This is so not only in books of history but—and above all—in popularizations, particularly in films. Historic films in Russia are as common as "westerns" are in the United States. In some cases, of course, the heroes have been re-interpreted and redecorated.

A typical case is that of Alexander Nevsky, Prince of

Novgorod, immortalized by the film of the same title by Sergei Eisenstein. This is how history knows the Prince. He was only twenty when he defeated the invading Swedes on the banks of the Neva in 1240, while the crusading order of the Teutonic knights had begun their advance on Russian lands. Alexander turned against them, and the crucial battle took place on April 5, 1242, on Lake Peipus. This being in Northland, the lake was still heavily covered with ice. Like an enormous battering ram, the massed forces of the mail-clad German knights struck at the Russian lines, which began to sag, but held long enough for Alexander Nevsky to execute an enveloping movement, assailing the flank of the foe. The Teutonic knights were routed, and in the monumental rush the spring ice cracked under their massive weight.

The battles Alexander fought were against Christians who, to be sure, were not part of the Orthodox branch of the Catholic faith. But, he too, considering himself the champion of Christ, did not fight the Mongols, who were "pagans." He was canonized by the Orthodox Church— Saint Alexander Nevsky. In spite of his championship of the Orthodox faith, he has been "canonized" by Soviet nationalism, too. As an historic Russian hero, he is a member of the Soviet pantheon, the Christian cross and all.

To the Soviets, Ivan the Terrible is no longer a monster. Today he is known as Ivan the Fourth, whose monstrous acts are glossed over, and he is venerated in Soviet texts as the sovereign who set Russia on the road toward a global expansion. The unification of Russia and not the demented personal life of Ivan is the main subject of another Eisenstein film classic. He is shown as a man of great singleness of purpose, a great and therefore lonely man. After having committed acts of unspeakable cruelty, he wanted to resign, the film shows, but was induced to

remain by the prayerful appeal of his people. He was
capricious, but so was heaven. Why else should the fields
be smitten with blight in the face of the ardent prayers of
the dedicated community? Part of the expansionist age of
Moscow, Ivan the Terrible, too, has been canonized by the
Soviets' nation-centered history.

Other "heroes" of exalted and less exalted lineage have
become venerable figures of Soviet texts and mass media.
Some of the Soviet heroes include even Russian churchmen who made their mark under the sign of the cross.
One of these is Patriarch Hermogen, a forceful person,
who fought the Poles. The time of troubles was the period
during which he acted, at the beginning of the seventeenth century. At that time the Kremlin was in the hands
of the Poles, and chaos reigned in the countryside, which
was scourged by famine and plague. It seemed as if the
country were falling apart. Then came the salvation,
wrought through the intercession of Princes of the
Church, who are the Soviets' heroes today. Patriarch
Hermogen was supported by Abbot Dionysus of the
national sanctuary, Holy Trinity-Saint Sergius Monastery.
The people responded to the call of the cross to resist the
Poles, also fighting under the sign of the cross.

Soviet history tells the story proudly. A crusader army
of the true Orthodox was set afoot against the "infidel"
Poles, who were Catholics, as the classes and the masses
found a common ground. Representing the classes was
Prince Dmitri Pozharsky, a veteran warrior, the incarnation of patriotism, the manifestation of crusading Moscow.
The masses were represented by Kuzma Minin, a butcher.
In the crusading army he was the treasurer-quarter-
master, the voice and conscience of the people. The
obviously virtuous Muscovites defeated the obviously
"monstrous" Poles. This was not the last time Russians
and Poles were at odds.

Another Soviet hero is Bogdan Chmielnicki. In mid-
seventeenth century he took his Slav Ukrainians into the
Russian Czar's camp. Under the Soviets, the Ukraine is
the second most important component republic, next to
Russia. Again the country had been on the verge of falling
apart, and again it was saved miraculously under the
sign of the cross. It was the symbol of the nation, and
national symbols of the past are dear to Soviet hearts
today.

Peter the Great would seem to lack qualifications for a
place in the Soviets' "hall of fame," since he was the very
embodiment of the spirit that the imperial order breathed.
But he strengthened the Czarist regime that endured for
another two centuries, and the Czarist regime was Russia.
To the Soviets he is the "Renovator," a proud figure in the
history of a proud nation. Perhaps Peter's record reminds
them of their own uncommon feat. With his superhuman
strength he shouldered Russia's burden, all its millions of
square miles, and shifted Russia closer to the modern
world. The Soviets did the same, as they see their historic
role. Strange as it may seem to us, the Kremlin sees an
affinity between Lenin the Commissar and Peter the Czar.

Czarist army leaders as Soviet heroes seem to be incongruous, at first blush, especially if their fame rests partly
on crushing popular revolts. But they were Russians, and
the revolters often were not—hence the regilded fame.
Field Marshal Count Aleksander Vasilyevich Suvorov is
such a nationalist Soviet hero. He crushed the uprising of
the Poles and Russian rebels with a cruelty that recalled
those of Genghis Khan. He fought the revolutionary
armies of France at the end of the eighteenth century. In
spite of all this, he is enshrined in the Soviet pantheon.
History produced no more loyal servant of the Czars than
Mikhail Ilarionovich Kutuzov, Prince of Smolensk. Yet it
can be said without much exaggeration that, but for

Lenin, few people have received more adulation from the Soviets than he.

His destruction of Napoleon's erstwhile *Grande Armée* in 1812 has been picturialized in several Soviet classics of the screen, particularly the fabulous seven-hour-long *War and Peace*. A field marshal of Alexander I, Emperor and Autocrat of all the Russians, he was the member of the most exalted social class, himself the son of a general of military engineering. Soviet historians cannot say enough of Kutuzov's historic roles. To top it all off, the Kutuzov Medal is among the highest military decorations of the U.S.S.R., and so are the Orders of Suvorov and Nevsky.

Thus, historic names of the Czarist regime have become the Soviets' heroes. Historic terms that were at first taboo in the internationalist stage of the Soviets, too parochially nationalistic, have been restored to places of high honor, as, for instance, *otechestvo,* the fatherland, the term for the native land, *rodina,* and the concept behind it, *sviashchenniya.* The glories of Holy Czarist Russia and of the Holy Soviet Union have become fused in an indissoluble, inextricable whole.

THE GREAT PATRIOTIC WAR

The greatest war in history it was, a real global conflict, with more casualties than in all previous holocausts. By what designation should it be known to posterity? The answer to this question was to be found by writers and statesmen. One of the statesmen was also one of the greatest phrase-coiners of the English language—Winston Churchill. In the end, it was agreed that its name should be World War II. It is the despair of man that words—especially names of great disasters—cannot be launched on tidal waves of emotions.

For the Soviet Union, however, it was not to be World
War II. The Kremlin needed a "tidal wave" designation;
the people were craving a name to express their emotions.
The Third International was still in existence; at the same
time, the Soviets were members of a world-wide alliance.
But the Kremlin people saw only their own country, and
that Mother Russia was in mortal danger, its sacred soil
despoiled. They did coin an emotionally charged term—
the Great Patriotic War. And this in a land dedicated to
internationalism.

"Comrades, Compatriots, Men and Women . . ." the
leader of embattled Russia, Stalin, addressed his countrymen. In the Western nationalist world the word "compatriots" would have sounded out of tune. Moscow was in
danger of being overrun. By a near miracle, it was saved.
In charge of its defenses was Georgi Konstantinovich
Zhukov. In other countries purple-patch, description-
loving journalists might have described him as a "hero."
In the Communist Soviet Union he was exalted as the
Spasitel, "Savior," of Moscow. "Hero," "heroic," "heroism"
were common words in the Soviets. "All our forces for the
support of our heroic Red Army and our glorious Red
Navy," Stalin exhorted his countrymen in a typical
phrase. "All forces of the people for the demolition of the
enemy! Forward, to our Victory!"

For an endless spell of time the course was backward,
to defeat. The reeling giant, Russia, one-sixth of the land
surface of the globe, was about to fall. Then the destiny of
the despoilers of Russia moved into reverse. This time,
patriotic harangues were superfluous. People rallied to the
defense of their Mother, Holy Russia, the consecrated
community, as they had done many times in their history.
They brought Hitler's presumably invincible war machine
to a halt on the banks of Russia's River of Sorrow, the
Volga, at Stalingrad. In addition to the regular army,

guerrillas began to sprout from the vernal soil behind the enemy lines. If caught, they were subjected to unspeakable torture, but that did not matter. Immense was the price the Russians paid for the defense of their *Mater dolorosa*. Again, as always in the past, patriotism was mixed with religion—the Russians' special brand of creed. The Communist's internationalism vanished out of sight. The Moscow International was dissolved.

RELIGION — A NEW PHASE

"In Russia, religion is the stimulant of the people," the Communists said under their breaths during the "Great Patriotic War," revising the famous axiom of Marx. They could not overlook any of the instruments to stimulate the patriotic fervor of their countrymen. The country's historic religion was one of these.

For over a generation they had sought to instill atheism into the younger generation, at school, through their unceasing propaganda, in the mass media, and, above all, on the screen and stage. The League of the Militant Godless had been brainwashing the people of the Soviets for decades. For the stalwart upholders of the pre-revolution ideology there was the "living church," the creation of the "innovators," in juxtaposition with the traditional Orthodox *ecclesia*, presumed to be the "dead church." In the traditional church, state and creed had mutually sanctified each other, inextricably intertwined, Russia equalling the church, and the church equalling Russia. In the living church the Soviets were the new *ecclesia*, no longer a mere promise, but the fulfillment of a blissful life, not in heaven but on earth—Paradise won.

Yet during the Great Patriotic War it was not to the

pseudo-religion that the authorities turned. They went to
Canossa, on the doorstep of the traditional Orthodox
Church. It was the pre-revolutionary church, built upon
the rock, Petrus, the Holy Russia of Peter the Great. It is
true though that meanwhile the "Rock" had been cut down
to size and become merely the "rock." Though it was
reduced in size, the Communist leaders called upon it
to help save their "Holy Land," the dwelling place of
the consecrated *sobornost*. Religion became respectable
again, and was spared further persecution.

Victory came to Russia at an exorbitant price. More
than twenty million people were missing; it had been the
greatest holocaust in history. The "black earth" of the
Ukraine was white with human bones, a charnel house.
What was going to happen to the Orthodox Church, now
that its stimulation for the war effort was not needed?
After all, opposition to religion was the "religion" of communism.

This is what happened: Emilian Yaroslavsky, president
of the League of the Militant Godless, felt compelled to
complain that two-thirds of the villagers and one-third of
the townspeople of the Soviets were still believers, and
this in spite of the fact that the government still lent its
hand to antichurch propaganda, although brutal persecution had ceased. Much publicity was given to the snide
statement of the first Soviet cosmonaut, the late Yuri
Gagarin: "In my journey through heaven, I have seen
neither God nor a single angel." Churchgoers were still
barred from Communist Party membership.

A new wave of nationalism had brought back the
church as an institution of eternal Russia. Church domes
remained the landmarks, especially in Moscow. Laborers
were at work restoring decrepit churches, their mosaics
and art work, regilding onion-shaped domes. Photogenic
St. Basil's in Moscow's Red Square was spic and span,
ready for the tourists' cameras. It was a tourist "must."

"Every ikon corner is a church," the prelate confided, and who could count them? The church organization was alive and on display. The patriarchate of Moscow—"The Vatican of the Russian Orthodox Church"—was now housed in the stately building that used to be the German Embassy. It was a busy place, visited by ecclesiastics and delegations from everywhere. Farmers and their wives, for instance, came to ask church authorities to let them keep their priests, about to be transferred to new posts. A bearded priest, passing through the large antechamber, was quickly surrounded by the villagers, who kissed his hand and asked his blessing.

At the same time, the Orthodox Church had been placed under diverse departments, for "protection," and also, no doubt, for surveillance: the Office of the Administration of Patriarchal Affairs; Office of External Relations; Directive Committee of Theological Education; Committee for Pensions; Publishing Service; Material and Supply Office.

Still, after all those years of martyrdom, there was the Orthodox Church, part of historic Russia. At the time of the fiftieth anniversary of the Soviet republic, Alexius, the Patriarch of all Russias, still a holdover from before the revolution, was ninety years old. He was supported by the Synod, which had dropped the attribute "Holy." The jurisdiction of these authorities still extended over 73 dioceses, governed by 7 metropolitans, 37 archbishops and a large number of bishops. There were still some 20,000 parishes, also some 3,000 chapels, 69 monasteries and convents. This left tens of thousands of communities of practising Russian Orthodox communicants. There were about 33,000 priests, 5,000 monks and nuns. But there were millions of consecrated ikon corners in the Russian consecrated land.

Perhaps the greatest compliment to the religious feelings of the Russians after half a century of Communist rule may be found in atheist propaganda complaints, as, for instance, this comment in a Ukrainian magazine:

Today we are still lulling ourselves with the illusion that many believers in our country have left their religion and the church. This is sheer self-deception. While over a large part of the territory of the Soviet Union there are no churches and no preachers, there still are believers. Cutting off access to the churches did not turn them into atheists. On the contrary, it seems to have strengthened peoples' leanings toward religion, while it embitters their hearts, to boot.

Russia has been Communist for only a little more than half a century, and Orthodox for a thousand years. The lives of countless generations were conditioned by the teachings, the art and history of the Church. Many of the Russian classics have reflected the influence of the Church by mirroring the people's lives. To many members of an entire generation these references to the ancestors' creed convey no meaning. Since the Church and state formed a "united front" in the past, many people today do not know the full history of their country because they are unfamiliar with its Orthodox creed. That is why the noted Soviet author of children's books Kornei I. Chukhovsky has been commissioned by the authorities to prepare a series of books of Bible stories for children. "It seems to me," he commented, "that our Soviet children who confront Biblical stories constantly in galleries, museums, and books should finally be able to get acquainted with them." Thus, the national history of religion is reaching children in a devious way.

While co-existing with the Russian Orthodox Church, the Communist Party has not abandoned hope of finding a substitute. If religion is the opium of the people from their point of view, what is their nectar? The Soviets are experimenting with a Code of Morality, incorporated in the 1966 Program of the Communist Party of the U.S.S.R.

It contains what have been called the "Twelve Commandments" of the Communist, among them devotion to the cause; conscientious labor for the good of society; sense of public duty; comradely reciprocal assistance; mutual respect; uncompromising opposition to injustice, greed, dishonesty and "careerism"; brotherhood among all the Soviet republics, combined with opposition to racial and national hatred; uncompromising opposition to the Communists' foes; and fraternal solidarity with the working people of all lands, to take the place of "brotherly love."

The substance of the twelve commandments is that man is a communal creature and should act in that sense. As a "loner" he is devoid of the basic traits of man, and he becomes human only in his social setting. "As he lit his famous lamp," the Russian writer Askold Shalayev commented on the commandments, "Diogenes set out in search of an honest man. Honesty is the substance of the Code of Morality. Perhaps the West would do better in comprehending the 'Russian soul,' if it knew that in search of the humanness of Man, the Soviets are determined to find the object of Diogenes' search."

The Communist twelve commandments make no mention, of course, of a supernatural God. Yet the very fact that these commandments have been framed points to the roots of Russian bolshevism in the national past. In presenting this program, the Kremlin has sought to re-establish contact, tenuous though it may be, with its historic *sobornost*.

A curious case of survival of religious feeling in the land was reported in the Soviet press in the spring of 1968. Involved in the affair were some sixty individuals, including university teachers, engineers, scientists, all members of the intelligentsia. They were active followers of an "All Russian Social-Christian Union for the Liberation of the People." Their program was a mixture of incongruous elements—incongruous, that is, everywhere

except in Russia. In politics, Union members advocated a
presidential form of government based on free elections to
a parliament. In economics, they espoused socialism, in
which the state would retain full ownership in heavy
industry only. The President and the assembly of this
renovated Soviet regime were to be subject to the control
of representatives of the Holy Russian Orthodox Church.
Several members of the group were apprehended, tried,
and convicted to long terms in labor camps.

What could be more Russian than this weird plot? The
plotters wanted to retain "socialism," the local term for
"communism." This communist system was, in turn, subject to the control of the Russian Orthodox Church. This,
after more than half a century of anti-religious propaganda! The intellectual plotters, evidently, decided to
ignore the reality of the recent past and to concentrate on
the Russian "eternity," the "Holy Orthodox Catholic Apostolic Eastern Church," instrument of an aspiration and
thus more real than reality, the incarnation of the consecrated community, *sobornost*. It was to thrive under a
communist economic system.

In the nationalist revival of Soviet communism, the
historic Orthodox Church still plays a role. Persecuted,
chastened, its wings clipped, it has turned out to be too
much a part of the Russian's personality to be completely
crushed. Eye-witness accounts of the advanced age of the
members of the congregations tell only a part of the story,
a very small part. Millions of Russian homes have remained private chapels with their ikon corners. The idea
is not yet dead that Eastern Orthodox and Russian are
interchangeable terms and that the true believers are
members of the historic "consecrated community,"
sobornost.

The much-noted neo-anti-Semitism in the Soviets is
largely the product of the resurgence of this aspect of

nationalism. In a community in which Orthodox Christian and Russian meant the same, the Jew was always an outsider, an "unconsecrated" person, and, therefore, an alien, a foe.

Russians born into the Jewish faith have played historic roles in the Soviets. That was during the "international" period of the country's history, when the Orthodox faith apparently had been all but stamped out. With the resurgence of nationalism, the Orthodox faith has staged its partial comeback and with it has returned the identification of Russianism with Orthodoxism. This, in turn, has revived the historical exclusivity of the Russian within the sanctuary of the Orthodox creed. The Jew, not of the "true faith," has been rejected as he was under the Czarist regime. This is a serious drawback of the restored link between nationalism and the spirit of *sobornost.*

6

"The Happy Science"

Communism was to eliminate the exploitation of man by man. Its pivotal point was economics—the mode of production, to use a term of Marx. The government was the people organized for the performance of specific tasks. By eliminating exploitation, the social stresses were removed—no sharecroppers at one extreme, and no Rockefellers at the other. This would be economic democracy—the basic democracy. From it would follow political democracy, naturally and inevitably. Social democracy would follow, too, not immediately, nor spontaneously. Social institutions are tradition-founded, and therefore change-resistant. But they would fall in line, eventually. This would be integrated democracy—the genuine one. "Dismal science" was the name attached to economics since the days of the Reverend Thomas Robert Malthus, who saw a race between the food supply and the people, in which the latter were to lose.

Yes, said the Communists, they were bound to lose if the conditions under which the Reverend Malthus lived were to continue. That was not to happen, however, under communism, in which the food supply and every other supply would cease to remain in greedy private hands and were to be transferred to the community. In communal hands the supplies were to increase to satisfy all needs. There were to be no occasions to withhold goods from the markets so as to increase profits. Economics was to become "the happy science."

"The surplus value" was the *bête-noire* according to communism, the part the capitalist retained for himself from the laborer's wages. It caused the accumulation of wealth, the social stresses, political oppression, and "slave labor." It was the original sin. Under the Communist system there was to be no such short-changing of labor, and the working man was to get the worth of his toil. The "law of value" was to prevail, as the price of goods and services was to represent monetized labor. No more thieving from the worker, and no more exploitation.

Wages had been the only return on production, and nothing more. Life was not to be as under capitalism. No rent to the landlord, the arch-exploiter who expropriates the gifts of nature. There were to be no landlords.

There was to be no interest to the capitalist, because there were to be no capitalists in a Communist commonwealth. Capital was to be the result of the accumulation of productive factors of a certain type needed for social purposes. And, above all, there was to be no profit, except for the community. There was to be no individual entrepreneur, no "profitariat," battening on the proletariat.

Communal production was to be more economical than private enterprise. There was to be no competition, because there were to be no business rivals. In the absence of such rivalry, there was to be no need of an endless series of ancillary services. There was to be no high-pressure advertising with its built-in exaggerations and duplicities. There were to be no intermediaries in the distribution of products, the entire gamut of superfluous services, from the producer downward by way of the wholesaler, the jobber, the retailer, with their hangers-on. In advanced capitalist countries far more money was spent on selling than on producing.

Nor were there to be private monopolies. There was to be one source of production, to be sure, and capitalist economists called this monopolistic production. But that, in Communist countries, was for the public benefit and not for its exploitation.

Above all, there was to be the *Gosplan*, the planning agency, the key to what the Communists expected to be their success. It was to show the world how much more effective and less expensive their mode of production was. With the *Gosplan* they were to win the world. It was to be shown that planning for production on the national level would introduce a new dimension into the life of the nations: work for all, unemployment for none, goods and services within the reach of all, no rich, no poor. Yes, no rich, because wealth is power, and that entails corruption. The ultimate aim: equality.

It did not work out that way. The rich were no more, but the poor were everywhere. There were the explanations—lots of them. The beginning was always hard, people were told. The Soviets had to start on a low plateau. Had life been better for the British worker during the first Industrial Revolution? Americans would not speak English if that revolution had not been cruelly hard. Perhaps there would be no New World either. There would have been no British immigrants.

Had life been better for Americans during the second Industrial Revolution? Look at the ghettos of the fabulous country, with its slum areas—far more slums than decent dwelling districts. Look at the American South, with its "tobacco roads," with its poverty-stricken areas within nodding distance of the twenty-first century.

And the third Industrial Revolution, the fabulous one, which enriched the world with the marvels of chemistry

—the one in Germany. Again the United States was the witness, with its millions of citizens of German descent. America had its slums, but its dinner pails were less empty than those of the working people of the Reich.

So, this was the explanation for the slow progress; at any rate, it was one of the explanations, and there were many others. The Soviets had to lift themselves out of position zero by their own bootstraps. No help was available for them from anywhere, as there had been for Czarist Russia. They were pariahs, considered to be outside the pale of the human community.

Then there was the human equation—perhaps the most important factor. The gnarled *muzhik* hands had not been prepared for the fine work of millionth parts of a millimeter of tolerance. A new generation had to be trained in new skills of the computer, *sputnik,* and nuclear energy.

The war, too, set the Soviets back immeasurably, causing havoc that would be compared only with that brought about by the Mongol "Golden Horde." So fantastic was the destruction that the Soviets revealed only parts of its details, for fear of encouraging new enmity aimed at their destruction. The full scale of devastation was divulged only after the Soviets had felt their life forces coursing. Some twenty million Russians were missing, most of them cut down in the full bloom of their youth.

NEW HORIZONS

"Millions of starving, ignorant, brainwashed Russians" appeared on the screens of the mental images of the people in the West, especially in America. To state that the Russians were no longer so ignorant and starving was equated with disloyalty to democracy. Then, a dozen years after the war, a new image of the Soviets floated within the vision of the West—the Sputnik. It showed the Russians ahead of Americans in one of the most complex fields of space exploration. America's age of innocence relating to Russia was over.

Visitors to Russia reported, though, that the people there did not look too well—many of them seemed to be overweight. But they were not starving. America, always inclined to saturation techniques, now found it to its advantage to engage in a massive study of the U.S.S.R. Soon the shelves of libraries were groaning under the countless volumes about that puzzling land. Has anything been overlooked about its ways? Its economic life was placed under the most highly polished magnifying glasses. The *Gosplan* was in the center of attention. How was that strange planned economy doing? Was the Soviet Union "overtaking and surpassing" America, as it had proclaimed?

The annual rate of growth of its industries in mid-century was found to be 10 percent; about three times higher than in the United States. This time the rate of growth was no longer computed from the narrow base of an underdeveloped nation. Still, obviously, the Soviets were decades behind the United States, which had entered an era of prosperity that broke all previous known records, perhaps the records of all times. Here, then, was the paradox. The economic "anarchy" of the capitalist world was still doing much better than the "orderly" procedures of the planned economy.

Planned economy was, of course, at the core of communism. It was not only the basic economic tenet of the regime, but also a dogma, an article of faith. After the death of Premier Joseph Stalin, however, a questioner and iconoclast, Nikita S. Khrushchev, ascended the party peak.

He questioned the methods, not the principle of planning. Was it possible for a country as large and highly industrialized as Russia to have every step of its economic work prescribed in one big building in Moscow's Gorky Street, headquarters of *Gosplan*? After having asked the question, he provided the answer: "Planning, *da;* integrated planning, *nyet.*" More than a hundred regional planning branches were established, therefore. They were familiar with local problems, and did not leave everything for the Gorky Street pilot-tower. Did the system work? Khrushchev said *da;* the others said *mozhet byt*—perhaps. They said that because they did not dare to say *nyet;* yet nobody was particularly happy with the experiment. Khrushchev lasted until the autumn of 1964, and then new men came in, ready to listen to new ideas.

THE PROFIT SYSTEM IN COMMUNISM

The thinking process may have begun before him, but it was a professor of economics, Yevsei Liberman, who became the father of the "revolutionary" new Soviet economics, with his book *Ways of Raising the Profitability of Socialist Enterprises*. Or was it a "counterrevolutionary" new Soviet economics? The work and the man made history, and the dictionary was enriched with a new word: "Libermanism." What was it?

Under the old systems, quotas of products were set for thousands of items at headquarters. Those quotas were established in anticipation of market demands, the needs as the planners saw them. Certain products formed parts of political indoctrination, and they were "needed." Books were needed, because they carried useful technical information or desirable doctrine. Therefore books were produced in large quantities. Their prices were set low—very low, according to our standards. Radios were needed because they transmitted propaganda. The prices of radios were low too.

Above all, housing was needed. Russia had been an "all-or-nothing" country under the old regime: the land of massive *palazzi* for the few and of ghetto dwellings for the majority. She had been a peasant country and became an industrial nation, and so housing was needed for the gigantic population influx into towns. Rents were set very low. The prices of social services were set at zero: medicine was completely socialized.

The people who streamed into the towns changed their social status and would have liked to flaunt it in the clothes they wore. But the regime assigned very low priority to clothing. As long as the people's bodies were covered, everything else was considered luxury. One suit would do for several years. Accordingly, the prices of garments were set high. And so on, up and down the line.

The managers of factories under this system operated to protect themselves. Since planning was a dogma they had to uphold, their main concern was to fulfill the production quotas. If they sold their goods, that was fine, and they had no storage problem. If they did not sell them, that was all right, too, since their quota had been fulfilled. They still received their promotions and more prestigious official cars, and their portraits were emblazoned in the mass media as "Heroes of Soviet Labor." Of course, they had the problem of storing the unsold goods.

Libermanism took its stand against this anomaly. "Often the enterprises concerned themselves primarily with increasing gross volume of output," said Liberman, "since their performance was judged above all by that and not by the amount of output sold."

After a while the Soviets entered the world market and

found that in spite of their "orderly" planning they were
not competitive, because they had been too orderly, producing according to unrealistic plans that had no yard-
stick. Yet such a measuring rod was needed. What was it
to be? Professor Liberman had the courage to utter the
term: the profit system.

Production should be for profit, he said, as simple as all
that. Since the planning bodies on their lofty perch on
Moscow's Gorky Street could not possibly work out profit-
producing programs for thousands of units, the final
decision would have to be left to the individual producing
units, just as in any capitalist country, with this difference, though: there was to be a broad overall plan on the
highest level, into which the individual plant projects
had to be fitted. Also, only the general wage scales and
prices were to be indicated by headquarters, leaving a
certain leeway to the producing units.

"Success in competition [with the West]," Liberman
continued, "could not be gained by the old method of
administrative and excessively centralized management."
It was necessary to change it so as to give the enterprises
themselves a material stake in the better utilization of
their assets and in providing the best possible service to
their consumers. To do this the enterprises had to be
relieved of the "excessive number of planned targets
. . ."

This all showed the way to the prophet of free enterprise, Adam Smith, and to the invisible hand of the
gendarme of capitalism, the purchaser. That hand kept
the economic system on the go, giving the green signal for
the production of goods it needed and flashing the red
signal to halt work on programs it did not need. Communism, by way of Libermanism, has made a momentous
discovery—known to countless generations—the law of
supply and demand.

Out of that law, profits were to grow, as in the capitalist world, and out of the profits, lots of things would grow, such as bonuses to the workers and to the management, reserves for future operations, funds for augmented social benefits, savings and tax payments for the government.

The Liberman plan went into effect in stages. About 5,500 factories were working under it by 1968, producing one-third of the Soviet industrial output. The other Communist countries followed the Russian lead. Poland grouped 2,700 key industrial enterprises into 130 associations, patterned on cartels; even the least industrialized country of the group, Bulgaria, turned to the autonomy of industrial enterprises. The Socialist bloc had moved away from dogmatic communism.

AND THE WEST?

While the Communist countries were shifting the emphasis from central to decentralized planning, the capitalist countries were moving in the opposite direction. John Kenneth Galbraith, in his best-selling book *The New Industrial State* had this to say:

"In the industrial enterprise, power rests with those who make the decisions. In the mature enterprise, this power has passed, inevitably and irrevocably, from the individual to the group." The new industrial state, according to him, was dominated by the supercorporation under the control of management (*Technostructure*), which plans the economy. This was caused by the highly sophisticated mechanism of modern industry, and characterized all modern economies using this technology. Galbraith said that now there may be less planning and more autonomy in the Soviet firm than in the American supercorporation. Full social authority by the stockholders, he said, was proclaimed in the United States. But who was the owner of General Electric, with its hundreds of thousands of stockholders? In the Soviet Union the party was paramount. But in practice it was the corporations that said the final word. "Galbraith sees a convergence between capitalist and Communist economies despite their opposing ideologies," the critics commented.

In their analysis of political power in the U.S.A. and U.S.S.R., Zbigniew Brzezinski and Samuel P. Huntington extended the analogy to the political systems. "Already there are signs that Soviet ideology and the Soviet system are less compatible. In fact, the Soviet leaders are showing signs of apprehension that in its own terms their ideology makes the party dictatorship in the Soviet system obsolescent. . . ." It is the managers who operate the levers that, according to Marxist doctrine, determine the social and economic pattern of society. And their power is constantly on the increase.

In this context, the following words from Toynbee, who has taken an ecumenical view of world events, are relevant: "From the standpoint of the employee, it is coming to make less and less practical difference what his country's official ideology is and whether he happens to be employed by a government or a commercial corporation."

THE COMECON

Among the capitalist countries there are international cartels. What about the Communist countries? Even though their economic systems are undergoing a change, the very nature of their operations would make it desirable for them to engage in specialization. Some of them may be well advanced in building heavy machines, while others would be good in producing precision instruments.

Internationalism was the theoretical framework of communism, and economics was its pivotal point. International-regional economics was on the agenda of the European Economic Community. The United States operated economically within a global framework, its financial bases scattered all over the world, in the form of direct investments in raw materials, plants, production, distribution, and sales. Economics was one of the arms of the Cold War, too.

The Communist countries—or Socialist countries, as they like to be called—had prime qualifications for international economic integration. Planning was the pivot of their economic existence, and international planning was its crux.

At first, however, several of them practiced bilateralism: joint companies in which the satellites teamed up with the Soviets. Naturally, the latter got the most out of these companies. It was against such exploitation and other sharp Kremlin practices that Tito rebelled. The Yugoslav defection weakened the hold of the joint concerns, and after Stalin's death they became moribund. The Hungarian uprising finally put them out of their misery. Still, *bona fide* integration might have made sense. Since the Socialist-bloc countries were ideologically related "fraternal" nations, why not strengthen their hands through systematic distribution of labor, drawing benefits from the "law of comparative advantages," as the economists call this type of planning?

The Soviets wanted such cooperation among the Socialist countries. But . . . there was the big *but*. These countries were suspicious of the Soviets. They had had experiences with the bilateral agreements. Crafty Khrushchev, at the helm, assured the fraternal countries: "This

is going to be different. This time, you will call the tune
and all of us will benefit." He recommended setting up
a supranational organization, Council for Mutual Economic Assistance, CMEA, which was to be known as
Comecon.

To assure the fraternal countries that the Soviets had
no designs to dominate the field, the exploratory conference was called in Budapest. The year was 1955, a singularly inauspicious one. Next year the streets of Budapest
became battlefields, and the time was most inappropriate
for fraternal back-slapping. A lot of water had to flow
down the Danube before confidence returned.

Two more years passed, and another meeting took
place. The conclusion arrived at was that the problem of
integration presented great difficulties because each of the
potential members had its own economic development
rate, traditional ways, technical and manpower problems.
Yet the composition of the organization *in spe* was decided
upon. The members were the Soviet Union, Poland,
Czechoslovakia, Hungary, East Germany, Rumania, and
Bulgaria. Mongolia was an observer at first and later a
member.

Another two years passed, and it was now 1960, and
another meeting took place. This one framed the statutes
of the Comecon. The final product did not gladden
Khrushchev's heart. It provided for the unconditional sovereignty of the component states. The Kremlin was not to
control the Comecon even by remote control. More than
that, each member retained the right to veto, and unanim-
ity was to be the rule.

Khrushchev was not the man to give up easily. Meanwhile, in the West, the European Economic Community
had made great strides toward becoming a truly supranational organ. It was, of course, American-oriented, and
the Soviets assumed that its success strengthened their op-

position. The Socialist countries were still disunited, facing two great monoliths. They had to try again.

Another Comecon meeting was called; it met in June 1962. It was a summit conference that produced a set of principles. The Russians liked to designate historic events with the names of months. There was the Decembrist Revolution early last century, the October Manifesto early this century. There were the April Theses of Lenin. The label attached to the result of the 1962 summit meeting was the "June Principles." It was only its name that seemed to wear the Soviet hallmark. The June Principles again stressed "voluntarism," the complete independence and national sovereignty of the member countries. At the same time a planning board and an executive committee were established, the latter manned by deputy premiers or their equivalents in charge of economic development.

In 1964 a Comecon Bank was established. It created a new accounting currency, known as the transfer ruble. The object of the Bank was to "balance the turnover of each participant of the multilateral cooperation."

Certain measures were taken to bring about the economic integration of the group members. Some of these were: a railway freight-car pool, in which all members of the group participated; Intermetal, a metallurgical combine, confined at the outset to Rumania, Hungary, Poland, and Czechoslovakia; an electric power grid, described as "an immense step toward strengthening the supply system of the area," which brought the western Ukraine, Poland, Hungary, East Germany, Czechoslovakia, Rumania, and Bulgaria under the same umbrella. The Soviet's Friendship Oil Pipeline extended from Russia's terminal station of Kuibyshev into the Communists' northern tier—Poland, Czechoslovakia, East Germany, and Hungary. Industrial output in the area increased dramatically. In 1966 it was close to ten times that of 1939, and the

average industrial rate of growth for all of these countries
was 10 percent a year. All of this was impressive, but it
was not the work of Comecon.

For the future there were additional plans. There was
the plan of the Danube-Oder-Elbe canal, linked up with
the Vistula, too, providing direct river transportation between the North and Black seas. It was to be begun in
1971 and completed in 1978. There was also an ambitious
Danubian power-plant program to be implemented between Bratislava and Mohács, to be completed in 1980.

While the countries wanted to get industrialized, and
they did, they did not want to become physiologically
united "Kremlin septuplets." They were nationalist first
and Communist second. Particularly opposed to full integration were the nations at the outset of their industrial
careers. Bulgaria, normally docile in heeding the Kremlin's word, wanted to have little to do with the concept of
comparative costs. Being inadequately industrialized, her
"advantages" would have kept her from full development.
Rumania's First Secretary of the Communist Party declared good and loud that she was going her way regard-
less of any comparisons. The Rumanian economic journal
Viata Economica took up the cudgel against a Kremlin
trial balloon in the form of an article in the magazine of
Moscow University by its professor of economic geography, E. B. Valev. The "Valev thesis" was a sophisticated
form of economic geography linking northern Bulgaria
with southern Rumania and southwesternmost Ukraine, a
region extending inland from the Black Sea, from Odessa
to Varna, by way of Constanta, with common interests in
maritime transportation and complementary mining, industrial, and agricultural bases. These three regions, economically integrated, would impart to it a higher
standard, the Russian sought to show. The Rumanian
economic journal's outraged shriek was heard all the way

to the Kremlin; Rumania wanted no part of such integrations. *Izvestia,* the Soviet government's news organ, had to hasten to disavow Professor Valev's ambitious thesis. "Revolutionary" countries can be most conservative when their economic interests are threatened.

Even Czechoslovakia, a very compactly industrialized country of the bloc, disliked the idea of the Comecon. And this in spite of the fact that the Czechs might have benefited from its operation economically, supplying the less industrialized Socialist countries with their wide variety of goods and getting raw materials in return. With the backing of the government, Otto Sik, the director of the Institute of Economics of the Academy of Sciences of Prague, went all the way in opposition to the Comecon. He proposed to abandon the entire central planning in production, applying it only in forecasting market conditions and laying down development trends. Hungary, another low-key country in opposing Kremlin advice, uttered a fervent "amen" to the statements of the more boisterous Czechs. She was not going to abandon her economic independence either.

There was a measure of give and take within the bloc, of course, in this respect too. The Hungarians, who had a world-wide market for their buses and could have turned also to the production of passenger automobiles, preferred to buy their cars from such established producers as the Soviets and the Czechs. In doing so, the comparative advantage was on their side. All in all, the Comecon and its bank played no important role in the economic integration the Soviets would have welcomed.

So here was the paradox. Within the nation-centered, capitalistic West, integration was proceeding apace. The European Economic Community—the Common Market— was working well. It was credited, at least in part, with the "European economic miracle" of full employment, which necessitated the import of massive doses of foreign labor, and a standard of living that surpassed all the previous records of all the previous ages.

The Socialist-bloc countries, on the other hand, remained largely within their national frameworks. And this in spite of the fact that regionalism among like-minded nations and internationalism among all countries formed a part of their dogma and creed.

While the nationalist countries were moving toward internationalism, the presumably internationalist countries were moving toward an accentuated form of nationalism. But, then, this development has been shown to be typical of their ways in other relations, in the political and social fields as well. The economic nationalism of the Eastern-bloc countries fits into the general pattern. And this accounts for the fiasco of the Comecon.

"We now see," said Milovan Djilas, the Yugoslav critic of Soviet communism, an ex-Communist leader himself, "that a revolution cannot change a nation, its tendencies, qualities, and traits. It only changes the form of power and property, but not the nation itself."

The Soviets' challenge, he added, has been significantly altered by the re-emergence of Czarist imperialist ambitions and the decline of Communist revolutionary ideology. And this adds up to the nationalization of communism.

7

Yugoslavia—
Where the Heresy Began

If," said the Austrian satirist Karl Kraus, "we could design a big enough saw to sever the Balkan Peninsula from Europe, what a great boon it would be to us. It might float across the Mediterranean and bump into Tripolitania. Perhaps the desert heat could cool off its people's ardor for wars."

Even today, "Balkans" implies not only a peninsula, but also trouble—neighbor's hand set against neighbor. Yugoslavia is in the heart of this trouble center. The heart of this Balkan core-land is Serbia, around which it was established. And what an inscrutable heart it is. It is the land of a proud peasantry that had the spunk to stand up to great powers—the Ottoman Empire, Austria, and Germany. It is also the land of unforgiving hatreds and vendettas, of regicides, of secret societies, of bloodthirsty patriots. It was no coincidence that a Serbian teen-ager's bullet shot into the heart of an Austrian Archduke had touched off the first World War.

Yugoslavia is not a country, the tourist guides intone. What is it then? It is a world—a world of an incredible variety of landscapes, peoples, civilizations, religions, economies, and ways of life. You will find the most primitive and the most sophisticated people dwelling together there.

Women in Skoplje and Sarajevo wore veils not long ago, and Belgrade, the capital, was a decrepit Balkan town. Today it has the gigantic traffic paralysis of "advanced" cultures. No two civilizations can be further apart than that of the Slovenes in the far west of the country and that of the Macedonians in its far east. No two groups fought each other as bitterly as the Croats and the Serbs, who spoke the same language, but thought different thoughts. Is there a common denominator in this rugged country? Can one describe the nature of its collective nationalism? Can one explain why it led the reformation within the Communist ecumenical universe?

The variety of Yugoslav life has to be seen to be appraised. How can one do that within the confines of a single chapter? How can one encompass this microcosm of the macrocosm? Surely, not by detailed examination. We have to use a plane for a glimpse of the salient features of the country. We have to draw back in time, to the inter-bellum period before Yugoslavia had been cast in the Communist mold—its special type of communism. The mold standardizes, perhaps unifies, or just masks the variety.

An airplane flight from west to east and thence south, across the length and breadth of the country, reveals its many faces and the strong contrasts of its cultures. It shows us a country of old towns with lingering traditions, and of haphazard mud villages seeking protection behind primitive walls. It is a land of forbidding mountains peopled with hobgoblins of superstition, and of silent plains over which the deceptive Fata Morgana rolls. It is a country of Alpine snows and subtropical climate under a dazzling sky. It is also a land of strong passions, where political opinions were accented with dagger and pistol. In other words, it is the heart of the heartless Balkans. So, let us take that look.

Ljubljana, capital of the Slovenian part of the republic, was known before the first World War as Laibach, where the Habsburgs ruled as long as they did in old Austria. It was the center of the Slovenian movement. The fortress of Schlossberg, standing guard over turrets and chimneys, reminds us of centuries of Habsburg rule. The churches are Italian renaissance and baroque, combining Slav austerity with Italian serenity. The glacier-topped Slovenian Alps are only a step away. Here the southern Slav comes closest to the West, and Italy is across the mountain range. The Slovenes' lips are sensuous and smiling— not a Balkan trait. But then, they, a component part of Balkan Yugoslavia, are not in the geographic Balkans. Who would not smile at the sight of the pines of Bled and the furious little streams racing down stone-strewn beds in a playful mood? They will swell the waters of the Danube, telling it about the winding mountain roads as merry as those of Lombardy and as tidy as those of Bavaria. The air is crystal clear, and the forts on the hills cannot be seen, since they are underground.

Ljubljana stands guard over a mountain gap into Italy —the historic Amber Road. Here Alaric fought his way across unyielding ranges on his way to Rome. Here the Huns justified their dreaded name by laying waste a thriving trading center on their ruthless march to the sea. The Magyars swept down the hills, following in the footsteps of their Hunnic brethren, destroying old cultures' fruits. Ottokar the Bohemian here chased the mirage of union of the Slavs of north and south. Indeed, for a brief historic moment he made them supreme in Danubia. Rudolph the Habsburg, seven centuries ago, blasted this dream and became the founder of one of the world's strongest and most lasting imperial rules.

We skirt the Julian Alps, the boundary between Yugoslavia and Italy. To take our minds off unpleasant

thoughts of underground forts we turn our eyes toward
the Adriatic Sea, a sheet of lazy blue, embracing emeralds.
The South Sea Islands cannot match these gems of enchantment a romantic jinni must have dropped into the
sea. Dalmatia is the narrow coastline leaning against the
mountains, another frontier. It is the land of palms and
Italian siestas, of oranges and southern dreams. It is a
magic haven that now shares the fate of highly touted
beauty spots. Cut off from its hinterland by the mountains, accessible mainly by sea, this narrow Slavic Eden is
still unspoiled. "The Pearl of the Adriatic," Dubrovnik,
once Ragusa, and a mighty city-state, looks coquettishly at
herself in the azure water under the bare limestone bulk
of Monte Sergio. She sees a mass of aloe palms, cypresses,
villas, Venetian ballustrades, churches, flowering trees,
and shrubs. Once this dream city was great, and its ships
plied the oceans as far as India. In the English language
its name is remembered as "argosy," recalling the far-
famed carracks of Ragusa, which Englishmen knew as
Argusa or Aragosa.

After this short detour to the Adriatic Sea, we turn to
the Danube in the north, away from the west and into the
past. Each minute of the flight takes the viewer closer to
yesteryear. The houses begin to shrink; the red roofs turn
black, and the tiles become slate. We are now in the Croat
part of the country, over which the Habsburgs ruled for as
long as Kings of Hungary. The Karst mountains loom up
as we leave the wooded slopes of Slovenia. They are limestone, which laps up the rain, and so they are naked. The
invading Venetians once entered fully into the spirit of the
nearby peninsula when they stripped the mountains of its
remaining forest verdure in protected spots. There are
green patches in the Karst, too, in sheltered gullies, proclaiming the triumph of life, defying the cold bora of the
north and the warm sirocco of the south. The frontier

culture of these green spots draws strength from fighting the elements.

Beyond the mountains is the center of Croatia, known before the war as the "Ireland of Yugoslavia." The country here is Catholic, a religion it received under Habsburg and Magyar rule. The man who led the Communist reformation, Marshal Tito, was born a Croatian. It is strange that the archrebel should belong to this branch of the Yugoslav world. Throughout history, the Croatians were far less rebellious and intolerant of foreign yoke than their neighbors, the Serbs.

The capital of Croatia, Zagreb, looks smug between the Sava and the Sljeme peak. The upper town, with its winding streets, and the lower town, with its many shops, are studies in contrast. At every turn Zagreb accentuates its attachment to the West. Its university, picture galleries, libraries, academies of science, botanical gardens, public parks, and monuments are signs and symbols of the Occident. Before the advent of communism, much of Zagreb's life pulsed on its café terraces in the rhythm of a south German town. Time was not money, but the medium of leisure.

The large number of Catholic churches in Croatia remind us of the historic conflict between the Croat and the Serb, now minimized. Catholicism, however, still means much to the Croat peasant, whose ancestors bled for it during many centuries. At every turn there is evidence of this conflict, and everywhere the Croats' resentment at the attempt to turn them into Orientals is on hand. Their Latin script itself is a challenge to the Cyrillic of the Serb.

On the eastward journey the viewer sees still another part of the country—Slavonia (not to be confused with Slovenia, farther west), which for centuries shared the Croats' fate. Here the Turkish invader stayed longer, and you can see his hallmark to this very day. "Where the

Turk trod, no grass grew." That was as true as the other famous adage: "Where the Roman trod, imperial roads sprouted." The Turks left ruins, and not many, even, of those, while the Romans left the traces of roads.

Still farther east we come into view of the plains, extension of the Magyar *Alfold*, Lowlands, the rich Voivodina, a part of the Hungarian granary before the Great War, and after it the black soil bread-basket of Yugoslavia. The streets are bordered with acacia trees, and the toylike peasant houses are blinding white. Before the war this was Hungary, and Hungarian settlements are all over the land. When nimble fingers strip the maize of autumnal husking bees, peasant girls weave tales about the magic of the soil, which is among the best of Europe's wheat lands.

At last, we approach old Serbia, the nucleus of the south Slav kingdom before the first World War. This was the sorest spot of the Balkans, and there that war began. When reaching the capital, one must stop for a moment's meditation. *Beli Grad*—White Town—should be called the "Red Town," a French writer once suggested, red because of the stream of blood it saw throughout its tragic Balkans life. For centuries it belonged to the Turks and was one of their most advanced bases in Europe. They called it *Darol-i-Jehad,* home of the wars for the faith, Islam. Sixteen times the town was destroyed and reconstructed. The gardens of Kalemegdan, a former Turkish citadel, command the towering heights above the Danube where it receives one of its main tributaries, the Sava. One feels the slow pulse of the Danube which, until the Communists took over, was enwrapped in the silence of ages, the deep silence of the erstwhile frontier, where one world ended and another began. The north wind brings the warm breath of the overheated ex-Hungarian plains, and also the breath of the west. The south wind from the

Balkans is as mysterious as that troubled peninsula. It carries a message that is that of a land still trying to find its soul.

Until the end of the second World War the East and West seemed to clash at every cornor of Belgrade's streets. It was a remarkable fusion of old and new, ambition and achievement. New buildings were going up, no less modern than those of New York and London. But at a street intersection in the hub of the center a ramshackle Albanian tavern stood. Its petroleum lamps were not much help in throwing light on its assortment of exotic food. In many side streets, cobblestones wrought havoc with rubber tires, while plaster houses, which looked as unsanitary as they did ageless, seemed to reel in all directions. In front of the *cavarnas* sat proud Serbs, drinking the mild spirit of plums, *shlivovitsa raki*. They may have come to town to transact business with a government organ or to shop for their village co-op. They looked dignified, and did not scrape and bow as did their Hungarian peasant neighbors. The Serb peasant never minced his words, and under the royal regime he called his King "thou."

The Turks who ruled here for more than five centuries did leave their mark on the land, after all. To the Turks all non-Moslem subjects were equal—all of them were "dirty dogs." Since all of them were persecuted, none could stand out, and the traditional stratification of the social classes came to an end. Hence the Serbian peasant —whether under the rule of a king or a commissar—is a born democrat. That cannot be said of the Croat, who lived for centuries under autocratic Christian rule, which maintained the social stratification.

Before the second World War the Yugoslav capital yielded to the new inch by inch. The name Russian Town recalls memories of the Ekaterinburg merchants who had

tried to corner the lower-Danube market in wheat. In their
meeting place, a center of Russian imperial intrigue, Apis,
the key man of the Black Hand secret society, was often
seen. The fateful assassination of Austrian Archduke
Franz Ferdinand, which touched off the great tragedy,
was conceived there.

Today Belgrade is a twentieth-century town, very Western bourgeois, capitalistic, as are all the up-and-coming
Communist hubs, and so one of its major problems is
traffic congestion. The visible status of Party membership
is a substantial car.

"Whoever is master of Singidunum [Belgrade's Latin
name] is master of the Balkans," may have been the
motto of many imperial regimes—Romans, Byzantians,
Austrians, Russians. This was also the view of the barbarians who seized the natural citadel overlooking the
Danube. Charlemagne's Franks, too, penetrated as far as
the confluence of the Danube and the Sava, chasing the
world-empire mirage. The Bulgarians held the town for
centuries, then the Greeks took it, and the Hungarians.
Sultan Suleiman seized it from the Magyars, and the
Turks had it, save for short intervals, until a century ago.
But for a small mosque, which the Yugoslav government
has maintained as a relic, most of the signs of the Turkish
rule have been effaced.

The deep Balkans face us as we look southward from
the capital. Pyramidal Mount Avala is crowned by the
ruins of a Roman fort, near the Tomb of the Unknown
Soldier. It makes one reflect that few small nations gave
so good an account of themselves when defending their
country as the Serbs. Pushed out of it during the first
World War, they continued the fight in neighboring
Greece, and helped to turn the tide. Their role in the
second World War became a saga. While nearly all of
Europe lay low in mortal dread of the Apocalyptic mon-

sters—the Fascist Axis of Germany and Italy—the Yugoslavs opened the first fighting front against the foe in occupied land. The cruelties perpetrated on those of them whom the enemy seized cannot be described, and in comparison with them the scenes of Dante's hell are pale. Sawing off a victim's head was one of the more "gentle" exercises of German *Kultur.*

Moving south, peaks rush at us threateningly, encroaching upon one another in a savage jumble, and thwarting man's free movement at every turn. This is the real Balkans of sinister fame. Unruly ranges cut off the sight of patches of fertile meadows on mountain slopes, running into other ranges, gashed by streams cascading down steep inclines, and vanishing in the security of rocky masses. The river Morava looms up, darting in one direction to avoid a hill, rushing headlong in the other direction to make up for lost time. The roads in the west are like chalked ribbons streaking across the green landscapes; here they become rarer and bolder too, climbing the heights and falling back into the valleys. Here the mountains are bleak and black, denuded of trees by the Turkish rulers of the past. Far from the steel tracks that are harbingers of progress, this part of the world began to catch up with the twentieth century just the other day.

Another short detour toward the sea brings the former Kingdom of Montenegro within view, the Black Mountains having sheltered it from sight. This was a Lilliputian kingdom before the first World War, ruled over by good King Nicholas, affectionately known as "Nikita"—little Nick—to whose quaint ways vaudeville writers were deeply indebted. If we fly low enough over Cetinje, the small-town capital of the former kingdom, we may yet see the ancient plane tree under which the late ruler administered justice and sometimes carried it out with his own hands. He had several daughters, tall royal beauties, wooed by royal mates at European courts. The printing press and the prison were unknown in this little country until about a century ago, and then they were introduced by Prince Peter II, autocrat and bard. He needed the press to print his poems, and the prison, it was suggested, for those who failed to like them.

Montenegro was so small that any major power could have snuffed it out. But the chivalry of the great powers placed such mini-countries under their protection in those days. Not even the smallest could find security after the Great War—chivalry was gone. The Yugoslav Kingdom absorbed the tiny Kingdom of Montenegro. Under the Communist regime it became one of the states of the federation. Several leading Communists came from this incubator of valor, political and otherwise, finding their way to the center of Yugoslav authority in the Dedinje section of the capital. The saying was "from Cetinje to Dedinje."

"Bosnia begins with the forest," a native adage says, "Herzegovina with the rock." "End of the world" might have been the proper designation for these parts of the republic. The provinces were isolated from both the east and the west. The *kapetans,* public officials, were so many sovereign princes, and serfdom was rampant. Up to the end of World War II Sarajevo, the Bosnian capital, had all the hallmarks of the Orient. There religious people still insisted: "If it is in the Koran, it is superfluous; if not, then it is a sacrilege." In smell and noise the bazaars, while smaller, were not much different from those of the authentic East. The coppersmiths' streets still echoed with the sounds that must have been familiar to Jacob's ears. The water boys still carried the gourds that Lot's wife would have greeted with joy. Veils and fezzes still dominated the scene.

The Austro-Hungarian Monarchy had risked a world

war when it annexed the two provinces from Turkey six years before the great conflict. Even though many of them were Moslems, the Bosnians were Slavs, speaking Serbo-Croatian. The Serbian neighbor shrieked: "The Habsburgs want to sever our jugular vein," "the Bosnians are our kinsmen." But Austria did not care; it had to show its strength at every turn because it was too weak.

Bosnia and Herzegovina are being opened up to the rest of Yugoslavia, and its mines are to serve as broader foundations of a large gamut of processing industries. Those mountains of rugged beauty are stocked with such valuable minerals as copper, chrome, zinc, mercury, cinnabar, iron, and coal. More valuable than these underground treasures is the spirit of the population. In crucial periods of the second World War it was there that the partisans maintained that fabulous front within the Fascist lines. There the future Marshal Tito laid the foundations of a new Yugoslav world.

The Kara Dagh floats into view farther south, and one reaches the deep Balkans—Macedonia, eye of the erstwhile hurricane. Macedonia is synonymous with mishmash, hodgepodge, chaos. It is the confluence of disunited nationalities, whose ancestors had sought sanctuary in the jumbled mountains—southern Slavs of all kinds, not only Serbs and Bulgarians, but also vestiges of vanished groups, Greeks, Albanians, Vlachs, Turks, Circassians, and Gypsies, settled along vague frontiers, overlapping and encroaching upon one anothers' lands. Here anarchy was the rule, because one neighbor could not or would not understand the other neighbor's tongue. The mountains are naked because the Turkish pashas in the distant past found that woods were worse enemies than the *comitadjis*, committee members with guns. So they lighted the forests, to flush out the foe.

In those days Turkish "justice" was worth its weight in

gold, and so the natives organized an outlaw judicial
system of their own. If the defendant was found guilty,
nobody bothered about a court of appeals. There were still
enough trees in the clumps of woods, and they served
their purpose no less effectively than a well-tailored gallows. If the accused was absent, the tribunal found him
guilty anyway, and when he was found the bullet did the
duty of the rope. No one can tell how many people were
killed in such a way. King Alexander I, killed in Mar-
seilles in 1934, was the most prominent victim of the
lawless law.

Things have changed in this part of the country since
the war. Before it, a village in this part of the kingdom
looked little different from a mountain hamlet centuries
ago. Here is an impression of such a village in the thirties
of the twentieth century:

There was the village wall of mud trying to keep together the struggling houses around a spacious clay man-
sion which once must have belonged to a *beg*. The village
had been built with native earth, blending into the landscape in the hope that marauders on the lookout for loot
might overlook it. If it was a Moslem village, the slender
minaret of the mosque stood out incongruously. Allah
must be given his due. Marauders, usually pious bands of
Moslems, might take pity on a hamlet of such deep piety.

The streets were unpaved and unlighted, and after a
rain, carts sank into the mud axle-deep. It did not really
matter, since the lanes were dead ends. If the village were
on the railway, part of the population met the local train,
staring wide-eyed at it, as if it were the miracle of the age.
As the train guard handed over the day's mail to the
the stationmaster—one letter—the villagers wondered
whether it brought word from afar of birth or death.

Today, Macedonia too has entered the industrial age,
and the ramshackle houses have been largely replaced.

Besides Yugoslavia, Macedonians live also in adjacent Bulgaria and Greece. Perhaps they would like to join their co-nationals. Today there are no midnight conclaves in the woods. There is a "Macedonian question": the Bulgarians claim that they are the authentic heirs of Macedonia. Bulgaria is a Communist country, like Yugoslavia, and as yet the disharmony is *sotto voce*.

This look at Yugoslavia shows that one cannot speak of one national trait. For centuries the Serbs had been under Turkish rule, and that left its mark on them. They had joined the Eastern Orthodox Church, and that stamped their culture with its own hallmark. The Turks had made the Serbs a democratic nation through their secular policy. The feudal landlords were eliminated one way or another, and only the *misera plebs contribuens*—the wretched taxpayers—remained. Among all the component parts of multi-national Yugoslavia, the Serbs shed more blood for what the contemporary world knows as human dignity than probably any other nation.

The second most important component of the republic did not share Serbia's fate for a full millennium. The Croats got their civilization from the West, under the influence of which they had fallen through their conversion to the Roman Church. For many centuries they lived in uneasy association with the Hungarians, who sought to dominate them on occasions and to fight alongside them at other times. When the Hungarians fell under the Habsburgs' sway—again for centuries—the Croats were sucked even more into the Western orbit. The Turks never penetrated into their heartland, and that was not good for their social institutions. Class and caste characterized Croat life, unlike that of the Serbs.

During the second World War a strange duality developed in the Croat land. It was a Croat Communist, Josip Broz, whom history came to know as Marshal Tito, who opened up a front behind the Nazi-Italian front, astounding a browbeaten world. No other country of Europe displayed this reckless courage. But, then, no other country in Europe had the backing of the Balkans, that jumble of mountains in which, it was said, not even God could find his way. The chaotic nature of the peninsula helped destroy the Axis.

There were other Croats, too, and they were as much dedicated to the Axis as Tito and his partisans were dedicated to their country's independence in its fight against Berlin and Rome. Judging by their wartime performance the Croats are a remarkably intense ethnic group. The henchmen of the Axis they produced were fanatic and, unfortunately, cruel beyond words. Cruelty was not in short supply during a war that broke out under the auspices of a demon who believed that terror and horror are the tools of government. He had his henchmen in Croatia, known as the *ustashi,* and they were the most hellish fanatics among all the sadistic fiends unleashed by the war.

The Croats' neighbors to the west, and the westernmost component element of Yugoslavia, Slovenia, displayed again a different temper. It was comparatively subdued, not engaged violently on either side. Through the centuries of Habsburg rule it acquired a measure of gentle indolence that kept it out of the camps of both extremes. Dalmatia, under its southern sun, accepted its fate, whatever it was to be. Bosnia and Herzegovina had to find their way first into the twentieth century, which they have now reached. The greatest surprise of the south Slav world was little Montenegro, a place that one could reach and leave only with the greatest difficulty, hemmed in by fantastically protective mountains, many miles from Western civilization. Quicker than any of the country's component parts, the Black Mountaineers adjusted themselves to the abstractions and realities of communism. For its size, the former miniature kingdom provided an inordinately large contingent of ruling elements. It was a Montenegrin, too, Milovan Djilas, who surprised the world with a scathing criticism of Communist bureaucracy, which he described as a cancerous and deadly product.

THUS THE NATIONAL CHARACTER WAS FORMED

"Emperor of the Serbs and Greeks, Eternal Life to Him!", the crowd shouted on Easter day 1346. The choice of day was not left to chance. Resurrection was the theme of the reign. The land of the Greeks had forsaken the religious rites of the ancestors, was moving close to Rome. In the heart of the Balkans, King-Emperor Dushan was to foster the ancestors' creed.

An even greater danger than that of Byzantium threatened the true faith—the infidels out of the depths of Anatolia, the land of Satan, the realm of the Turks, extending all the way to the limits of the earth, to the great ocean. The Turks had vaulted the Dardanelles, bypassed Constantinople, and were headed into the land of the *giaour*, the infidel. The ruler of the Empire of Serbs and Greeks after Dushan was Lazar, attended by many bold knights, one of whom was Kobil, "the bloodmare's son," Voyvode Milosh, and no man was more contemptuous of life than he—the life of others and his own. We will hear about him in a while.

The Turks descended as an endless swarm of locusts, voracious beyond belief. For a Turk to kill a Christian was bliss, and to kill a hundred *giaours* was ecstasy. Christians did not believe in Allah, the All Merciful, and therefore they should be wiped out without mercy. "Field of the Blackbirds" was the name of the place of battle, and the historic date was June 15, 1389. To say that Lazar's hosts were outnumbered by the Turks would not be literally true. Sultan Murad I had a vast army, to be sure, and he had the reputation of being a great warrior—intelligent, perceptive, strong, and ruthless. But his Christian opponents were sure that all the hosts of heaven stood on Lazar's side, and their number was myriad.

The Field of Blackbirds, *Kossovo Polye*, became the mass grave of the Christian valiants. With that June day, the country, the Balkans, and, in the end, Constantinople, were lost. Lazar's body, too, became the feasting ground of blackbirds. The Turks were now in a position to establish themselves in Europe, and from there they merely had to follow the Danube to penetrate into the heart of the continent. This was the darkest day of Christianity. The great Sultan's invincible arms had Allah's backing.

In the moment of the great triumph of the Grand Turk, a messenger, announced as a Christian defector, appeared before his tent to transmit a secret. Was the secret to be the Sultan's key to the breaching of imperial Vienna's walls? The messenger turned out to be Kobil, Voyvode Milosh, and his "secret" was the Balkans' intense feelings against the foe. He was shown into the imperial tent, and seconds later Murad the Invincible was a corpse. In spite of that, the Turks established themselves in the Balkans. They stayed there for five centuries.

Infidels were *rayah*, cattle, to the Turk, to be milked. The milking device was the *haratch*, capitation tax, from which nobody was exempt, be he sick, famished, or beset by plague. That very word entered the languages of many countries, and is used to this very day. Another word that entered Balkan languages was *yatagan*, curved sword, to be used on people who lacked the "milk."

The Turks were good psychologists. They cut down the leaders—feudal lords and aristocrats—leaving the people without guides. That established a pattern among the Serbs: no aristocracy, and therefore no inequality. This created the democracy of the lowly. One cannot treat the Serb peasant lightly even today. The Soviets were to learn this, centuries after the tragic outcome of the battle on the Blackbirds' Field.

The Turks had endless trouble with the Balkan natives because, according to legend, the Earth Giant had had a no-holds-barred quarrel with his vixen wife ages before. In his savage rage, the giant tore open the entrails of the earth, tossing mountains around, until the area became a maze of rocks. Thus the Balkans were created.

In the wild mountain areas the human cattle turned into human beings, using savage nature to torment their tormentors. The natives knew their country, and had the protection of fellow refugees, *haiduks*. Centuries later, this ancestral training stood them in good stead when they, simple Balkans peasants, were able to challenge the "impregnable" Nazi Third Reich, during the second World War.

There were traitors among the Serbs, too, who attached themselves to the winning Turkish cause. One of them was George Brankovich, whom a Turkish pasha had set up as the despot over his countrymen. He felt slighted by an underling, Michael Szilagyi, and only blood could remove the stain. A duel by the sword was arranged, a long-lasting affair in which two lives were in the balance. In the end, Brankovich was wounded, and eventually he succumbed. At the time of this duel, he was ninety years of age. This was the Balkans, in which age did not count. Had the "despot" been a century old, could he have ignored the slight?

RELIGION TURNS TO NATIONALISM

Nationalism at the outset was an unknown concept in the Balkans. Known was the abyss between religions—the Orthodox, which the Serbs considered the true creed, and Islam, the only true faith to the Turk. Past history and traditions were all linked to the creed.

The Balkan Peninsula was then "Asia in Europe"—Asia because the Turks were Asian, and Europe because of the facts of geography. After a while, Europe began to move into the Balkans: the dominant thought of the West, its ideology, its ecumenical creed—nationalism—came to replace the ecclesiastic creed. It did not sweep into the Balkans, it merely percolated into it slowly. On its way from France, where the revolution became its banner-bearer, it moved eastward, finally reaching the Balkans. By that time, the belief in the strength of the Turk had begun to fade. The Ottoman Empire's hieratic orientation was unfit for the new age of nationalism. And this brings us to the story of Black George.

Czernydjordje to the Serbs and Karajordje to the Turks, he was black inside and out. His skin was so dark that he could have been taken for a Gypsy, and his heart was black, too. If one wanted to get on the top one had to have a black heart in the Balkans, ruled, as they were, by the unspeakably cruel Turk, especially cruel now that he had to fight for his waning power.

Black George began his career by killing fellow-Christian rivals to demonstrate his strength among would-be freedom leaders. This made him feared among the fellow Christians, dreaded and respected. Being respected, he acquired a retinue that followed him through thick and thin. He led his people against the Kalimegdan, the fort overlooking the Danube on top of a landmark bluff. The defenders of the fort were the rulers of Turkey, *janissaries,* New Troops, of Christian origin, converted to Islam, their masters' creed. These troops outdid even the Moslems in their cruelty toward the Christians over whom they ruled. At the beginning of the nineteenth century, they were bloated with food, loot, and lust. The paunchiest among them, successful looters, became the pashas. The followers of Black George, on the other hand, were trim. Even though outnumbered by their fat foes, they overpowered them. Black George became a hero. This was the beginning of the end of the Turks in the Balkans heartland. Their rule in Belgrade, the site of the Kalimegdan, was replaced by a national council—an anticipation of the Soviet meeting on December 26, 1808, an important date in the country's history. A portion of the land had now been cleared of what Black George called "Turkish filth." There was much more cleaning to be done. Again the detergent was blood.

The council swore to abide by Black George—Karageorge Petrovic—and his lawful descendants as the rulers of the land. Other leaders held the time opportune to make their bid for power. Black George disagreed and ordered some 125 of his "followers" killed. Among these was his father, who wanted to assert his paternal authority. Also, he not only had his brother hanged, but watched him die on the gallows, and went so far as to forbid their mother to bury his body. Undeterred by sentiment and kinship, he was admired as a truly strong man.

The Turks were out of the Kalimegdan fort, but they were still masters of the Balkans. Black George knew that his people alone could not clear the Turks out of the region. He hoped to be able to do it with Russian aid. They were fellow-Slavs, also Greek Orthodox. To the Russians, the Balkans was a natural outlet to warm waters.

The international situation required that the Russians should execute a sudden turnabout and make up with the Turks, as a bribe. Serbia received a measure of autonomy under Turkish control. The *janissaries* returned to the Belgrade fort, while Karageorge cleared out.

Heading the *janissaries,* Suleiman Skopljak Pasha brought in hundreds of pales and had them stuck into the ground where they could best be seen. Each pale was the witness of the agony of a patriot. Serbia became the martyr country. This insane cruelty incensed the people, who sent word to Black George to return. To escape the pale, he did so in disguise, again taking up the cudgel against the Turks. The Turks responded by setting up a puppet government, headed by one of Black George's former underlings, Milosh Obrenovich. Milosh played a double game—Turk collaborator on stage, and friend of the Russians behind the scenes. As soon as word reached the Turks about the return of Black George to his native land, they wanted to test Milosh. They demanded that he deliver the head of George to them on the occasion of the Moslem holiday Ramadan. Should he fail to do so, they would demand a substitute head—his own.

At the appointed time, during Ramadan, Black George's head, sent him by Milosh Obrenovich the Serb, adorned the Sultan's table. The head had been severed from the torso while George was asleep. Without delay, Milosh Obrenovich was appointed *Vrhovni Knez,* Supreme Chief of Serbia under Turkish rule. It was because of these events that the world came to call the Balkans the powder keg.

Even though George was dead, his family continued to play important roles in Serb history. For over a century the two families, Karageorgevich and Obrenovich, rotated in office, through regicide and otherwise. The ruggedness of the country, aggressive neighbors, and historic memories brought about the "Balkan curse."

COURAGE AND REGICIDE

Serbia, located next to Austria, looked like the proverbial mouse in the lion's paws. It was, in this case, the mouse that roared, while the lion caved in. The murder of Austrian Archduke Franz Ferdinand and his wife in the Bosnian town of Sarajevo was the work of a Serbian secret organization with the blood-curdling name of Black Hand. It was not, however, the work of the Serb government, as is definitely known now. Austria used this tragic incident to intimidate and mutilate Serbia. She stood up to the challenge. While the Serbs lost all the battles in the first World War, they won the war. Serbia expanded into the land of the south Slavs, Yugoslavia today.

New problems arose, however, attended by new tragedies. Within the new south two ideologies collided, those of the West and the East. The Croats had been rotating in the Western orbit, and were Catholics. The Serbs had been rotating in the Eastern orbit, the Ottoman Empire, and most of them were Greek Orthodox. The Serbs considered themselves the nation builders and acted accordingly. In the spirit of the time and location, political assassinations were routine. The Croat peasant leader Stefan Radic was assassinated. His death was followed by regicide, the 1934 murder of Alexander I Karageorgevich, descendant of Black George.

A movement of basic violence now swept into Europe—fascism. It glorified strength, was dictatorial, jingoistic, and expansionist. Italy's dictator, Benito Mussolini, called the Mediterranean *mare nostrum,* and saw his country as the successor of classical Rome. In Germany, Adolf Hitler, the Fuehrer, called for a new order under which "superior blood," Nordic, particularly German, was to rule over *oestliche Untermenschen*, "eastern subhumans." The Balkan Peninsula was considered the dwelling place of an inferior breed.

In the face of this challenge, the Yugoslavs closed ranks. The Serbs and Croats reached an agreement of peaceful coexistence in their unified country. A week after this agreement was signed, the Germans invaded Poland. The second World War, which had begun in Poland, spread to the west, and now reached the Balkans.

The Yugoslavs had observed what happened to France, a great power. The civilized world was then under the impression that not since Genghis Khan, the Terrible Tartar, had mankind seen a force as formidable as Hitler's. There was more to this parallel, too, than a mere figure of speech. The Nazis too drove unbounded terror into the people's hearts, as had the Mongol Khan. Hitler's terms were accepted by Yugoslavia's neighbors, Hungary, Bulgaria, and Rumania, not because they saw eye to eye with him, but because they dreaded his wrath. The Serbs were of a different fiber, ready to resist the Nazis. Resistance of invaders was their historical heritage.

The latter-day Genghis Khan swept into the country with low-diving Stuka bombers, against which the Serbs had no defense. The bombers massacred thousands in Belgrade's streets. The Yugoslavs continued to resist, longer than had France. "At noon," Nazi headquarters announced on April 19, "firing ceased in the Serbian theater of war."

THE "AWAKENERS" AND THE DEAD

"The Serbian theater of war," the Nazi bulletin specified, and not the Yugoslav one. The country split into its component units. Serbia was set up as a Nazi satrapy. The number of collaborators in that area were few. A "Free Croatia" was set up, and its "throne" was offered to a cousin of the Italian King, to become King Tomislav II. The royal cousin preferred not to occupy his throne. Within Croatia, *ustashi,* a terrorist organization, emerged. The "Awakeners" were extreme nationalist anti-Serbian Fascists, who introduced a reign of terror that would have put Genghis Khan to shame. *Ustashi's* members were not content with having their enemies, political opponents and Serb patriots, merely shot. In many instances they had them bend over stumps of trees on which the patriots' heads were sawn off. Often the victims were surrounded by amused *ustashis*. So proud were they of their deed that they had photographs without number perpetuate the memory of some of the foulest actions in Balkan history.

During the long Turkish rule bands of freedom fighters had fought their tormentors in the jumbled mountain region. These were the *chetniks.* Now, all of a sudden, *chetniks* emerged again in the forests, swiftly pouncing upon Axis-held strongholds. Few other parts of the Balkans favored guerrillas as much as Yugoslavia did, particularly the mountains of Bosnia, Herzegovina, Macedonia, and, above all, Montenegro. In these areas daring foot soldiers had the advantage over Axis military hardware, which could tackle neither the mountains nor the trackless wastes. Drazha Mihailovich, a former Serbian army officer, assumed command of the guerrillas. He was a dour, unsmiling soldier, who attracted patriotic mountaineers and peasants dispossessed by the invading armies, seeking revenge for the death of their kin.

It took considerable time before the outside world took notice of this unique event. Looking like the horsemen of the Apocalypse, the Axis armies were terrorizing Europe, while opposition to them was stirring in the Balkans. The Serbs punched a deep hole into the Axis' protective walls.

THEN CAME TITO

The details of what was happening in those dark woods will forever remain a mystery. Again, as in the past, Serb was at the throat of Serb, while also fighting the Axis. Suspicions became rife that the leader of the *chetniks* had reached an understanding with the Germans and Italians. A new force had arisen in the tangle of the Balkan mountains, calling themselves Partisans. And they were Communists. Who had heard of the name of its leader? Nobody, except the criminal courts of the pre-war Kingdom of Yugoslavia. His name was Tito.

Gradually it became known that this was not his real name. It was Josip Broz (perhaps Brozovich). He was a Croatian, born in Kumrovac, near Zagreb. During the first World War he was drafted for military service in the Austro-Hungarian army, in which he fought against the Russians. With the emergence of the Soviets, he became converted to communism and fought its foes after the Russian revolution. As a Communist organizer he returned to Yugoslavia in 1924; he was jailed and, after his release, had an adventurous life, ducking out of sight at the approach of the police.

Suddenly, during the war, he appeared as the leader of a National People's Army known as Partisans, arousing more enthusiasm in the mountains than Mihailovich. He was far more successful too. While ardently pro-Serb, Mihailovich was as much very intensely anti-Communist. In the course of time, he came to fight the Communist Tito with more fervor than he had fought the Axis. By that time the United States was in the war, too, and both America and Britain shifted their support to Tito, who proved to be more effective in fighting the Axis. He also got Soviet aid. Gradually, Mihailovich sank into half-light, "sulking in his tent," while Tito became the hero of freedom-fighting Yugoslavia, hailed the world over.

Now there were two freedom fighters, lovers of liberty and haters of each other. Ready to offer their lives for their country, and their political adversaries' lives for the satisfaction of their personal piques, they recalled the early days of Serbian history, the feud of Black George and Milos Obrenovich. Being more effective in fighting the Axis, Tito now called the tune. He invested himself with the rank of general and then with that of field marshal. The Partisans set up a provisional government, a parliament in Hitler's Europe, in which resistance was considered espionage, the penalty for which was very much like the pale of the Turks of another day.

The tide of war turned on the Volga and North Africa, and German resistance was fading away. By the autumn of 1944 it was completely on the wane. Soviet and Yugoslav forces stormed into Belgrade. Quickly, it became a shambles, witnessing one of the most inhuman hand-to-hand battles. This was the Balkans' curse. In the end, power came to the Communists.

Yugoslavia was the first country to become Communist after World War II. Like Russia, she was a Slavic country, and an underdeveloped one at that. Therefore, farming and the extractive industries accounted for the bulk of her national products. But there were also dissimilarities between the two countries. For centuries Russia had been outside the mainstream of European life. Not so, though, those parts of Yugoslavia that had been parts of the Austro-Hungarian Monarchy, a Westernized realm. Communism penetrated into Europe.

During the war there had been a comradeship of arms between the two hostile ideologies of capitalism and communism. Now they were torn apart, intensely jealous and fearful of each other, devising each other's downfall. The Cold War was on.

COMMUNISM IN THE BALKANS

The Federal People's Republic of Yugoslavia was established on the Soviet model, consisting of six component republics, and the League of Yugoslav Communists set the pattern. It dominated the Socialist Alliance of the Working People, a Popular-Front device, including not only outright Communists, but also fellow-travelers. A Federal Assembly was set up, composed of five chambers, dealing with economic, health, cultural, and nationality problems. There were no ministries set up, as there had been no ministries in the salad days of the Soviet Union. There had been Commissariats in the Soviets; in Yugoslavia there were Secretariats. Ministries were thought to be organs of the state, and these were to fade away after the triumph of communism, Karl Marx had thought. In reality, the only difference between ministries and secretariats was the terminology.

The Yugoslavs were supposed to ape the Soviet Union, "motherland of the proletariat," and to hate the United States, "arch-imperialist." Communist Russia was to Communist Yugoslavia what the Holy Orthodox Church had been to the Serbs during the Turkish regime. And the United States was what the Ottoman Empire had been during the Balkans' endless night.

An American C-47 was shot down over Yugoslavia on August 19, 1946, by Tito's fighter bombers. The boiling point seemed to have been reached in East-West relations. Suddenly, the world recalled that the Great War had broken out in that area. Was the third world war to erupt in the Balkans too? The United States indicted Belgrade at the forum of the world in the United Nations. Belgrade, in turn, indicted the United States at the same forum, claiming that 228 unauthorized and provocative American flights had taken place over Yugoslav territory within the previous five weeks.

A visitor to Yugoslavia in those days saw evidences of the hatred of America and of Soviet-Yugoslav friendship everywhere—posters, banners, and propaganda headlines. They hailed the "Glorious Soviet Fatherland of the Proletariat." Portraits of two world leaders—the Soviet's Stalin and Yugoslavia's Tito—were displayed everywhere, Russia's dictator beaming at the Marshal, who was wreathed in smiles.

The following anecdote, current in those days, illustrates the relations of Yugoslavia and Russia. It is the story of a befuddled Serb peasant, paying a visit to the capital, Belgrade. The names of the thoroughfares had been changed recently from those of the royalist regime to those of the Communists, causing confusion. The countryman, according to the story, asked for a ticket to King Peter's Square and was rebuked by the conductor. The new name was Stalin Square. The following day the same incident occurred, except that the names were Prince Alexander Boulevard, and Avenue of the Glorious Soviet Army. The third day the countryman wanted to go to the terminal on the Danube, but this time he knew his lesson.

"Comrade, conductor," said he, "please give me a ticket to the Volga."

Holding up the United States as a nightmare land of oppressive capitalism occasionally boomeranged. It did in at least one notable instance.

The Yugoslav authorities exhibited the American film *The Grapes of Wrath,* a film of national calamities compounded of despair and man's inhumanity to man. All these points were made in the film. What did the Yugoslav viewers see in it? They saw only that in the United States even the poorest of the poor had motorcars, and they were impressed. After seeing the film even more of them would have bolted to America, if the gate had been open.

THE NATIONALIST HERESY

Three years after the war, outside of the Soviet Union, there were eight Communist countries: the European satellites, in eastern central Europe and in the Balkans. Yugoslavia had become Communist in the wake of the Partisans, because of their war work, while the other countries were engulfed by Bolshevik-controlled Popular Fronts. Communist leaders formed coalitions including non-Communist, anti-Fascist groups. Quickly, they were sliced up and either absorbed or eliminated.

Before the second World War, this swath of countries from the Baltic to the Adriatic formed units of a Western defense shield against the Soviets—*cordon sanitaire*. The West considered Soviet communism a plague to be quarantined. Now the "sanitary cordon" was turned against its designers and became a protective shield for the Soviets, as well as a possible staging area for further advance. A year later, hundreds of millions of Chinese were added to the Communist bloc, at the other end of the globe.

At this time, the Kremlin was under the rule of Joseph Stalin, in his dotage. His will-power was as hard as his arteries. Deified in an atheistic country, he was surveying the Communist world with the savage complacency of senility. He was the ruler of all this vast world because *he* was the Soviet Union and the Soviet Union was the pioneer, the master teacher, the global icebreaker in the frozen Cold War. The cause of the Soviet Union was that of the world proletariat, and it was the duty of all Communists to hurry to the aid of the cause. Were this to happen, Stalin would have his final triumph over his brilliant antagonist, Leon Trotsky, who had maintained that Russia alone could not construct communism.

That unfortunate "bungler" had maintained that communism in Russia could not prevail for two main reasons: the Russians lacked organizational skills, and the non-Communist countries had the strength to crush the regime, denying its basic values.

In the great controversy Stalin had said communism could succeed in Russia alone. He also had said that the success of Russia would attract other countries to communism. Russia was successful. Now it was the turn of the other countries to join the victor. To encourage them to do so, the solidarity of the Communist countries under Soviet leadership had to be shown. The motto was no longer merely: Proletarians of all Countries—Unite. It was: Proletarian Countries of all the World—Unite, and recognize the dominance of the Soviet Union. What could be done in Russia could also be done elsewhere if all the "fraternal countries" remained united.

Marshal Tito was as good a Communist as any, a dedicated one, who believed in the common cause. He was also a patriotic Yugoslav. Russia had suffered a tremendous bloodletting, but so had Yugoslavia. It was the only country in the bloc that had freed itself mainly through its own efforts. It could not afford the sacrifices required for the benefit of the Soviet Union. Tito rebelled against the Kremlin's "Man of Steel."

The headquarters of the Communist Information Bureau, Cominform, had been set up in Belgrade. It was the new Comintern. In view of what happened, it is pertinent to ask why, since the Yugoslav capital was geographically peripheral to the Communist bloc. The headquarters of the original Comintern had been Moscow. Now, however, Stalin shied away from making the ideological dominance of the Soviets too obvious. But why Belgrade? Perhaps because it was the most important country of the bloc, Communist by its own right and not through coercion, as were the others. Belgrade was closer to the West, too, than other satellite countries, and that advantage might favor propaganda. There was much admiration abroad for the Serbs because of their wartime deeds. Of speculations there is no end. Suddenly, they unleashed a cataclysmic event within the Communist world. It was the schism, heresy, break with the ecumenical orthodox "communist church," with the third Rome on the Moskva. It was the "reformation" in the Eastern bloc. It was June 28, 1948, recalling All Saints' Day in 1517. In this instance there was no Schlosskirche and no Wittenberg with its ninety-five points. The day was an anniversary, that of the outbreak of the first World War, in the same country, now Yugoslavia.

The anathema was contained in the leading Communist newspaper of Prague, Rude Pravo. Yugoslavia had been expelled from the Cominform, it announced. This was the excommunication of a country from the Communist ecumenical church, and it shook the world. What were the grounds for this unprecedented event?

The newspaper article told the story, and it sounded like the explosion of an apoplectic wrath, at the point of puncturing an artery. The ninety-five articles of Moscow verged on incoherence. One point was made, then another one, with scarcely a connecting link. The postulate of the indictment was the international party line, the dogma. Diverging from it was considered heresy, denounced as "revisionism," an unforgivable sin. The Kremlin leveled the charge of revisionism against the Yugoslavs. It was paired with "liquidatorism," a concept supposed to mean an attempt to liquidate the tenets of communism. Tito, according to the charge, said that in Yugoslavia the National Front had drawn up the program the nation was to follow, and not the League of Communists. This was "blatant and brazen revisionism."

Within the league itself there was no democracy, the indictment charged. Party officials were appointed in the way of self-perpetuating bureaucracies, and not elected. No criticism was permitted within the party ranks. Also the league was "secretive," especially in its relations with the Communist Party of the Soviet Union.

The Yugoslavs said, the article charged, that they themselves had liberated their country and were therefore under no obligation to the Soviet Red Army. This was "megalomania," the Russians said. The Yugoslavs had not done any more to liberate their country from the Axis forces than other nations and "less than the French and Italian comrades." It was presumptuous, too, for the south Slav, the indictment confirmed, to take umbrage at the work of the Soviet intelligence in their country. Intelligence was active there because the subversive work of the "Western imperialists" was ubiquitous, and common effort was needed to scotch it.

Visiting Soviet officials, the Kremlin charged further, had been kept under surveillance in Yugoslavia. Particularly obnoxious was the work of the principal sleuth, Colonel-General Aleksander Rankovich. The newspaper article also denounced Vladimir Velebit, the Yugoslav Assistant Foreign "Minister," and Ljubo Leontich, Ambassador in London, naming them as "British spies."

Economic deviations formed the third part of the indictment. The Yugoslavs had said that the pillars of their

Mao

country were the peasants. "This was in complete contradiction with the principles of Marxism-Leninism that the industrial workers—not the peasants—represented the revolutionary advance-guard." Nor was it true, as the south Slavs claimed, that the peasants formed a homogeneous class. They included the ruthless rich farmers, *kulaks*, too. The south Slavs assumed that it was possible for capitalism to merge with socialism. This was arrant "Bukharinism," named after Nikolai Bukharin, an "old Bolshevik," and a victim of Stalin's blood purges.

THE SKY TURNED BLACK

What did the man in the Kremlin expect from this blast? He expected Tito, the heretic, to go to Canossa—Moscow—on his knees, at two hundred miles per hour in the fastest plane. For a true Communist, and Tito was one of them, to be read out of the party was equivalent to being thrust out of the Church in the Middle Ages, forsaken by God and man. Death was better than life away from the community of fellow believers.

Tito did not go to Canossa. He remained in his Dedinje palace, the Martin Luther of the ecumenical Communist church. His theses were presented in the official program of the Yugoslav League of Communists. Under Stalin, the theses said in a disputatious way, the state dominated in all areas of life. According to Marx, it was to wither away. "To the apparatus of this state is assigned too vast a part in the construction of socialism and in the solutions of the inner contradictions of the interim period, a role that is bound to obstruct the development of the socialist forces in society."

The struggle for socialism must go on, said the Yugoslav theses. The working class of one or another country may become the standard-bearer of the working class in this struggle for victory, but this did not mean that the working class of any one country should acquire a position of monopoly. "Only among equals has cooperation been possible in the labor movement, past experience reveals."

Internationalism was originally one of the main tenets of socialism and communism. The nation was then an adversary to the working man, the bourgeoisie's fighting front. But conditions changed, especially within the socialist countries, and one could not force the tempo of history. Before reaching the stage of internationalism, nations will have to pass through the organic stages of nationalism. These stages cannot be skipped even in socialism.

"The general aims of socialism are common," said the Yugoslav Manifesto, "but the tempo and forms of the movement toward these aims must be different, depending upon actual conditions in the individual countries. Consequently, freedom of internal socialist development and absence of any imposition of standardized forms, noninterference in the internal life and progress of various movements, a free exchange of experience and socialist thought must be the basic principles of relations among the socialist countries . . ."

The nation is the people, the Yugoslavs asserted, but it can also degenerate into a bureaucracy. This tendency can be combated through close contact with the working people and their elected organizations. In the struggle for the strengthening of socialism, continued the Yugoslav Manifesto, the "Communists must constantly verify the right political line through their increasing responsibility to the broad masses of the working people." The Yugoslav Communists wanted to make it clear to Moscow that they did not wish to gain power through the use of a bureaucratic apparatus. They wanted to do it through the working class itself, because its interests—and those alone—were the agents of social progress.

By rights, the land should be collectivized, the Yugoslav Communists conceded. Being the gift of nature, it should have never been acquired as private property, because it belongs to all. Such possession by the people necessitates its being turned into collectives. So it was in Yugoslavia, too, in her early history. But land had been seized by individuals as their private property, and this created a "cash nexus" between man and land. While this was wrong, it was a fact that could not be ignored. Private property in land became a mode of life. Small holdings were common in the Serbian part of the country under the royal regime. Through their secular rule, the Turks had eliminated the owners of large estates. Croatia, however, had been linked to Hungary for nearly a millennium, during which the feudal type of holdings flourished. The Communist regime recognized the farmer's right to own land as his own private property, but his holdings were limited to 24.71 arable acres. On larger units of land the cultivators could use machinery. Therefore, the government encouraged the creation of peasant cooperatives.

Yugoslavia was set now to establish its own way of national communism, continuing its traditional ways, adjusting them to the precepts of the teachers Marx, Engels, and Lenin. These differed from Stalin's doctrines. His teaching centered around an ecumenical system pivoted on the Soviet Union, the pioneer, entitled to its leadership role because of its longer experience. Also, advantage accrued to an ideological world empire opposing the "decadent" capitalists, who, in their agony, reached the outer limits of irresponsibility.

For an understanding of what followed in the wake of

the Yugoslav heresy we must recall that Stalin, who exhibited remarkable strength during the war, had become mentally deranged. He acted like a maniac in the face of the Tito heresy.

To him, communism was either unified, international, or it was no communism at all, and the unified "church" must be responsive to the Kremlin's commands. All the interests of all the other countries had therefore to be subordinated to those of Moscow. In some instances this postulate grew out of wartime conditions. Some of the new Communist countries had been enemies—East Germany, Hungary, Rumania, Bulgaria. Poland and Yugoslavia, on the other hand, had been allies, overrun by the Germans, while Yugoslavia was a special case. Irrespective of their starting points, all the former friends and foes had the duty to help rebuild the fatherland of communism, the Soviet Union, now their bastion and shield. This was exploitation, of course, but not as seen from the Kremlin.

Stalin saw that quick action was needed to stem the tide of heresy. The neighbors of Yugoslavia were ordered to shrink back from the pariah, Yugoslavia, and then to move ahead, to mow her down, to put her out of her misery. At the Kremlin's instigation, border incidents were created on fictitious issues, and the frontiers with the fraternal countries rang with the shootings of trigger-happy guards. The Kremlin satellites were bent on provoking an international incident.

This was the question haunting the Kremlin's despot: if Yugoslavia got away with her "declaration of independence" what was to keep the other fraternal countries from following suit? And if they did so, the Soviet Union would stand alone facing the hostile world. In that condition, the imperialist powers might move from cold to hot war. Stalin knew that Russia was weak because of the unprecedented wartime bloodletting. Every measure would, therefore, have to be taken to keep the satellites from following Tito's example. To discourage the explosion of Titoist heresy, bloc-country Stalinists launched a reign of terror.

This time the terror was directed against Communists suspected of nationalist deviation. These were thoroughbred Communists, whom Stalin suspected of considering the problems of their countries, too, not merely those of Russia. Their "crime" was home-baked communism.

It began in Hungary, and its first victim was the Minister of Interior, Laszlo Rajk, a dedicated Communist, but, unlike other leaders, not a "Muscovite." It would not be far-fetched to call him a "Budapester." Russia, he agreed, was entitled to special treatment among the fraternal countries but Hungary's problems could not be neglected, either. Rajk would have never dared to express such blasphemous thoughts in public, of course. But the people with X-ray eyes in the Kremlin knew what he thought. A farcical trial found him guilty, and, convicted by several judges, he was hanged. Other grass-roots Hungarian Communists were rounded up, tortured, and put away for years. One of these was Janos Kadar, who seemed to be doomed, too. Eventually, his life was spared, but not his body nor his human pride. He was one of the few who had a strange reincarnation. About that in another context.

The same grisly scenarios were enacted in the other Communist countries too. In Rumania the most prominent victim was a former minister of justice, a loyal Communist, Lucretiu Patrascanu. He was convicted of espionage, as were many defendants in these "Tito trials." The Muscovites, headed by Gheorghe Gheorghiu-Dej, Teohari Gergescu, Vasile Luca, and Ana Pauker, formed the Stalinite "star chamber."

Espionage was the charge against Rudolf Slansky, Secretary General of the Czechoslovak Communist Party.

He, and then other leaders, was sentenced to death and hanged. Slansky and seven of the others were Jews, condemned as Zionists, Trotskyites, and Stalin's foes. Years later it became known that Stalin himself had ordered the purges in 1952 and sent Anastas I. Mikoyan to Prague to supervise the trials.

In Poland the grass-roots Communists, headed by Wladyslaw Gomulka, were arrested and placed under detention. Gomulka was another one of those who had a reincarnation in years to come. In Yugoslavia's neighboring country, Bulgaria, top Communist Traicho Kostov was hanged. In Albania, another Yugoslav neighbor, Koce Xoxe, was the victim.

In these years of terror, many observers had the impression that it was the aim of Communists to root out Communists. Large was the number of those who were tortured and placed in jails for years. Some of them survived; others did not. Those that survived were to wear the scar for life. Many of these managed to sneak out of their countries—especially the Hungarians at the time of their uprising—and former dedicated Communists became the most dedicated anti-Communists. This was one of the important products of the witch hunt.

THE DRAGON SEED

The heresy was halted for a time. The reign of terror succeeded in isolating Yugoslavia and keeping the faithful in line. In 1953 Stalin died. Gradually the thaw set in, although in some cases it took years. In the unique case of Czechoslovakia, de-Stalinization did not set in until fourteen years later. It was only in the late sixties that a revolutionary new age began in the Communist bloc.

Meanwhile, Yugoslavia had not been forced off her

course. The anathema pronounced against Tito did him
no harm at all. On the contrary, it introduced a fruitful
era for his country.

Two years after the war, the historical record shows us,
it had looked as if the United States and Yugoslavia were
on a collision course. It was then that the Yugoslavs shot
down an American military plane, with a serious loss of
lives. The "great heresy" opened the way for Yugoslavia to
be accepted into the bosom of the anti-Communist world
in spite of this tragic event. Tito continued to be a Communist, but not of the Kremlin variety. The avowed aim of
the United States was then to weaken and, if possible, to
destroy "international communism." Since Yugoslavia was
no longer a satellite, it was in the interest of the United
States to keep it there and to encourage others to join the
dissidents. Perhaps this would lead to their "conversion" to
the American creed of laissez-faire and even anti-commu-
nism. Experience has taught that erstwhile Communists
are likely to become fanatic anti-Communists.

Economic advantage was the lure America held out.
Yugoslavia became the beneficiary of the largess of the
United States, military and civilian aid, grants, food, and
even the most-favored-nation treatment in foreign trade.

Years after Stalin's death, Yugoslavia learned how to
get the best of both worlds. She resumed friendly, but not
satellite, relations with Russia. Now she received aid not
only from America, but also from the Soviets—again,
military and civilian aids, grants, food, and the equivalent
of the Western most-favored-nation treatment. Clearly, it
was profitable to keep on good terms with the two antagonistic worlds.

The good omen was noticed by the developing nations.
They noted the jealousy of the two superpowers, who
were ready to grant aid to nations to keep them out of the
rival camp. Thus the weak manipulated the strong, and

thus the south Slavs' national-communism fertilized the
fancy of other lands. Their motto was: communism—yes;
internationalism—no. In the end, it was: communism—
yes; internationalism—yes, a different type of internationalism. That end was beyond the horizon as yet. Was
not all the world to be one, in the end?

Meanwhile, in Yugoslavia the guide-motive was *liberal-
izatsia*, liberalization, on all fronts. But, the process was
slow. In 1963, many years after the break with the Kremlin, a liberalized new constitution was adopted. It provided
for a parliament, which, however, was a rubber-stamp.
On the other hand, there were to be elections, with a
choice of candidates accepted by the party machine. There
were also checks and balances incorporated in the parliamentary system. These included legislative committees
exercising some influence, and effecting compromises between the federal government and the states. The legislatures occasionally mounted debates. A court was to
adjudicate disputes among governmental bodies.

The Politbureau (Executive Committee) was disbanded, replaced by the larger, thirty-five-man Presidium,
charged with policy planning, and a new eleven-man
Executive Committee was formed, to execute the party
Central Committee decisions. The structure was much
like that of large business corporations in the capitalist
world: the management, and the board of directors. How
did one become a member of the Central and Executive
Committees, of the Presidium, in Communist Yugoslavia?
Very much the same way in which one becomes a member of the management and the board of trustees of an
American business corporation. The ingredients were similar too: ability, aggressiveness, connections, chance, and,
above all, luck.

The Marxist-Leninist dogma in Yugoslavia was modified after the break with the Cominform, and in came

"Titoism," reared on the Marxist understructure. Reality superseded aspirations, and the nation was reality. Aspiration was a united world community. One of Tito's early close co-workers, Milovan Djilas, claimed that bureaucracy was a reality too, and that it was the new ruling class. He also claimed that bureaucracy corrupted, it being power, and absolute bureaucracy corrupted absolutely. While knowing that this was true, Tito could not admit it. Djilas had years to ponder over this truth in jail.

In the late sixties even more critical views than those of Djilas were expressed in the Yugoslav press, sometimes without landing their authors in jail. It was possible to pass critical judgment on "petrified ideology and ideologized sciences," as Belgrade university professor Djuro Susnjic did, without being marched off to jail. Nor did the sky collapse when he criticized the "loquacious demagogues" who, he asserted, were now in full retreat, suffering defeat at the hands of people who were no longer willing to put up with the mouthings of unsubstantiated ideologies. "Ideologies are always absolutist," he dared to say. "The most frequent aim of every ideological resistance is the retention of a monopoly over social values . . ."

THE CASE OF RANKOVICH

The Yugoslavs and the Serbs, above all, might have gone into the underground, this time against the Tito regime, as they had done against the Axis, during the war. They did not do that. Even though many of them disliked communism, they were better off now than under the previous regimes. The peasants got land, which they retained as their private property, and they benefited from a

broad spectrum of social services. As Yugoslavia entered
the industrial age, living standards rose, and there was
hope for an even better day.

To keep discontent plugged up there was also the SDB,
the Security Police. Above all, there was Aleksander
Rankovich, the super-sleuth, the Scarpia of the regime. He
had not merely two ears, but thousands of them, in the
shape of bugging devices. He must have been amused to
hear the uncontrolled words of people about himself and
even about the *Stari*, the "old man," Tito. Rankovich also
had the *Stari* bugged. Security-police organs take no
chances; that of Yugoslavia was ever vigilant. But this
was no longer the age of big brother, and Rankovich was
relieved of his post. There was no bloodshed, not even
jailings, only demotions. Yugoslavia's national *liberalizat-
sia* was an accomplished fact. It was fostered by the rise
in living standards.

The injustice communism had come into the world to
rectify, according to its devotees, was this: the few had
too much, while the many had too little. The grasping
were rewarded, while the decent were penalized. There
was the exploitation of man by his fellow man. The
greatest injustices were, allegedly, perpetrated and perpetuated through the "surplus value," the excess of labor
performance producing surplus profits for the employer:
the exploitation of the worker.

Therefore, individual employers in Yugoslavia, too, had
been removed, and the means of production were nation-
alized. Since the nation was the people, and the owners of
the means of production were the people too, they would
exploit themselves by exploiting the toilers. That employers and employees had identical interests became a
party dogma. It was indeed a dogma in international
communism, but in Yugoslavia it was a national one. In
Yugoslavia positions are adjusted to the local scene; the

nation experiments, and even, sometimes, returns to previous positions. Yugoslavia herself being an experiment, the people have learned to grope their way to acceptable adjustments.

Yugoslav communism did indeed abandon the rigid position inherited from the Soviets that the individual as an employer is intrinsically an exploiter. Exploitation, Titoism held, could be averted through corrective social institutions. At the same time, the south Slavs reached the conclusion that the public corporation, working through governmental agencies, was preferable to private corporations pursuing private profits.

In the late sixties the Yugoslav government introduced the economic reform that marked the break with previous party dogma. Authorization was given to private persons to employ a maximum of five workers. Incorporating small handicraft industries and trading operations in governmental bureaucracies would have caused institutional elephantiasis. Also, some workers—especially in handicrafts—were at their best when working for themselves. Care had to be taken, though, that they should not overreach themselves and lay the foundations of new economic empires. The limitation of the maximum working force to five was to accomplish that. "Individual ownership," said the south Slav party, "is not abolished in socialism. It must be protected, and it may even be judiciously expanded."

The uniqueness of the Yugoslav system was expressed in one word, a long one, at that—*samoupravljanja*, self-management. Its substance is this: it is not the state, not the bureaucracy, that runs the enterprise, but the workers themselves. In the struggle to strengthen socialism, says the party, Communists must constantly verify their political line "through their increasing responsibility to the broad masses of the working people." Chief responsibility to run the enterprise was assigned to elected workers' councils. These, in turn, were linked to management boards and to their appointed directors.

This being a Communist system, even though a nationalist one, planning remained central, gaining the benefits of a regime from which frictions and rivalries were removed. Within this system, however, limited competition was restored to the extent that it might strengthen the workers' initiative. Each enterprise thus became a self-governing body with its own cost-accounting, and within the broader cadre each unit was to function competitively. Prices were not to be centrally determined, either, as under the regime of dogmatic communism. On the contrary, they were determined through the free interaction of supply and demand, as in the capitalist market-place. Wages were not determined centrally, either, and they became the functions of unit profitability. The higher the profit, the higher rose the wages, this resulting in an incentive system. Thus Marx made place for Adam Smith in a Communist country, resulting in a hybrid economy. While the market remained Marxist strategically, it came close to free enterprise tactically. It was a paradoxical laissez-faire socialism.

How did the Yugoslav system work? Particularly, what about the most characteristic feature of the regime, its self-management? Obviously, it takes time before such revolutionary changes exert their full influence. Can they ever reach their objective? The Yugoslav Communist regime is not quite sure of that even now. A famous cartoon in *Vjesnik*, a Zagreb paper, expressed doubts about the proper operation of the system. It showed an industrial manager responding to a worker's stricture:

"What? You protest that there is no self-management in my enterprise, and you all know that I myself manage it."

A "nation of many nations" is a pat description of Yugoslavia. From the beginning, her nucleus and power fulcrum has been Serbia—the core. Her historic fight against the Turks, the Habsburgs, and the "Axis" was the expression of a collective will. Inevitably, it led to the Reformation Movement, the Titoist heresy, within the Communist Ecumene. It was the outward manifestation of the new wave in history, the breaking up of the presumably international communism into a superlative degree of nationalism. It was no coincidence that it should have happened in the Balkans, the peninsula of dissidence.

In leaving the prescribed road of orthodox communism, Yugoslavia has acted in character. The south Slavs, and most particularly the Serbs, are not the people to toe arbitrary lines. They want to be shown and to be convinced. The government has had to adjust itself many times to the peoples' way of thinking. Had it not done so, those rugged mountains in the Balkans might have witnessed another manifestation of dissidence. National communism originated in Yugoslavia, and therefore it is the country that should be observed with particular care for other manifestations of basic changes in other parts of the Communist world. "As Yugoslavia, so goes the Communist world," is a statement that may be only partially true as yet. But it is not far-fetched to say: "Watch Yugoslavia for future trends in the Communist portion of the globe."

8

Hungary—A Destiny

The nationalist reformation of communism began in Yugoslavia, while in Hungary nationalism and communism had a head-on collision. It was a notable event, attracting world-wide attention. History explains the Hungarians' special place within the Eastern bloc.

The Hungarians, together with the Finns, are the displaced people of Europe, a Finnish-Ugrian language group in the midst of Indo-Europeans. To the north and south of the Hungarians are the Slavs, people propelled by an enormous power of expansion and integration. The Hungarians, who are not Slavs, keep them apart geographically. To the west of Hungary are German-speaking people, who, like the Slavs, are endowed with a dynamic force, the erstwhile Habsburg Empire, and the German Reich. Many times they sought to subdue and overwhelm the Hungarians, but they are still there, and likely to remain. To the east of them are the Rumanians, speaking a Latin language, likewise aliens to the Hungarians. They have been even more successful than the Slavs, north and south, and the Germans, in penetrating into Hungary. Though reduced in strength, the Hungarians have been standing their ground.

With great pride, they call themselves Magyars after a

legendary hero of olden times. Being a small nation, surrounded by the Slavic vastness, they acquired the reputation of being arrogant and proud. "If the earth is the hat of God," one of their favorite songs says, "Hungary is the bouquet on it." Their Latin-speaking nobility was once in the habit of saying: *Extra Hungariam non est vita, si est vita non est ita.* To them, at any rate, there was no life outside of their country, and if there was life, it was not the same.

THE MIRACLE OF HUNGARY

They swept into the Danubian valley a thousand years ago—horsemen, nomads from the east. They happened to reach their present location when it was a power vacuum, at the end of an era, and before the beginning of another one. It was a miraculous stroke of luck, because the land they found is fabulously rich. It is part of the Danubian bread basket. Today, too, no other country except Denmark has, proportionately, as much good land as Hungary. For a thousand years, she had also a protective shield, a magnificent wreath of mountains, from the Carpathians to the Transylvanian Alps. She was girded by mountains on all sides except the west. That fact determined her fate. The Magyars settled in a dreamland.

But it was also an explosive land, situated on the dividing line between the Eastern Christian Church, headquartered at Constantinople on the Golden Horn, and the Western Christian Church, with its Vatican on the river Tiber in Rome. That gap in the mountains to the west determined Hungary's future. She adopted the Roman faith, and Western civilization.

Because the Magyars' country was located on rich soil

and in an area of conflict, its history was a succession of traumatic events. In the face of them, the Magyars have stood their ground. Their present condition can be understood only by taking a look at their past.

They resisted all the pressures to cast them out as usurpers of the best land in Central Europe. Behind their protective mountain shield, they challenged the world, until one day word reached them through missionary travelers about the approach of the horsemen of the Apocalypse. Out of the parched east on the confines of the Gobi came the irresistible human tornadoes, the mounted devils of the "Perfect Warrior," Ghenghis Khan. Their fabulous success, we have seen, was due to several factors: unity brought about by a master organizer, swift horses, the incentive of hunger in the drought-ridden east, superior generalship, and an irresistible new weapon— fear, fueled by terror, and the futility of resistance to human-faced monsters who lived by others' death. The Tatars penetrated deep into Hungary, leaving gruesome markers along their line of march, white skeletons picked clean by vultures that blackened the sun. To this day the Hungarian word for a cataclysmic event is *tatárjárás,* Tatar invasion.

Not even this disaster destroyed the land. On the contrary, it created new defenses, which were to leave their mark on Hungary. The memory of the horror they survived encouraged the nobles to build strong castles, which served as redoubts. The nobles were to serve the King against invaders. They were also invested with many privileges to strengthen their hands. The result was an extreme form of social stratification. The nobles acquired near-royal powers to be exercised within their feudal jurisdiction. The Hungarians called them "little kings," *kis királyok.* At the same time, the population, decimated by the disaster, had to be replaced, and so new settlers were induced to dwell on the land, Slavs from north and south, Germans from the west. The original dark-colored Asian Magyars were replaced by fair-haired people. Since they came in large groups and were settled collectively, they retained their native tongues and separate ways. Thus, the solving of an old problem created a new one—the national minorities became the majority. Still, the Magyar supremacy continued; the lords of the manor, the Hungarian little kings, saw to that. The newcomers adjusted themselves to the ways of the ruling caste, and in spite of the generous infusion of new blood, Hungary never lost her identity.

The reconstruction took years, while wars continued intermittently. At the beginning of the fourteenth century, the native dynasty, the Arpads, died out. After them, diplomatic machinations, dynastic marriages, coups, counter-coups, and great-power interference kept the mid-Danubian cauldron boiling. Intermittently, Magyarland acquired strength to act as a great power, expanding to the Adriatic, and even to the Baltic. The fate of the country was determined by the character of the ruler.

The Renaissance made its mark on the institutions of the country. King Mátyás Hunyadi gave the land a place in the sun of history: power, prestige, an effective army, and, above all, social justice. His death was lamented: "Dead is *Mátyás Király* [King Mátyás], and justice is gone."

Greatness was gone too, and so also was the peoples' freedom. This time, too, out of the east came another swarm of locusts, the Turks, lured by the weakness of the West, which was engaged in religious disputations. The Turks burst into mid-Danubia in the first half of the sixteenth century and stayed in Hungary for a century and a half. They were destructive people, living on loot, unimaginative conquerors whose robber-baron ways caused the lush fields to be overrun with weeds.

Their uncreative rule resulted in the torpor of apathy that eventually made them targets for a stronger force, the House of Habsburg, of German-Swiss origin, German-speaking, anational, dynastic, engaged in a Christian crusade against the Turk. Just as quickly as Turkish power had soared, so it now collapsed. If the European powers had been able to agree among themselves they could have wiped out the Turks altogether, to share the Tatars' fate. But the powers could not agree, and so the Turks remained in Europe, even though no longer in Hungary.

"Carcasslike famished dogs haunt the lanes," a roving monk reported about the Hungarian state of affairs at that time. The peasants were famished, too, in their ramshackle huts, in mountain caves, and in the woods. They dragged their skeletal bodies to work in mid-Danubia, a land that had the best soil, the black humus of the Backa and the Banat—a blessed soil, now accursed with famine, in the wake of endless wars.

The Habsburgs moved into the country in pursuit of the Turks, and they tarried in the land for centuries as "Apostolic Kings," "Their Most Christian Majesties." They too were oppressing, killing, and torturing their Hungarian fellow-Christians. The war of religions was on, followed by the Counter-Reformation. Then a strange thing happened in this remote corner of Europe; the Habsburgs were less successful in reconverting their subjects than in the far more advanced Western crown lands of the German Reich, Austria. Calvinism and Lutheranism—in one word, Protestantism—retained their toe hold in Hungary. In particular, they retained their toe hold beyond the forests, in Transylvania, the "Far East of the land," wooded, mountainous, proud, and lovely. They retained their grip also in the devastated steppe of the *Magyar puszta*. Centered around the city of Debrecen, the new faith maintained itself with particular force. To the Magyars that city is known as the Calvinist Rome.

A HISTORIC PARALLEL

The little kings of Hungary had survived the rules of
Turks and Tatars, as many of them had made their peace
with the pashas, served them for a time, and, when they
weakened, turned against them. Behind the stout walls of
their castles they ruled like kings in a land where local
authority substituted for national power. This had to be
so, because the land was a wilderness, and means of
transportation were lacking.

The country was so run-down that the Habsburgs,
global rulers at the time, should have been able to attach
it to their crown lands, as they had done with the Tyrol,
and were going to do with Bohemia, Moravia, Galicia, and
other lands. That would have been the end of the "intruders," these Magyars, who had survived on the land
that had destroyed other tribes. Although the Habsburgs
moved in, Hungary was not crushed, and Magyarland
maintained its unique identity. It was the arrogant little
kings, Magyars themselves, in their fortified castles, who
continued to rule, as stewards of the Habsburgs, but more
often as sovereign liege lords. Their arrogance or stiff-
neckedness, as the Habsburgs called it, saved Hungary's
national identity.

The country was again depopulated after the ravages of
the Turks and those of the religious wars. Should the
steppe be abandoned to the drifting sand of the Horto-
bágy, which was constantly expanding? Should it be left
to the ravages of malaria, which threatened to become a
national calamity in the drainage area of the Danube, its
main tributary, the Tisza, and the countless small streams
that seemed to be in a hurry to reach the broad bosom of

the mother stream, so as not to see the devastation all
around? Death lurked in the sands in portions of the
country, and in the swamps. Again people were needed to
resuscitate the land.

As after the Tatar invasion, so now, after the expulsion of the Turks, the call went out to peasants in foreign
lands to move into Hungary and take possession of the
land, not all of which was plagued by sand and swamp.
There was still enough of the black soil to be had. There
was also aid from the authorities to heal the ravaged soil.

The immigrant peasants came from all directions.
Many of them descended from the northern hills. These
were the Slavs: Slovaks, Ruthenians, and their kin. From
the Transylvanian Alps came the people who were to call
themselves Rumanians, the dwellers of Bucovina, Moldavia, Wallachia, as far as the Dobrudja. From the south
came the South Slavs, known under many names: Slovenes, Croats, Serbs, and the people of Slavonia. It seemed
almost as if the advance of the Slavs from north and
south were to jeopardize Hungary's mission to keep these
northern and southern groups apart. The Germans
crossed the Leitha river in the west, settled in the region to
be known as Burgenland, and from there penetrated into
the interior of the Magyars' country, forming compact
settlements in the towns.

Many of the newcomers were absorbed by the Magyars,
but more of them retained their native traits. A distinction
was later made in foreign lands between Hungarians and
Magyars. The former included all the ethnic groups living
in Hungary, while the latter embraced the "basic" Hungarians, the presumed descendants of the "conquerors."
Since the minorities formed the majority, they presented
a problem, which became nearly fatal after the twentieth
century's first World War.

In this respect, there was a parallel between the American dilemma and the Magyar dilemma. America's dilemma was the Negro, while the Magyar's dilemma was the minority-majority. Negroes and Hungarian minorities were discriminated against. In Hungary they were not considered full-fledged citizens, and to them many fields were closed. On the other hand, in the absence of obvious distinguishing marks, they could join the dominant Magyar group. Several of these nationalities lived back-to-back with their co-nationals across Hungary's frontiers. The day was to come when they joined their kin.

This was a challenge to the Hungarians, who feared being divested of their national identity. But they had a strong sense of attachment to their land, fortified by many conflicts in which they had to reassert themselves. It was these challenges that prepared Hungary's historic response to the Soviets in the middle of the twentieth century.

AN ARROGANT NATION

The Hungarians acquired the reputation of being arrogant. They had to be that to hold their ground, and they were that to their nationalities. They were that also to their Habsburg rulers. It was their arrogance that kept them from being absorbed. They were even more arrogant in the revolutionary years of 1848 and 1849, another historic landmark.

This time they, the backward peasant folk, rose against Europe's greatest dynasty, the Habsburgs. Under their leader, Lajos Kossuth, they proclaimed the dethronement of the Habsburgs in the Calvinist Rome, Debrecen, in 1849. The fabulous Lajos Kossuth captured their fancy more than any other historic personality, more, even, than King Mátyás the Just.

Lajos Kossuth was a phenomenal leader who turned the Hungarian peasant into *ember*, a human being, filling him with national pride and forging an army out of inchoate dreams. It was Hungary's greatest moment.

So invincible was the "rebellious rabble," as the Habsburgs called Kossuth's volunteer army, that they, masters of the Danubian core land, had to call in the Russians to help. Finally, two of the world's greatest powers subdued the embattled freedom fighters. The Magyars' special aversion to the Russians dates from that time. Indeed, it was more than an aversion; it was a deep contempt, reflected in the name the Hungarians gave the Russians— *muszka*, Muscovite, a derogatory term.

The Hungarians were defeated by the united Russian and Austrian forces but were not crushed. Austrian rule was imposed upon them. They were biding their time. They knew that the Austrian Empire was an anachronism in the second part of the nineteenth century, a dynastic realm in the age of nationalism. The Habsburgs ruled over a conglomerate of nationalities whose loyalty was due to the dynasty. The weakness of the system was revealed when growing nationalism defeated the Habsburgs in crucial wars, and they had to make their peace with the "stiff-necked" Magyars, the strongest nationality in the inlands. Vienna could not afford to score another "victory" against them, such as the one it had scored with Russian aid. This time the Russians would not have helped. This led to one of the great historic moments of the Danube valley. Textbooks call it the *Ausgleich*, compromise. The unitary Austrian Empire now became the Dual Monarchy of Austria-Hungary, a partnership. This was the reward of the Hungarians, "orphans on the Danube," for having retained their historic arrogance and strength. Some of the other Habsburg nationalities were more advanced than the Magyars, the Bohemians, for instance, and the

Czechs. They had not been promoted to the Hungarians'
status. They were not so stiff-necked.

The Hungarian dilemma, the problem of the majority
minorities, found no solution at this time. The Magyars'
arrogance prevented their extending their hands to the
Slovaks, Rumanians, Serbs, and many other groups. Their
country had been in existence for a thousand years in an
alien environment behind its national frontiers, and they
were determined to have it remain that way.

It was not to remain that way. The Habsburg anachronism was terminated with the first World War, and the
dynasty was dethroned. The loser, Hungary, lost her millennial frontiers, two-thirds of her territory, retaining only
a small core land. Millions of Hungarians felt now what it
was to be a minority, as they were incorporated in the
territories of the victors. The Hungarians reacted to this
tragedy in their traditional way. While they had to sign
the peace treaty, since they were in the hands of alien
masters, they never accepted its provisions. Their reaction
was expressed in the Hungarian words the world was to
learn: *nem, nem, soha*—no, no, never. They who had
survived the Tatars, Turks, and Habsburgs without territorial loss could not accept their fate. They would not bow
to the Rumanians, Czechs, and Serbs, whom they considered inferior breeds. The Magyars lost most of their
country but not their arrogance.

THE EXISTENTIALIST MOMENT

Meanwhile the Russians, scorned by the Hungarians,
had turned to communism, and that made them hated in
Hungary even more. Three-fourths of the Hungarians
were Catholics, and revulsion toward atheistic commu-

nism was in their bones. The Catholic priesthood had a particularly strong hold on the peasant, and Hungary was then predominantly an agricultural land.

The hole in the western mountain range which linked the Hungarians to the Occident made their higher social classes Western-minded. Their greatest poet in the nineteenth century, Sándor Petőfi, translated not Russian or German classics, but English and French ones. The poetic genius of Endre Ady, in our century, attracted him to the Seine, about which he sang in ecstasy, and not to the Volga. Hungarians made their pilgrimages to London, Paris, and the Italian cities, but never to St. Petersburg or Moscow.

Now the West had forsaken them, as shown by the peace pact. The Treaty of Trianon, which despoiled them of their millennial heritage, had been signed in France, and the main signatories were the Western powers. Where were they to turn? This was the moment of despondency, numbing their senses, and they were ready to heed the counsels of despair. The contemptible *muszka,* the Muscovite, was rebelling against the values of the Western order, aiming to change not only the institutions of his nation, but also those of the world. Perhaps the Soviets could help the Hungarians in their revolt against the injustice? In this moment of the despair, their existentialist moment, the Magyars turned toward the East. In the spring of 1919 Hungary set up its own *tanácsköztársaság*—Soviet Republic.

If it had not been a tragic event, it would have been comic. It was a republic of utter confusion. The Commissar of Finances did not know how to endorse a check. Other members of the cabinet were as incompetent. Several of them were frustrated intellectuals. One of them was an unsuccessful playwright whose first move was to have his drama performed in the prestigious National

Theatre. Golden tongues were in great abundance, but
everything else was brass. After floundering for three
months, the regime collapsed.

It was followed by an era of reaction, headed by Admiral Nicholas Horthy, and Hungary had neither a navy
nor a seacoast. It lasted for a quarter of a century. It
began with the outlawing of Communists, then it turned
to anti-Semitism, anti-liberalism, and anti-laborism. As the
years passed, its extremes were tempered and it remained
merely an unimaginative regime, maintaining law and
order and little else. Some improvements were introduced,
just the same, as a result of the communist challenge and
the democratization of the Western world.

Basically, the social structure of Hungary, too, remained stable. The little kings of previous ages were
transformed into the big shots of the big bureaucracy of
an authoritarian regime. For a quarter of a century the
sun stood nearly still over the Hungarian countryside. The
word *paraszt*, peasant, remained a derogatory term. While
feudalism was gone, its vestiges weighed down the common people. On the richest soil of Europe there lived
many peasants who were emaciated because they were on
short rations; farm laborers were working other people's
lands. More than a third of the farm population vegetated
at the lowest level of existence, to be treated by wealthy
landlords as an inferior breed.

THEN ANOTHER WAR

Although Admiral Horthy was an unimaginative man,
he saw that it was not in Hungary's interest to go into the
second World War on Hitler's side. This in spite of the
fact that he was consumed by zeal to rectify the injustice

perpetrated at Trianon. The Germans of the Third Reich
pushed Hungary into the war. The capital's imperishable
wits quipped: "Now we know who will lose the war. We
are always on the losing side."

True to ancient tradition, the Hungarians were indeed
on the losing side. The Russians were the winners, and
they moved in. They could have incorporated Hungary
and her neighbors into their country, as they have done
with the Baltic nations, but they refrained from that
move. Hungary merely became a satellite.

THE RUSSIANS WERE COMING

The elections held in the shadow of the Soviet bayonets
failed to intimidate the country, and so the Communist
Party was merely an also-ran, while the Smallholders'
Party ran a strong first. A drastic land reform was
effected, which divested the estate owners of their holdings and vested the small peasant with ownership rights.
Unfortunately, there was not enough land for all. And the
new landowners lacked the means for profitable farming.
The plots were too small for effective utilization.

Meanwhile the stalwarts of the old regime, noticing the
warning on the wall, bolted out of the country, with the
aid of Western Allied personnel, often military, immune
to border search. Old-regime funds were whisked across
the frontiers to capitalist strongholds. Swiss and American banks became acquainted with tongue-twisting Magyar names.

The clumsy ones, unable to fly the coop, were stripped
of their historic prerogatives. Long after feudalism had
disappeared in the rest of Europe, the quasi-feudal Magyar system was on the wane. A currency inflation, artifi-

cially induced, devalued the local currency so fast that
four hundred thousand quadrillion pengoes (clinkers)
barely bought a single American dollar. Many holdings in
the local currency could now be used as wallpaper. The
old regime of status and money was dead.

RÉMURALOM

Nobody could have looked less heroic than Mátyás
Rákosi. The top of his head looked like an outsize billiard
ball; he was short; he had an abrasive personality. Yet, he
was the object of a demonstrative personality cult. When-
ever he uttered his tired clichés in public he faced a
spellbound audience, and what he said were tired clichés.
But he had shown courage during the Horthy regime,
returning to Hungary from Russia to reorganize the Communist underground. Caught, he was sentenced to death.
In response to foreign reaction, his sentence was com-
muted to life imprisonment. Pardoned after years in jail,
he returned to Russia, and at the end of the war he
arrived in his native Hungary on the Soviet bandwagon.
He became the party's top man, the Stalin of Budapest.

In his coldly intelligent way he was a fanatic for a
cause, which was a disembodied concept, only casually
linked to man. His mind was filled with Marxist dogma, as
interpreted by the Kremlin prophet. Rákosi received peremptory word from the Kremlin that the nationalist
heresy must be stamped out before bursting into the open.
That is why Lászlo Rajk, one of the devout Communists,
and so many other Communists, had to die, accused of
heresy. Loyalty was due to the Kremlin and its lack
indicated treason. Patriotism was equated with subversion.

Rémuralom, reign of horror, was the term the Hungarians used for this phase of their history. It *was* a reign of horror. Horror haunted the country, there was fear of the dark, of the dreaded knock on the door, and of the brutal examination in the barracks of the A.V.O., the political police.

In a Communist country it was just as dangerous to be a Communist, in those days, as to be a non-Communist. Tito, the national heretic, claimed to be a true believer too.

Stalin died on March 5, 1953. It took three endless years for a new age—the thaw—to incubate. The new First Secretary of the Central Committee of the Communist Party in the Soviet Union, Nikita Khrushchev, made a "secret speech" to the Party Congress in 1956, a speech that shook the world. Stalin, he said, had been a tyrant engaged in the non-Marxist "cult of personality" and the subversion of party aims. The despot's embalmed body, next to Lenin's in the mausoleum on Red Square, was removed.

The Hungarian reaction to the secret speech was in character. The despot was dead; long live freedom. Seldom has the world witnessed anything like this: a tiny nation challenging a super-power. In no time the nation was up in arms, ready to wrest its rights from faltering Russian hands. Remarkable was the composition of the freedom fighters: mainly students and industrial workers, cheered on by all the others. These students had been selected from underprivileged families, to replace the overprivileged student generation. The industrial workers, too, were the darlings of the regime. What induced them now to turn against their presumed benefactors at the cost of their lives in this late fall of 1956?

The inducement was that something intangible we call national ways, compounded of memories, legends, and

bravado. It was also the result of exhortations from the
West, the natural reaction to the age of horror, and the
inchoate expectation of a better day. Above all, it was the
result of the mating of the Hungarian character with an
atavistic romanticism. Hungarian poetry and music provided much of the explanation, a challenge to fate.

More attention was paid to this Hungarian uprising
than to any other contemporary event. Yet, the Western
world missed the main point. It said that the Hungarians
were fighting for their traditional freedoms. That was not
so. Never had they been the darlings of fate, and only
their frustration was traditional. This time they were
fighting for freedoms they never had before, freedoms of a
new age of humanism.

They lost the battle but won the war. They lost, as so
many times before, since they had been a tiny dot on the
outskirts of a near-global empire. They won because Moscow could not afford to pay the price of its victory. Until
then Budapest was constantly giving, while Moscow was
receiving. Now the traffic was reversed. Having shown
their nature, the Hungarians had to be appeased.

THE NATIONALIST EXPLOSION

The new head of the Hungarian Workers' Party (Communists) was János Kádár. Accused of nationalist heresy,
he had been one of Rákosi's victims. A dedicated Communist in spite of this martyrdom, he continued to believe in
the ecumenical proletariat. He saw Hungary as an historic
segment of that proletariat. But that proletariat was far
from monolithic. The Hungarian branch was the product
of a thousand years of history. It was the history of a
unique nation, which required a unique treatment. Be-

cause of her historic development, way of life, literary and
artistic heritage, and the necessities flowing from its geographic location, Hungary's problems had to be different
from those of other fraternal nations. They called for
national solutions.

A decade after the uprising an *ex-cathedra* statement
was made on this subject by the top party expert, Zoltán
Komocsin, secretary for international and interparty
affairs. Speaking for the party, he stated that "national
unity, developed on social foundations, is a new trait in
our history and continues to be the source and encouragement of socialist patriotic awareness."

János Kádár himself provided this interpretation of
socialist patriotism in an interview with an American
correspondent in the summer of 1966: "Nationalism has
developed over the course of centuries, especially in the
way of the thinking of the peoples of Europe . . ." It
cannot be ignored, he added, and can be reconciled with
the international ideology of Marxism. Just as the individual has unique traits unduplicated in any other person,
so the nation has characteristics that cannot be dupli-
cated by others. "Every nation has its own problems calling for special solutions."

The new regime under Kádár had learned the lesson of
the 1956 trauma. For fear of another outbreak, and to
appease the Hungarians, the Soviets now began to pour
money into the country, instead of taking it away. How
much it was cannot be ascertained because of Moscow's
secrecy and the Soviet's monetary conversion. A Western
source estimated that Hungary received about 400 million
dollars from the Soviets in six post-revolutionary years
alone.

The most important innovation in the economic management of the country was the change in the ratio of
consumer articles to industrial equipment. Housing re-

ceived high priority. New industrial centers were constructed, including Hungary's Pittsburgh, in Dunaujváros,
"Danubian New Town." Manufacturing plants were
scattered in many parts of the country, helping farm
workers to obtain employment during their slack season.
More than before, mid-Danubia's "sickle" yielded to the
"hammer."

There were fewer brainwashing operations, too, while
more fringe benefits were added. These included not only
free medical services but also better government-financed
vacations and workers' sanatoria. Urbanization grew
apace, not only in the metropolitan areas, but also in the
attitude of people, especially the young. Peasant girls and
lads, having become workers in "open-air grain factories,"
no longer looked different from their city-bred peers. All
along the line, the life of the toilers was eased. A few
short years after the uprising the Hungarians knew who
had won. Nor did Kádár want all his countrymen to
become Communists. He expected them merely not to be
anti-Communists.

NATIONALISM TAKES OVER

The Hungarians have an inveterate habit of grumbling,
a way of life, for valid cause. They had the Turk, the
Tatar, and the Habsburgs on their necks, for centuries.
Above all, they had their kiskirályok, little kings. They
were the victims of their public servants, who, in Hungary, were public masters.

During the Rákosi reign of terror people did not dare to
complain even in their sleep. The very walls had keen
ears, and there was that ominous midnight knock on the
door, followed by the interrogation of the A.V.O., the
dreadful political police.

Now again Hungarians felt free to grumble, and that was a hopeful sign. Endlessly, they complained about their government, and that made them feel good all over, stimulated to grumble some more. Happily, they indulged in the national pastime of feeling unhappy. Still more significant, they felt free to complain about the Soviets too.

The institution of which the Hungarians have long been proud is their Parliament. They like to say that their "Golden Bull" was coeval with England's Magna Carta. The photogenic Parliament Building on the Danube embankment in Budapest has long been the most popular aim of camera lenses in the uncommonly attractive Hungarian capital. Hungarians do not like to mention the fact that the appearance of their Parliament is more impressive than its substance. The majority party supporting the government nearly always called the tune. Yet, Parliament also served as the opposition's sounding board, carrying on the Hungarian tradition of grumbling. Occasionally, the government, tired of complaints, yielded to the opposition.

Under the Rákosi Communists there was no audible grumbling in or out of Parliament. An atmosphere of sweetness and light pervaded the Solons' chambers. Everything was calm and orderly, and the governmental measures were approved with no demur. Parliament was Budapest's magnificent gothic rubber stamp.

As the regime became national, all of this changed, too. Hungarian tradition asserted itself. Here is an example of the changed role of Parliament: the Minister of Justice submitted to it a bill on certain offenses, containing significant changes from the prevailing pattern. Under the previous system, all the deputies would have said "aye," and the bill would have become law. This time, in the spring of 1968, the Parliamentary response was different.

Members of the House took the floor and recommended several amendments, which the government did not ignore. The movers of the amendments met with the Minister of Justice and with members of the permanent Legal and Administrative Committee of the House, and as a result of these meetings the amendments were incorporated in the pending law. In Communist Hungary this was considered a significant departure from the routine.

One of the traditions of the pre-Communist Hungarian parliament was "question time," known as *interpellacio*, interpellation, during which cabinet members faced a barrage of legislative interrogation.

During the Kádár regime, it was revived in the national assembly, as a kind of third degree for the government. As a result of such interpellations, the government was known to take action that it may not have otherwise. Another national institution had been saved.

In the words of a "Radio Free Europe" (anti-Communist) commentator on April 5, 1968:

It is impossible to overlook the fact that Parliament is slowly emerging from the "Ice Age" of its existence, gradually engaging in more meaningful activity. It is reasonable to assume that it will be the Central Committee of the Party which will remain the supreme council of the regime. . . . At the same time, it is still true that the House is in a position to supply something that the highest collective body of the regime cannot give, i.e., a public platform for open discussion, where not only members of the party, but also non-party people, have an opportunity to air their views.

This is precisely the Hungarian national tradition—a parliament following governmental guidance closely while, at the same time, giving a chance to the opposition to have its views aired. Respectability again was covering the grumbler with its mantle.

THE LIVELIHOOD OF THE PEOPLE

In the beginning there was free enterprise, which goes back to that famous apple trade in Eden. Trade gradually became unfree because of the domination of the monolithic corporations. This is the Communist version of economic history. The Communist state therefore had to tackle the economic problems, to solve them in the interest of all the people, instead of the particular holders of stocks. Thus began the new era of planned economy. And now there was again a new age in Hungary, too, as in the rest of the bloc. The monolithic system had become too cumbersome, and the individuals were no longer ready to put up with the period of austerity that was to lead to the much-promised age of socialist plenty.

At the plenary session of the Central Committee of the Hungarian Socialist Workers' Party on May 25–27, 1966, a long-awaited system of reforms was heralding the new age accepted in Hungary. This entailed an historic retreat from the advanced positions of austerity, communism. Was this the beginning of a movement toward the Yugoslav line and beyond? What did the reform contain?

First, there were certain features it did not contain. The principal means of production and distribution continued to be held by the state. To abandon them would have been tantamount to relinquishing both communism and socialism. Central planning retained its pivotal place.

The significant innovations were these:

The law of supply and demand was restored to its proper place. Economic methods similar to those of the capitalists were emphasized. No longer were goods dumped or withheld because of the arbitrary will of the

planning center. The customer was king, up to a certain
point, to be sure. Within the overall plan the directors of
the individual plants were free to act, no longer hobbled
by the decisions of distant authority. As in the capitalist
countries, the manager was supposed to know best. In line
with these changes, the structures of prices and wages
were remodeled, and in doing so the national interests had
to be brought into line with those of the individual consumers and wage earners. Greater emphasis was accorded
to agriculture, hitherto the stepchild of the regime, considered an atavistic survival of the past. Now it was
accepted as an organic segment of economic life. The
private sector was enlarged, and the issuance of private
trade licenses eased. The one-man store as part of a vast
bureaucratic mechanism was to yield to individual ownership. Thus the source of much inefficiency and petty
corruption was to be erased.

The most basic changes were these. No more than the
long-range objectives were to be contained in the master
plan. The details of the implementation were to be left
flexible, adjustable to the requirements of the prevailing
conditions. Enterprises were informed of the amount of
money they were expected to contribute to the national
budget, but even this was flexible. Profits remaining to
them could be used at their discretion. The price structure
was to be brought into harmony with the world market,
which was predominantly capitalistic.

More in detail, three categories of consumer prices were
introduced. In one of these, prices remained free to follow
market fluctuations, just as in the United States. In the
second category, a certain latitude was set by establishing
maximum-minimum prices. Finally, in the third category
(which had to do with the satisfaction of basic needs),
prices remained fixed, and this included most foodstuffs,
clothing, and building material for private use.

In agriculture, too, compulsory production targets were removed. In that area, too, the government encouraged initiative on the part of managers. National publicity was given to the suggestion of Imre Tar, the economist, that a merit system be introduced on the farms, resulting in good workers being given larger private-property allotments, so-called household plots, and the government providing them with free small farm machinery, chemicals, and seeds. This suggestion appears to have been stimulated by the government. These were bold measures in a Communist country. What results were foreseen?

Competition among the enterprises was bound to result in some of them winning and others losing in mergers, and perhaps a new phenomenon, a Communist type of bankruptcy. The inducement, also envisaged in the new system, would lead to wage differentials, which, in turn, might lead to claims, counterclaims, bargaining, and, inevitably, to strikes.

Improved quality was expected to provide surpluses in the form of increased exports, countered with more imports and greater participation in foreign trade. As a result, there might be success in hardening the currency to the point where the country would have a favorable trade balance, exports in excess of imports, and, perhaps, a favorable balance of payment, more money moving in than moving out.

The success of the supply-and-demand sector, which is the capitalist segment of the Communist system, might lead to the reduction of the importance of the two other price categories. In the end, the law of supply and demand might prevail along the entire line; and when these twins prevail, can capitalism be far behind? "New Economic Model" was the name the Hungarians gave to this system.

Yet it might be jumping the gun to expect the final decline of the socialist method of production in Hungary.

In spite of all the changes, the principal means of production and distribution were bound to remain in the hands of the state, while in capitalist countries they were bound to remain in stockholders' hands. But, in the end, the gap between the two may not be as wide as it seems.

Were the Hungarians satisfied with this New Economic Model, their NEM?

"I have looked for this NEM," one Budapester told the other, "but could not find it."

"Under what letter were you looking?"

"Under *N*, naturally."

"That was wrong."

"Under what letter should I have been looking?"

"Under *C*, naturally."

"Why *C*?"

"Under *catastrophe*."

Can one ever satisfy a Hungarian, the eternal grumbler?

RELIGION IS THE ELIXIR OF THE PEOPLE

Churches are the landmarks of the Hungarian countryside. They thrust their imploring fingers toward the sky. "Spiritual lightning conductors," a Hungarian poet has called the church steeple, shields against celestial wrath. The church is the community center, surrounded by dwellings that are clustered close to it for protection. Thus it was before the Communists, and thus it is under their reign.

Church reconstruction commanded high priority after the war. The floodlighted tower of the Matthias Coronation Church, on the Fisher Bastion of Buda, is a prime tourist attraction. The regilded inscription on the monumental front of the Basilica of Budapest still proclaims the basic Christian faith: *Ego Sum Via Veritas et Vita.* The Cathedral of Esztergom, the seat of the Cardinal Primate, occupies its prominent position as the Hungarian equivalent of Rome's St. Peter's. The historic frescoes by Niccolo di Tommaso in the Esztergom Chapel and its Renaissance Bakocz Chapter are proudly exhibited as glories of medieval architecture, and so are the ruins of the thirteenth-century Romanesque church at Zsambek, and other vestiges of an ecclesiastical age. The tall steeples of the Dome of Szeged on the bank of Tisza, famed as the "most Hungarian river," and the great Calvinist Church of Debrecen, the "most Hungarian city," continue to top the list of photogenic public buildings.

The religious procession, perpetuating the traditions of another age in the Communist world, is as much a part of the Hungarian countryside as the village steeple. Also kept alive are the plaintive church songs, which may be as old as Christianity in Hungary. Processions sustain the festive fashion of the pagan past in which they originated.

Religion in Hungary is part of the national way of life, the way of a nation that has always considered itself Christ's shield against the Oriental infidel, mainly Islam, but also the Eastern Christian, the Greek Orthodox. The Transylvanian Alps of pre-World War I Greater Hungary demarcated the easternmost position of Protestantism.

The founder of Hungary, her principal missionary, King Stephen, a saint of the Roman Catholic Church, is also the country's blessed patron. His son, St. Emery, gained fame in Italian-speaking Europe under the name of Amerigo. Hungarians like to boast that their favorite saint gave his name to America. Saint Elizabeth of Hungary, daughter of Andrew II, King of the Magyars, wife of

Louis IV of Thuringia, became one of the most venerated and one of the most pictorialized saints of the Catholic Church. Her portraits by Fra Angelico, Hans Holbein the Younger, Murillo, and Simone Martini carried her fame to all parts of the Christian world. It received more impetus in the English-speaking world through Charles Kingsley's poem "The Saint's Tragedy." The heroic exploits of John Hunyadi in stemming the Turkish tide associated Hungary's name with the defense of the faith of Christ.

The link between the religious and the secular in Hungary was especially symbolized by the Magyars' Holy Crown. Its upper portion, consisting of two bent bands of gold surmounted by a cross, was presented to King Stephen by Pope Sylvester, with the title of Apostolic King. The lower portion of the crown, a broad round band of gold, was presented to King Geza I by the Byzantine Emperor Michael Dukas. The two crowns fashioned into one became the most sacred Magyar relic. The crown became not only a sacred symbol but also part of the Magyar mystique. Since there was only one crown, there could be only one ruler, and this fact was particularly important in feudal days, when authority exhibited a tendency to proliferate. In time a body of doctrine emerged attributing innate powers of sanctity, combined with sovereignty, to the Holy Crown. "The Hungarian people," wrote Akos von Timon, law professor at Budapest University and best-known exponent of this doctrine, "regard the state as a society organized in the interests of the whole, incorporated in the Holy Crown. . . . Public power is present in the crown as a mystery. Each factor of state life is in immediate touch with the Holy Crown and obtains its function from it. It is the source of all power and prerogative."

More than that, the crown was presumed to be the legal possessor of the land, the source of all property rights.

Thus it was not the King himself that represented the highest authority, but the "jurisdiction of the Holy Crown of the Kingdom," and the power inherent in it, as exercised by the "legal" nation.

Until the end of World War II the crown was kept under the supervision of an honorary guard in a separate structure. At the end of the second World War the crown was spirited out of the country by the Hungarian Nazi regime and turned over to the American forces in the West, so as to keep the sacred symbol out of Soviet hands. At the time of writing it is in the possession of the United States at an undisclosed location presumed to be Fort Knox. The Communist government of Hungary is believed to be striving to get back the Holy Crown. It is also anxious to repatriate other religious relics linked to Hungary's history. The writer of this book happened to encounter a representative of the Budapest government, a clergyman, engaged in negotiations to repatriate a part of the skull of St. Stephen, allegedly discovered on the Dalmatian coast. It was not clear how it could be identified after so many centuries. But, then, after all, both the Holy Crown and the part of the skull form portions of a mystique that defies rational explanations.

When Hungary became a Communist country, after World War II, religion, as such, was neither persecuted nor promoted there. The League of Atheists of the earlier Soviets had no counterpart in Hungary. Nor did the Magyars indulge in the "church-wrecking" of the Soviets. Individual churchmen believed to be hostile to the regime were persecuted. One of these was Cardinal Archbishop Joseph Mindszenty. On the whole, the church in Hungary was accepted as part of the historic past, surrounded by a traditional aura.

With the new accent on nationalism, religion was brought into a new relationship to Marxism by the most

prestigious Hungarian Marxist scholar, György Lukács, a
man of far-ranging fame. The Paulist Society for Christian Marxists heard this notable Hungarian express some
uncommon views at its international conference at
Marienbad, in Czechoslovakia, in the late sixties. "In the
process of human development," said Lukács, "the desires
and endeavors expressed in Christianity also belonged to
the traditions of humanism. The aim in both cases is the
development of personality and social justice. A world
must be created in which the full development of fraternal love, sustained by Christianity, is supported by the
social structure. . . ."

Professor Lukács did not subscribe to the view that it
is unnatural for people to believe in the supernatural.
The dynamic elements of Christianity, he set forth, could
be employed to help overcome static attitudes and to stress
man's active role in the formation of his society-based
future. Thus concrete historic tasks may be more readily
performed through the interlinking of Marxism and
Christianity.

"Without Christianity there would be no Marxism," said
another participant at the Marienbad conference. The
Marxist scholars appeared to agree that Christianity was
part of the Hungarian tradition. Clearly this was due to
the new intellectual climate of the country, which took
pride in its patriotic past.

THE HISTORIC MEMORY

Hungary's Soviet-oriented historiography began in
1945, the year of Russian victory. Beginning with that
year, the Magyars' history was linked to that of the Soviets
in an indissoluble whole. After the 1956 uprising, however, Hungarian history acquired an entirely new dimen-

sion, a nationalist one. History no longer began in 1945. Now it began in 986, the year of the conquest. Before 1956 it had been best to forget the past. After it, the past of the nation became respectable, designed to stimulate self-respect. There was much in the Hungarian past of which the nation could be proud, the pundits now proclaimed. A few illustrations of this new trend will try to prove the point.

"Just because a person happened to be an aristocrat," an article in a highbrow magazine, *Élet és Irodalom* (*Life and Literature*), by Pal E. Fehér points out, "he need not be a villain. Also, just because a person happens to be a Communist, he need not be a hero." Mihály Károlyi, the president of a short-lived republic, the author continues, was an aristocrat and the poor people's friend. György Dózsa, a member of the nobility, fought and died a grisly death in the sixteenth-century peasant revolt. Lajos Kossuth, the fabulous patriot in Hungary's mid-nineteenth-century independence, was a member of the gentry, but he also had a strong social conscience. And so had many others, Hungarians all, and members of the higher classes, endowed with deep human feelings and social sense. The Communists hail them as akin in soul.

During the ten years from the end of the second World War to the uprising, the new breed of Communist patriots say, Hungarian history was shrouded in black, as people were encouraged to be ashamed of their national past, weighted down with tyranny and abuse. Shame was not what Hungarians should feel. Their very survival, say the authors, was a near-miracle of surviving in the storm center of the world. Any nation that could survive the Hungarian tragedy was heroic. "Yes, this nation has performed heroic deeds, achieving results that justify this claim. Heroic is the appropriate term for Hungarian history."

A similar view was expressed in a national poll. What

do the Hungarians think of themselves as a nation? This was asked ten years after the uprising in the periodical *Kortárs* (*Contemporary*). While the respondents expressed divergent views on many points of the broad-spectrum poll, they agreed on one point, and, considering the country's ideological framework, a highly significant point it was. They expressed the view that the Hungarians were patriotic, above everything else. Quarrel among themselves they may, and have often done, but to outsiders they close the ranks. The constant need to remain alert against perennial aggression has infused them with patriotism.

Public-opinion polls have become as popular in Hungary as in the United States. Under the *ancien régime* of Rákosi and Gerö, public-opinion polls would have been inconceivable. Even more inconceivable would have been the answers published in the press, particularly of a certain type. Secondary-school students were asked to what nation, next to Hungary, they would like to belong. Their answer was highly significant. After years of brainwashing, only 3 percent of them selected the *muszka,* Muscovite. At the head of the list of their favorites was *la grande nation,* France, in line with the traditional orientation of the Hungarian. To him, France has meant the West. Also, being far, she was no danger. Next in line came the British, even farther and therefore liked, but not of the Continent, and therefore of a different breed. The Swiss, the Swedes, and the Germans received high priorities too. On the other hand, the next-door neighbor, Austria, won no popularity prize. Whether the regime is pro- or anti-Communist, Hungary's past quarrels with Vienna are recalled. It is more surprising that America ceased to be the Hungarian's dreamland: too many headlines linked it to violence. It was left for Communist writers to warn the xenophile Hungarian, "Don't fall flat on your face in the presence of a person from abroad. Don't underrate your own nation's achievements."

Increasingly, a quasi-evangelical fervor creeps into party preachments about Hungary's harassed past:

"Cultivate the historic and cultural traditions of the nation," writes Istvan Soter, history and literature professor of distinction, and president of the Hungarian P.E.N. Club, "and above all, outdo yourself in cultivating our native language. This is necessitated by the need to equalize the intellectual disequilibrium fomented by an overtechnical civilization." Professor Soter did not agree with the secondary-school students' rejection of the United States. He saw in the diversity of America's group traits a stimulating force. "Inner-directed nationalism," as he sees it, "stimulates individual maturation, while its outer-directed version fosters enmity."

"Nationalism is so essential," according to Jozsef Darvas, a party spokesman, "that Socialist countries will win only with its aid. The propelling force of nationalism, and that alone, will enable the countries to be lifted to the higher level of socialism. This entails neither uniformization, nor the liquidation of diversities, and least of all the termination of national growth."

Jozsef Darvas went farthest in his exaltation of nationalism. Lacking the experience of being an active nationalist, one could not become an effective internationalist, he said. Nationalism was the first stage of internationalism.

"National apathy is the danger, not nationalism." Echoing this concept, János Kádár, the party secretary, elevated it into a party dogma: "Our foremost duty is to build socialism in our country. . . . Only as our system gains in weight, shall we be able to stand by others."

In Hungary, the ideological guidelines of the Central Committee Plenum were drawn up in March 1965. The guidelines extolled "socialist patriotism," which they described as the refinement of the past's "democratic patriotism," the second step toward communism. The summit will be reached with "Communist patriotism." While nationalism without socialism had been denounced as a vestige of the discredited past, socialist patriotism was extolled as the correct way of promoting the cause of one's country and that of the toiling masses of the world. Zoltán Komocsin, the chief ideologue, declared that only national unity on socialist foundations represented the consummation of patriotic awareness, the ultimate goal.

The trivial sometimes casts its light on the lofty. When the "maxi-hair" reached Hungary on its inevitable march of triumph, it was given a nationalist coloration by reference to the portrait of Ferenc Rákóczi, the seventeenth-century patriot who anticipated twentieth-century hippies with his extra-length mane. The flower-printed garments had their ancestry in the Hungarian peasant attire. Proudly some Hungarians intoned: "The original hippies were our gypsies."

The legendary uprising of the Hungarians in 1956 against the Soviets best expresses their will. It was the logical sequel of their millennial history. In the midst of an alien world, the pressure of their environment hardened them into an irrefragable force. "Kremlinism" forced upon them has not affected their transcendent nationalism. They still believe—perhaps more than before—that Hungary is the flower on "God's hat"—the earth.

The march of Hungarian nationalism was summed up long ago in Sir Walter Raleigh's notable axiom, "History hath triumphed over time."

9

The Czechs—
Perhaps a New Era

Whoever is master of Bohemia is master of Europe," said the perceptive Iron Chancellor, Prince Bismarck. Bohemia was, in his day, a mere geographic expression, a historic memory, a land of the Habsburg realm. A generation later, at the end of the first World War, it became the core of Czechoslovakia. Under its statesman philosopher, Thomas Garrigue Masaryk, it began its career as the only democratic republic in Eastern Europe.

Czechoslovakia is the westernmost promontory of the Slav world, projecting into the core land of German-speaking Europe. Some of the historic battles of German and Slav were conducted on her soil. In the past, almost invariably, the Germans scored. Then the dramatic change, as the Slavs forged ahead, after the second World War, with the victory of the Russians, who swept the Czechs into the Communist camp. Clinging to this pivot was important for the Russians, who know history. "Either we or they," history told them. The Germans were the "anti-we"; the "they."

History taught them this lesson: Czechoslovakia cannot stand alone in the midst of the German world, but must be attached to the global Slav from the Pacific to the river Elbe.

"Only from the historical view of earlier centuries and from my experience in this one," writes Marcia Davenport in her autobiography, *Too Strong for Fantasy*, "did I finally learn that the twenty years of the Masaryk Republic were a sublime interlude in the long history of subjection, subjugation, and proof of the adage that the master of Bohemia is the master of Europe."

THEN THE HUSSITE WARS

In 1968 the Czechs took steps to assert their national identity. Their strongest historic impression was the Hussite war, in the first part of the fifteenth century. It was this war they now recalled.

That war was the climactic act the Czechs' ancestors, the Bohemians, played, as protagonists of the Reformation of the Catholic Church. Withal, it was their stand against the German, bent on the domination of the Czechs' pivotal land.

Let us look for a moment at the martyrdom of John Huss, rector of the university of *Zlata Praha*, Golden Prague. The national hero of the Czechs he was, and their inspiration in resisting Soviet encroachments, too, in centuries to come. He was nationalism personified in the local church. A century before Luther, Huss wanted the Church purged of politics and venality. His ideal was the religion of the early Christians, a creed of broad humanity proclaiming all men brethren before the throne of God. To the clear waters of Biblical teachings he wanted to guide his flock. An orthodox Catholic, not a reformer of mere dogma and doctrine, he professed to be. Religion was action to him, not formality, and so he set out to succour the poor, who were impoverished by the exactions of secular and ecclesiastical lords. Huss preached that having divested themselves of divine guidance, sinful oppressors should be neither obeyed nor revered. He averred it was a profanity for the Archbishop of Prague to own four hundred towns and for the church in Bohemia to hold one third of all arable land. "He who lives according to reason is a God-fearing man, while he who follows his lust is a beast."

For the authorities, this was blasphemy, and the preachings of Huss were declared an abomination in the eyes of the Lord. "The regularly designated authorities must be obeyed, not because they are good but because they govern by virtue of the powers conferred upon them as stewards of the law." Authority, the opposing camp proclaimed, was divine even when lacking in charity. The opponents hailed institutionalized virtue in lieu of individual worth. They claimed that the holy offices had been created to counteract man's weakness. If all had the right to judge if the Church were just, what would be the fate of authority?

The Emperor summoned Huss to the Council of Constance, promising him safe-conduct, full freedom to defend his views, and permission to return home unharmed. But Huss had a premonition as he took leave of his worried disciples: "Should my death be to His glory and your welfare, may He grant me my plea to face it with no fear."

Immediately upon his arrival at Constance, the Church authorities detained him. The Emperor protested mildly against this violation of his pledge, but the Council had the proper answer. Heretics, it said, stood beyond the pale of law; those who gainsaid them were friends of the fiend.

Huss dared to express his opinions, which he considered self-evident truths. He stood up to his judges invested with the majesty of law, human and divine, telling them: " 'Tis better to be vanquished while speaking the truth than vanquished while lying." In jail he cried out in agony: "Many spoke angrily against me without any reason. My kind deeds were repaid with evil and my love of them with hate. Many dogs have surrounded me." It was on a July morning in 1415 that the flames devoured his body at the stake. Thomas Carlyle said this about his end: "His truthful voice had to be burned out of *this* world."

John Huss became the father of Bohemian, later Czech, nationalism, and his motto, *Pravda vitezi*, "truth wins," the maxim of Czechoslovakia. In the midst of the flames, he could not have foreseen that he was to become his nation's hero, nor that his words were to be quoted with reverence at the time the Czechs infused their communism with nationalism. Nor could he foresee in the midst of the flames that it was he who put the torch to the ideology of his foes. His heroic fate aroused his countrymen and the Hussite wars ensued.

One of those men was Jan Zizka de Trocnov, the one-eyed nobleman who saw all. He saw that religion meant more than adherence to outworn forms and the recital of prayers in a foreign tongue. Only on the surface was the Hussite war he commanded against the Romanists. Basically, it was also against the social conditions; it was an ideological conflict unique in the Western world. Zizka signed himself "Chief of the Taborites, in the Hope of God," and called his soldiers "God's warriors." He was also a Bohemian patriot. His crusade was a crucial phase of the conflict between German and Slav. His foe was the German encroachment against the Slav. The Hussite armies turned back six attacks by German emperors. This they did against fearful odds, from 1420 to 1433, as a proof of Bohemian dedication to a religious and national cause.

The Hussite leaders fought their own crusades with

armies of peasants, the simple folk. Theirs was to be a
religious democracy, patterned on the early Christians'
ways. So great was the momentum of the Hussites that
they pushed beyond Bohemia's borders on what they
called *Spanile Jizdy,* lovely rides, thrusting up to twenty-
five miles a day into Poland, Bavaria, Saxony, Silesia,
Hungary, all the way to the Baltic Sea, chanting ecstati-
cally that they were the "fighters of good—blessed is each
who stands up for truth; fear not the foe; ignore his
numbers; with the good Lord you get a good ride." These
"truth-spreading raids of the Hussite field armies" were
recalled 550 years later, when Czech nationalism swept
the Communist bloc and the Prague radio stations echoed
the Hussite battle song, which, according to fifteenth-
century eyewitnesses, cast "panicky terror into the opponents."

"Czechoslovak liberals do not have maces and spears,
like the men of Zizka," a Prague newspaper editor said in
1968, "but every one of our commentaries is a spearhead
for truth, and the mighty weapon today is the press."

"We are not as far as Hussites in carrying ideas abroad
with cavalry raids," said Igor Hajek, editor of the *Literarni
Listy,* "but our radio, television, and press are the Hussite
brand." A Czech historian characterized this neo-Hussit-
ism as "devotion to an idea, readiness for sacrifice, determination, loyalty to principles, and, above all, a base in
the transcendental."

THE BATTLE OF THE WHITE MOUNTAIN

Two centuries after the Hussite raids, the German won
against the Slav. The crucial battle lasted only a few
hours on a hill overlooking Prague, the White Mountain.
Golden no longer, the *Zlata Praha* of the past exhaled the

stench of death. The imperial Habsburg troops knew no
mercy. "Murder them all, without exception, the Hussite
brood," the Emperor's councilors advised. "The unholy
nation should be extirpated," Madrid admonished Vienna.
Leading nobles were executed, while others fled the hang-
man, their estates falling into Habsburg hands. The peasants that escaped death at the enemies' hands succumbed
to epidemics. After America opened up to the Moravian
Brethren from Bohemia's eastern marches, they sought
refuge in the protectively forested areas of Pennsylvania,
where they constructed a new Bethlehem in the promised
land overseas. At home, the Czech language was all but
forgotten except by the rustics, and German triumphed.
Bohemia was an island in the German sea. The battle of
the Slav outpost against the German was lost. Bohemia's
population of two million dropped to less than a million.

The name Bohemian subsequently underwent a weird
transformation. It came to mean an easygoing, jolly, irre-
sponsible creature, the reverse of the Bohemian national
trait. This image was fashioned on the pattern of refugees
who had to stir abroad, eking out a livelihood. To Balzac,
the merry students of the Latin Quarter were the "Princes
of Bohemia," while to Walter Scott, a Bohemian was a
homeless minstrel. The immortal "Bohemians" of Gia-
como Puccini were impecunious artists.

The Bohemians in their homeland had no cause to be
gay. The hands of their Habsburg masters were heavy on
their lives. Yet the people learned to take the inevitable in
their stride. How they did it was told by the celebrated
Prague humorist Jaroslav Hasek, in the classic *The Good
Soldier Schweik*. The good soldier, drafted into the
Austrian army, always said "aye, aye," and acted "nay,
nay"; he was the incarnation of Czech passive resistance
to the alien overlords.

It was under the Austrians that the Bohemians, proud

of their Slav heritage, began to call themselves Czechs. With the coming of the Industrial Revolution they began to soar. Their part of the Austrian empire was rich in raw materials, was strategically located over land and along vital waterways. Both they and the German-speaking people in their midst were keen, literate, and skilled folks. The world was the market of many industries of the region, including weaponry, glassware, costume jewelry, paper, mineral products, and the far-famed Pilsen beer.

The Czechs, still a displaced people under alien rule, were groping back to a realization of their nationhood. Writers and artists were in the forefront of the national movement. Although the majority of the people did not read a single volume of the monumental five-volume *History of Bohemia* by Frantisek Palacky, the nationalist ideas it contained percolated to workers toiling in their fields and plants. Whose heart did not beat faster to the strains of Bedrich Smetana's *My Country, Ma Vlast?*

Nationalism was in the scented air of the woods and plains. As the Habsburgs grew weaker, overcome by age, Czech patriotism grew stronger. The Czechs were ready for a great change when the first World War broke out.

THE CZECHS CHANGE SIDES

We saw it happen. *We* were Austro-Hungarian soldiers in the first World War, dug into the clay of Volhynia, facing the Russians. There were other eyewitnesses to what we did not see; and then there were the results.

As Austrian subjects, the Czechs were drafted into the Habsburg army. During the training period they were the most pliable soldiers. We called them "aye, aye." They seemed to know no word beside the German *jawohl.* But

reaching the front, across from the Russians, suddenly
they became "nay, nay." In compact units, they marched
across no-man's land with their regimental bands. They
were not averse to fighting. Indeed, they wanted to do
precisely that, but not for the despoilers of their land.
They wanted to fight at the side of the Russians, fellow
Slavs, and so they formed the Czech Legion, to help defeat
the Habsburgs. Their country, extinguished three centuries before, was to be rebuilt.

It was reconstructed in the wake of the Allies' first
World War victory. The Habsburgs lost the war, and the
Czechs had their country. Its original name had been
Bohemia. Her eastern marches were Moravia. Now Slo-
vakia was added to them, extending Czechoslovakia into
eastern Europe. Ruthenia, in the Carpathian Mountains,
was added to it too. The German-speaking people of
Czechoslovakia on the wreath of mountains, pivoted on
the Sudeten range, became incorporated in the new Slav
country. Blended in the new country were also two million
Magyars, occupying the region all the way to the Danube.
The river was the natural frontier of the new republic; it
was unnatural to the Hungarians. The country's first
President was the philosopher-statesman Thomas Garrigue Masaryk, its principal architect. He was assisted by
his disciple, Edward Beneš, another scholar-statesman.
Plato would have rejoiced in seeing his Utopia come true;
it was a country ruled by philosopher-kings.

When all the countries were surveyed after the first
World War, the surveyors found that only one nation in
that portion of the world had democratic institutions—
Czechoslovakia, with a multi-party system, an effective
Parliament to which the government owed accounting. Its
elections were honestly conducted, and government members were picked with care. It dispensed justice impar-
tially. The country produced a model of good government.

The treatment of their minorities provided the proof of the good intentions of the government. There were minorities other than German and Magyar. They had their own schools and could use their tongues in government offices. They were not happy, of course, since minorities seldom are, especially if they had been majorities, but they were better off than other similar groups in Danubian Europe.

"THE SLOVAK IS NOT HUMAN"

The Hungarians used to say about the Slovaks: *A tot nem ember*—a Slovak is not human. They treated them accordingly for a thousand years.

They treated the Slovaks as Brahmans treated pariahs in India. The Slovaks had only limited access to vernacular schools. They were answerable to Magyar judges and bureaucrats. Even if there had been a popular-based parliament in Budapest, it would not have been responsible to the Slovaks, who were peasants and shepherds, and, therefore, as itinerant workers, unqualified to have their say. Seeking recognition as human creatures, a large number of them had gone to America, to work in mines, a type of work to which they were unused, which enabled them to be on their own, and to say *A tot ember*—the Slovak is human too.

When Bohemia was hooked up with Slovakia, the relationship between the two was similar to that of the locomotive and the freight car. The Slovaks lacked the dynamism the Czechs had managed to sustain under the less repressive Austrian rule. Ironically, the relationship between the two parts of the country should have fostered equality. But, then, can the freight car complain against the locomotive on account of discrimination?

The Slovaks denied that they were freight cars and resented the supremacy of the Czechs, who were to raise them to their level. This was paternalism the Slovaks resented! In due time a Slovak became the Premier, but his co-nationals remained unimpressed. One swallow did not make the spring. Did Prague think that they could be perverted with this sop? The nationalist dissonance weakened the country. The unity Masaryk had sought was unreal.

THEN THE GOETTERDAEMMERUNG

Then came Hitler, and in 1938 Czechoslovakia had its new battle of the White Mountain, at Munich. There the Sudetenland was detached from the country and attached to the Reich. Subsequently "Bohemia" became a German protectorate and Slovakia a Nazi satrapy. The Magyars got some frontier rectifications from Adolf Hitler, lord of continental Europe, and his Italian satellite, Benito Mussolini. Today, his was the land of Czechs and "tomorrow the world." Arrogantly he announced that his realm was to last a thousand years. Who could gainsay the Nazi on his Mount Sinai, in the Berchtesgaden of Bavaria? At the end of twelve years, his "eternal" realm ended.

Toward the end of World War II it was agreed that the Soviets should clear out the Germans from Czechoslovakia. This was done, and the former model democracy was set to continue a unique experience. The pre-war governmental team was back; all were champions of the common man. More attention was to be paid to the Slovaks, too. The Foreign Minister of the country was Jan Masaryk, son of the nation-builder and of an American mother. President of the country was Edward Beneš, the disciple of the nation-builder. Again the philosopher-statesmen were at the helm. The reaction to the Nazi rule was incandescent. In a wave of resentment, most of the Germans of the country were expelled. The Danubian frontier was restored. The Russians collected their fee, and they attached Ruthenia, the country's easternmost region, to have a common frontier with Hungary. The Soviet presence in Danubian Europe became a fact of life. What did that mean to the Czechs?

That was the question I took with me to the Hotel Claridge in Paris, where Jan Masaryk was staying during the 1946 peace conference that was to draw up treaties for the minor defeated nations. Masaryk was the spokesman for the Czechs.

The Cold War was already in full blast. What did Masaryk think of it and of its consequences for his country? What were the causes and the portent? The causes, he answered, may have been ignorance and innocence. Both the United States and the Soviet Union were novices in the field, dedicated to principles and ultimate solutions; they were missionaries viewing problems as absolutes of right or wrong: "My side is right, yours is wrong." They did not see that compromise was the only solution, and that it was diplomacy. Compromise looked like heresy to them. Their dedication was heightened by the unrelenting presence of public opinion watchdogs, the mass media, the radio and the press. The public thought that yielding an inch even for gaining a mile comported bargaining away basic principles. How could democracy operate in this ambiance?

Did Masaryk think that Czechoslovakia, because of her location and ideology, could act as a bridge between East and West? In his waggish way he reacted quickly: "A bridge? You know what horses are doing on it?" Mediation, as he saw it, was not a natural role for his country.

This was a battle of giants, and pygmies had better keep out of the way. The ultimate solution was a modus vivendi. The ideological concepts of the two sides should get less crusading and more accommodating. The Soviets were jittery for twenty million reasons . . . and more, because of their more than twenty million wartime dead. The United States, too, should get weary of its crusading role. Because of their size and strength the two countries either lived together or died together. They would have to learn a geographic lesson—that they occupied parts of the same planet, and that that meant coexistence. Capitalism was a fact, but so was communism. Even nations should be intelligent enough to recognize the facts. The first task of the two countries was to learn the obvious lesson of history—among all the conflicts there was nothing more dangerous than religious wars.

THE FLAME BURNS OUT

Not many months after this meeting, Masaryk was dead. Suicide? Murder? Twenty years later both hypotheses were maintained by near-witnesses of the tragic event. According to one view, Stalin had ordered Masaryk's liquidation. According to the other, Masaryk reacted impulsively to a moment of despondency. To be sure, he had conveyed the impression of being a jovial man, but on the diplomatic stage he was a character actor. In his private life he was often overwhelmed by gloom.

Simultaneously with this tragedy in February 1948, the Communists carried out a coup. At the national elections two years before they had come out on top, with more than one third of the votes. The Premier was a Communist, Klement Gottwald, who now ousted the non-party

members from the cabinet. For a time Beneš continued to
be a figurehead President, and then he resigned. His place
was taken by Gottwald, who was a dogmatic Communist,
as was the new Premier, Antonin Zapotocky. They now
proceeded to apply the classical method of slicing up the
opposition, the "salami technique." The Socialists were
absorbed by the Communists, and the country was on the
road toward uncompromising authoritarianism.

Censorship was established, and the Czechs' colorful
press became the instrument of party propaganda, colorless and dull. Drastic party purges were undertaken, to
combat "heresy" and to get even with rivals. Forced-labor
camps began to grow like weeds. The death penalty was
provided for "sabotage, espionage, and other crimes
against the state." The drive against nonconformist Catholic churchmen was launched, and a "national"—that is,
Communist—inspired hierarchy was fostered. Czechoslovakia, the model of democracy in eastern-central Europe,
had become a dictatorship. Nothing could have been more
out of character with her basic ways.

Clearly, the Soviet Union was pulling the strings, and
the Western world was aroused. Since the Communist
Party in Czechoslovakia was paramount, why not leave
the country alone? The Finns were also the Soviets' neighbors, and the Kremlin let them be. Why not leave alone
their fellow-Slavs, the Czechs?

The answer to this question was not provided in official
documents, but it could be read between the lines. The
Czechs were swept into the Communist camp because of
Germany. The land of the Czechs was a salient into the
land of the Germans, which, the historic episodes of the
White Mountain and Munich proved, the latter could not
tolerate. Granted that the *furor Teutonicus* had been
blunted, it yielded place of honor to the United States.
"American Germany" was the entering wedge of unre-

pentant imperialism into the Slavic world. That was the Kremlin's view—therefore the satellite status for the Czechs.

Their land now became a "People's Democracy," subsequently to be promoted to the status of a "Socialist Republic." To maintain the semblance of respectability, the vestiges of political organizations were retained—the Socialist Party, Peoples' Party, Freedom Party, Slovak Rehabilitation Party, National Regeneration-Freedom Party, the Revolutionary Trades Unions, and the Union of Czechoslovak Youth, under the umbrella of the "National Front," a pseudonym for communism.

The President of Czechoslovakia, Klement Gottwald, died in 1953, the year of Stalin's death. Antonin Zapotocky, the First Secretary of the Communist Party, became the head of state. Antonin Novotny became the First Secretary, occupying the key position in the country. For fifteen years Czechoslovakia was "Novotnyland."

THE AGE OF NOVOTNY

The thaw had set in in other Communist countries but not in the land of the Czechs. Novotny combined his top party function with that of the presidency, and he moved into historic Hradcany Castle, which people came to dub the "Little Kremlin." "There are people," President Novotny said on the tenth anniversary of his assumption of power, "and they come and go." Many of them went, but he stayed. . . . Many of those who went were old Communists. The revolution was devouring its children, as it has been doing through history. One did not expect a reign of terror among the Czechs, gentle people, careful of human life. It was difficult to fancy Czechs as jailors and hangmen. But there they were, acting out of the national character but in the character of the age, which was ruthless. That ruthlessness was very un-Czech, but, evidently, it was the *Zeitgeist, the spirit of the times.* German-speaking inhabitants in Prague muttered under their breath: *Zeitungeist*—inhuman spirit of the times.

It was estimated that about a million people were affected by the terror. Jail became the fate of some 130,000 politicals, and of these some 30,000 were Communists, victims of the jealousy of job grabbers. About 160 Czechs ended their lives on the gallows. Hundreds of thousands of them were reduced to lower posts, lost their livelihoods, and became "unmen."

On top of the pile was Antonin Novotny, "the Neanderthal Man." People called him that. They said that he could not look in people's eyes, and that all new ideas glanced off his thick skull. He was the *Law*, which was the *Word*. The age of Novotny was Czechoslovakia's iron age.

Czechoslovakia had been the most advanced nation of the region. Under the momentum of her past, she was advancing economically but slower than the other members of the group. Here are a few impressions of the country in 1964, a couple of years before the great change, which, alas, became the great frustration.

ON VACLAVSKA NAMESTI

The car left Vienna far behind, headed for the Austrian-Czech frontier, its ultimate destination Prague. The traffic thinned out rapidly as the frontier was approached. The gate barrier was painted red-white-red, the colors of Austria. Beyond it began another world.

The passports had to be processed, and the Austrian

frontier guards took their time. They had plenty of it, since ours was the only car on the road set to enter Czechoslovakia at that point. Meticulously and with bureaucratic nonchalance they entered the names. Since our presence broke the monotony of a boring day, who would blame them for their nonchalance?

We were lounging, meanwhile, outside the guardhouse, being caressed by the summer's twilight breeze. We looked at the other world, a hundred feet away—there was the flag of Czechoslovakia, with the blue triangle and the white-red bands. To the right and left of it there was the signal and the symbol of that other world, the hostile bristle of barbed wire. A short distance beyond the barbed wire, the rolling landscape displayed rashes, observation towers for the Czech guards, to see that the boundary was to be the dividing line of two worlds. The cosmic silence, bucolic and peaceful, bathed in the redolence of the rain-washed earth, was suddenly rent by the peremptory staccato of an imperious machine gun. Czech guards must have suspected an uncommon stirring of life where there should have been no animation. One of the Austrian guards emerged from the house, puzzled: "Why should people inflict such abuse upon themselves? They have turned their country into a K.Z. [concentration camp], with barbed wire, machine guns and all." He fell silent, and we were set to cross the line to that other world. Next we halted in front of the Czech gate.

The incongruity of the sequel turned out to be amusing. In the suspicious presence of all the paraphernalia of global division we were now eye to eye with a gangling young Czech frontier guard who did his best to look forbidding. But he was too young, and, besides, few Czechs were made for the role. He was not one of them. Sternly, he eyed the luggage of our group, piled up in the rear of a bus that followed our car, evidence of overseas opulence.

As if he wanted to fathom their secrets, his eyes pierced the luggage. Then, he turned his back on the pile, defeated. He was after all, a gentle Czech youngster.

His knowledge of Czech was no help in fathoming our passports' secrets. He solicited help and proffered eager thanks for the aid. Finally, a relaxed wave of his hand and his bon voyage wishes set us off. The entire procedure lasted only a few minutes. The young man was more pleased to be rid of us than we of him. This was all so incongruous—the forbidding sight, the gun, the observation tower, and the gentle young man putting on a show for our sake, and failing.

We were now on our way to Prague, on one of the country's major roads. Darkness had descended meanwhile, and rural quiet shrouded the towns we passed— Trebon, Veseli, Sobeslav, and then historic Tabor, headquarters of the Hussites, who had not been so gentle as the latter-day Czechs, and who memorialized their names in their country's annals with blood shed for religious freedom. Life was barely breathing under the nocturnal sky, and one would have never guessed that we were traveling on a major highway of one of the highly industrialized countries of Central Europe. Czechoslovakia was lying low.

Barely breathing, too, was the capital, golden Prague. The hour was well advanced, but the quiet was oppressive and revealing. As we passed through the center of the town it was obvious that it was short on night life. That it was short also on courtesy was revealed by the reception in the nominally first-class hotel. Our first impression was confirmed. Normally gentle and kind, many Czechs reacted to the hard times, and appeared to be resentful.

We went to Prague at the tail end of an extended tour of the other Communist countries, including Rumania,

Bulgaria, Poland, and Hungary. Included in the itinerary
was also a visit of Yugoslavia, not a chunk of the bloc, but
Communist just the same. In each of these countries we
detected the stirring of new life in response to what at the
time appeared to be a more relaxed atmosphere. The
change in the other "bloc" nations was written on people
and their towns. Many of them walked with a new bounce,
swinging their arms more boldly. Some of them were
better dressed than on previous occasions. The display
windows showed more a spirit of adventure, a desire on
the part of the managers of the store not merely to *have*
the windows, but to *use* them for display. What was the
situation in Prague and in the rest of the country?

The center of Prague, the magnificent Vaclavska
Namesti, was crowded in the morning with men carrying
briefcases and women with bags. They seemed to be
changed inside, laden down with cares. The clothes of the
men were shabby, shining with overuse. The dresses of
women lacked distinction—embarrassingly threadbare,
too. Their faces were bland and noncommittal, the faces
of people who had learned not to get involved. These were
the features of the good soldier Schweik—thus the Czechs
must have looked under the Habsburg rule. Unhappy
then, the Czechs were probably even unhappier now. The
spirit of Novotny was brooding in the land. That was our
impression in other parts of the land too.

Like other parts of that region, Czechoslovakia has long
been a part of the world in which grumbling is a respected tradition and way of life. In other bloc countries
people were grumbling too, with zest and verve. Not so,
though, in Czechoslovakia, where they saw no light at the
end of the tunnel, and were complaining with resignation.
Czechoslovakia, the most productive of the Socialist countries, was the least creative of hope.

THE CZECH REFORMATION MOVEMENT

How long could this situation last? The country was lagging far behind the other satellite nations in economic development, political suppleness, and, above all, in cultural freedom. Historic changes occur when two factors are compounded: the disposition and the triggering effect. The disposition was for all the world to see, the end-of-the-world sentiment, and the feeling was that a way must be found. The triggering effect was the conscience of the nation, of the readers of thoughts, the prophets of aspirations, the inner voice.

Czechoslovakia was unique because she was not the product of men of politics and of war. She was the creation of religious leaders, poets, historians, philosophers —the creation of John Huss, whose ashes more than anything else fertilized the soil; of Jan Neruda, poet of "Cosmic Songs"; of Frantisek Palacky, the historian; and, above all, of Thomas Garrigue Masaryk, profound thinker.

This time, too, writers were the conscience of the nation. One of the first to be heard was Ludvik Vaculik, who was to enter history as the author of the *Two Thousand Words,* a rousing proclamation of freedom, about which a word will be said. He had looked at life *de profundis,* he was an explorer of life's depths, and a manual worker. He was seeking the realization of his ideals in communism, but failed to find it. His disenchantment was analyzed in his noted novel *The Axe.* The terror accompanying forced farm collectivization was the subject of *An Hour of Quiet,* by Ivan Klima, a representative writer of the generation of the thirties. Another spokesman of the grumblers was Vaclav Havel, whose plays, particularly *A Garden Party* and *The Memorandum,* were widely performed on stages of the capitalist world. Also well known to the West was Bohumil Hrabal, whose film scenario *Closely Watched Trains* was overwhelmed with first prizes and Oscars in many parts of the world. Widely known also was the work of Edward Goldstücker, who reintroduced Kafka to his fellow Czechs. Readers found much similarity between the nightmare world of Kafka and that of the Stalin regime.

It was in a roundabout way that the Czechs found their road to a stronger stand against the Novotny age. From behind their barbed wire they learned how much the rest of the world was admiring them for their uncommonly absorbing artistic films, which became the vogue all over the West, and for their national autobiography presented to the world in Montreal's Expo 67. "The 'new wave' from abroad in 1967," said an authoritative source, "was Czechoslovakian." Following the critical and popular successes of the Academy Award winner *The Shop on Main Street,* there appeared in quick succession *Loves of a Blonde, Daisies, Do You Keep a Lion at Home?, Lemonade Joe,* and, above all, that admirable mixing of poetry, comedy, and realism, *Closely Watched Trains.* The Czechs were wondering, as news of their successes reached them, why they seemed to be recognized everywhere except at home.

The great sensation of the Montreal world exposition was the Czech pavilion. People who found it hard to pronounce the name of the country, and could not have spotted it on the map within a thousand miles, were standing in line for hours on end to get into the pavilion, which was a treasure-trove of enchantment. Once inside, they learned much about the genius of a small nation's arts, skills, and taste, the beauty of its natural setting, its history and traditions. "The Czech pavilion," one of the authoritative sources wrote, "concealed a brilliantly smooth display of socialism and national heritage, calmly taking in multiscreen films of modern industry by Joseph Svoboda with photographs of baroque architecture and an immense nineteenth-century wooden model of Bethlehem." And according to another prestige publication: "Of the small pavilions at Expo 67, the most outstanding was the Czechoslovakian. An immensely popular feature was its unique audience-participation film, *Kino-automat*. Also on display were fine Bohemian glassware and lace." Widespread recognition of Czech achievements bolstered Czech self-confidence.

At home, meanwhile, grievances were compounded. The widespread malaise of youth spread also to Prague, where university students staged demonstrations, demanding that the regime should take note. Because of inadequate light and heat, the young people complained, they were hampered in their work. They were fettered also in the selection of research material. The regime should not overlook them because they were young.

The young people were turning to the thoughts of Thomas Masaryk, a "nation-builder" to objective history, but merely a "bourgeois-nationalist" to the Novotny regime. September 14, 1967, was the thirtieth anniversary of his death, and a literary journal issued a commemorative issue with a large portrait on its front page. It fell victim to the censor's arbitrary whim. The students had another major grievance on their list.

Trouble erupted on still another front. Almost since the inception of the republic, the Slovaks had been restless. While Russia was the Big Brother of the Czech, the Slovak was his little brother. For a thousand years the Slovak had been ruled by the Magyar, who had said that he was not a man. To the Czech, the Slovak felt, he was half a man. The Slovaks felt that, having been separated from the

Czechs for a millennium, they had developed their own
traditions, dialects, and ways of life, their own problems
and even idiosyncrasies. They did not want to be led on
the Czechs' leading strings. They insisted that they should
have their autonomy, that their affairs should be handled
by a government of their own, in Bratislava, the Slovak
metropolis on the Danube. Czechoslovakia was to be
transformed into a federation—*Czecho-Slovakia*, with a
hyphen.

As the explosive material accumulated, the target was
found for the opposition shafts. He was Antonin Novotny,
head of state, and First Secretary of the Communist Party.
As the opposition was gathering strength, his own forces
were waning. He was, after all, the Bourbon atavism, a
throwback to the *ancien régime*. For many years the top
party instrument, the Politbureau, was his sounding
board. Now the sound of the opposition became stronger.
Frank words were addressed to him; he was called inflexible, immovable, out of tune with the age. Other Socialist
countries were on the new wave-length, while his was
lagging far behind. Historic forces in the country's past
were gathering momentum. The Hussite wars, the Czechs'
quiet progress to the fore as an industrial nation, their
magnificent experiment in democracy between the two
wars, their ability to stage their impressive post-World
War II comeback—these memories were beginning to
inform present realities.

GATHERING HOPE

"Our past had prepared us for democracy," the inter-
bellum founding father, Thomas G. Masaryk, had said.
"The foundations of the modern humane and democratic

ideal had been led by our Hussite reformation, in which, as Palacky shows, the Bohemian Brotherhood Church was especially significant. . . ." And in another part of his book *The Making of a State,* a confession and a revelation: "In our democratic republic, freedom of conscience and toleration must not be merely codified but realized in every domain of public life."

In Czechoslovakia, democracy was not merely a political instrument, but a way of life, coloring all fields of human activity. It was more than a way of life—it was nearly a religion. The time was ripe now to turn to the Czech way of life, the Bohemian creed.

The Central Committee of the Communist Party met on January 5, 1968, at which the past and present clashed, the new present inspired by the Czechs' tradition. At that meeting, Antonin Novotny was no longer the "word" and the "voice," the word of atavism and the voice of the Kremlin. He was on the defensive for the first time in his political life. The offensive was launched by a new breed of Communists, the progressives. Their spokesman was a Slovak, not a Czech, Alexander Dubček. He was a believer in Marx and Lenin, and much of his background had been in the Soviet Union. But he was a native Communist, not of the Kremlin variety. He was a low-keyed man, quick to smile—unlike the dour Novotny—but he spoke forcefully, weighing every word. He made his points in the language fellow-Communists would understand, giving priority to economics.

Czechoslovakia had had a head start over all the other Socialist countries, with a large infrastructure, great diversity of technical skills, well-organized plants. Yet she was lagging behind the other countries within the bloc. This lag was man-made, and its cause was lack of initiative and imagination. The past became a sacred cow. Also, the Party became a sanctuary for tired bureaucrats, who expended their energy on shielding their posts. Within the party there was the debility of conformity, and nothing of the "dialectics"—the dialogue—of Marxism. Genuine communism was grass-roots democracy, the modernizers claimed, and the Czechs were a democratic folk. The infusion of new blood was a must.

Culturally also the country was behind the times. To combat the enemies of the proletarian state, press censorship may have been needed at the outset. But now its existence was an insult to class consciousness. It deprived the nation of the intellectual energies of an articulate people. The creative forces of the nation had to be released by striking off the ideological fetters. The grievances of the university youth were well-founded and must be faced.

Then, too, there was the Slovak problem, the special status of a region with its own historic background and ways of life. The Slovaks' constructive potentialities had been less used, even, than those of the Czechs.

Exact details of the *in camera* meeting were lacking, but the result became quickly known. An age—the era of Novotny—was at an end. He had to vacate his place as First Secretary of the Party. It was filled by the spokesman of the vocal opposition, youthful-looking Alexander Dubček, the Slovak progressive. For a day or two Novotny retained his ceremonial position as the head of the state, and then he had to yield that too. The strong man of yesterday became the weak man of today. "If he wants to influence people," a writer quipped, "he will have to ring bells from door to door." A Western commentator summed up the situation: "What is happening in Czechoslovakia is nothing less than a revolution without bloodshed."

Some of the "damned of the earth" now became the "exalted of the earth." Novotny was replaced as head of the state by Ludvik Svoboda, a former army general, one of the former damned of the earth. During the savage period of the Stalin-Novotny reign he had been imprisoned. Freed, he worked as a bookkeeper on a collective farm. Rehabilitated, he became head of the Military Academy, but had had to resign when he reached the retirement age. Now he was retrieved from limbo, and his elevation to the Presidency indicated the progressives' victory along the entire line.

The "Magna Carta" of the Czech reform movement was the Action Program adopted at the April 5, 1968, Central Committee Plenum. Although couched in the party jargon, it did come to grips with the new reality. These were some of the main points it made:

Socialism should enable the citizen to unfold the full potentiality of his unique personality, more than bourgeois democracy. The free expression of one's opinions should be guaranteed to all, including the minorities. Under no condition should the creative work of the artist be subject to censorship. The new socialist society must be adjusted to the nation's ways, a goal that could not be reached by the antiquated road of the past, which thwarted progress.

The political system must be completely reformed, permitting the dynamic development of the synthesis of socialism and democracy. . . . There must be firm guarantees against the recurrence of "subjectivism" and high-handed autocracy. The republic must become the home of two nations of equal standing, Czechs and Slovaks; all social groups must be treated equally, class antagonism must be shunned. Outdated methods of the economic system must be rejected and new ones introduced, giving leeway to socially responsible individual initiative. "We must, through the entire legal system, gradually settle the question of how we can better and

more effectively protect the personal rights and property
of the citizens." Socialism must not attempt to do without
the spirit of enterprise. The economic democratization
program must involve the granting of independence to
enterprises and their relative freedom from state control.
It will be necessary to establish democratic organs in enterprises to which the managers should be responsible.
The creation of the national economic policy must be
subordinated to the national assembly's democratic control. The gradual opening of the economy to the world
market must be carried out.

Then the cultural factors: "We advocate both the international and the specifically national character of our
culture." And, insistently, equality for Slovakia: "We regard it as indispensable to adopt immediately effective
cultural measures in Slovakia, so that the area will have
the same conditions and opportunities as does Bohemia."
Then the independence of the country in foreign affairs:
"Our Republic will formulate its own stand on basic issues
of world policy. . . . " At the same time the pledge was
repeated that reformed Czechoslovakia was not to break
away from the fraternal nations, and that economic cooperation with the Soviets was to be maintained in full
force, and, indeed, intensified.

TWO THOUSAND WORDS

Writers had much to do with these developments—
they, the conscience of their country. One of the leading
authors, Ludvik Vaculik, drew up a manifesto, and had it
signed by seventy representative people of his country. It
was published on June 27 in the *Literary Gazette*, which
was sold out in a matter of hours. "I have written it," said
Vaculik, "because the partial freedom we have won is

menaced. The 'Novotnyists' are raring to go, to revenge
themselves. Free elections are indispensable, as are other
forms of struggle against the return of tyranny, if
needed." People began to quote parts of the manifesto. In
no time, it became a classic. The author's son took time to
count its words—two thousand. It became known as "two
thousand words." These words became important parts of
history.

The two thousand words were not directed against the
Communists:

We give the assurance to our allies that we shall respect
our treaties of friendship, alliance and commerce. The Communist Party scheduled the election of a new Central Committee. It should be better than the old one. The Party should
declare that its supremacy—which the Manifesto accepted
—should be based on the citizens' confidence and not on
force. The people should form committees for the defense of
the freedom of expression. With other countries we should be
on a footing of equality. This spring, as after the war, we
have a great opportunity. Again we have the chance to take
our common cause in hand . . . the possibility to give it a
form corresponding to the good reputation we had and to
the relatively good opinion we inspired in those days.

The new party chief, Dubček, struck the keynote: "The
party does not exist above or outside society, but is its
integral part. All attempts must be resisted to assert
authoritarian party influence. The party must act in a cir-
cumspect and tactful way, and must head off administrative domination."

Important steps were taken in quick succession. The
press censorship was lifted, and the newspapers began to
blossom. They reported events of all fields without any
restrictions. The editorials were often bold. Developments
of the world were freely transmitted over the radio and TV
channels also. Now it was possible in the country to be
well-informed.

No longer was a Czech to be Big Brother and the Slovak
Little Brother. The party itself was to have two wings of
equal importance, Czech and Slovak. There were to be two
national budgets and two sets of ministries. The federal-
ization of the country was going on apace.

Masaryk, whom another generation had hailed as the
nation-builder, was no longer an "un-man." He was given
his due, constantly quoted in the press, his books displayed, his photographs in countless stores. The photos of
his son Jan were to be seen everywhere too. His tragic
death became an issue. Had he been killed, and, if so, by
whom? Was the hand that pushed him out of the window
responding to an order from Moscow? Had Communist
Czechs been involved in this tragic event? Or had he committed suicide in a moment of irresistible despondency?

The new head of state invited formerly ousted Princes
of the Catholic Church as his guests in Hradcany Castle.
They were treated as respected guests. Bishops ousted by
Novotny were restored to their seats.

The livelihood of the people was to be given a boost.
More freedom was to be given to industrial enterprises,
and the peasants, too, were to receive greater leeway. In
the pre-Communist bourgeois past, when Czechoslovakia
was considered part of the Occident, the bulk of the
country's exports, sometimes as much as 90 percent, went
to the West. Under the Novotny regime the trend was
reversed and 70 percent of the trade was destined for the
East. The country was a member of the Soviet bloc's
Council of Mutual Assistance, Comecon. The new regime
now sought to divert more trade to the West—possibly a
fifty-fifty arrangement. In economic matters, too, dogma-
tism was to yield to a modified form of laissez faire,
socialist planning combined with capitalist competition.
Thus Czechoslovakia, too, was to break a new path—the
"Third Way."

Prague now also asked that the Warsaw Pact be revised. It was the Soviet-sponsored military alliance, the counterpart of the N.A.T.O. of the West. The commander of that body was always an officer in the Soviet armed forces. The head of the military department of the party's Central Committee in Prague, Lieutenant General Vaclav Prchlik, now made two basic recommendations: that the top command among the member countries should be rotated, and that the pact should not be used for political instead of military ends.

The recommendations of the two thousand words began to take effect. Czechs and Slovaks now began to form committees and clubs in the pursuit of common interests. One of these was called "Club 231," that being the number of the government ordinance under which political prisoners had been detained under the Novotny regime. "Our prison guards had been Gestapo auxiliaries," said the president of the club, an ex-diplomat.

More significant was the formation of the K.A.N., Club of Non-Party Members. "The Communist Party has opened the door by its liberalization program," said the prospectus of this organization, "and we are going through the door." The group asserted that it stood on the basic program of the non-Communist party coalitions begun half a century before, subscribing to the principles of free political self-expression, based upon the bill of rights. The group proclaimed that its goal was to "counterbalance the superior strength of the Communist Party."

That was just the point. If there were to be free elections, the Communists might be snowed under. And that would be the end of the Soviets' influence in the country. Another possibility: a popular front of many parties, so manipulated by the Communists as to retain the whip hand. In the mid-forties George Orwell remarked that, though he could not see how it would happen, it was clear that the Communist regimes must "democratize or perish." This was their chance to democratize and live. Carried away by euphoria, many people, even non-Communists, foresaw a new era for mankind. They expressed the assumption that economically communism was on the correct wave length. Planning in the modern world of mass production was unavoidable, and there was no reason why honestly run governments could not do it as well as the super-corporations. Corporation socialism and government socialism were not far apart. "Communism could become human, you know," a non-Communist Czech told the author of this book. Political democracy in an economically planned society was the issue.

THE ECHO IN THE WORLD

Proudly, Radio Prague commentator Milan Weiner noted that once again Czechoslovakia was in the center of world attention. Prague hotel registers, he observed, looked like the almanacs of the representative press organs, TV, and radio stations of the world, especially the West.

The Czechoslovak dawn was hailed on many sides. Particularly notable was the reaction of Marshal Tito, who two decades before led his country out of the Soviet promised land, which he had found all promise and no fulfillment. In his Dedinje residence, on the outskirts of Belgrade, he was interviewed by the chief correspondent of *The New York Times,* C. L. Sulzberger. The correspondent spoke about Czech "Titoism." The Marshal riposted:

What is involved is not "Titoism," as you call it but democratization in Czechoslovakia. That country has embarked upon a process of democratization of its internal life and elimination of old forms that have hampered its social progress so far. What is involved is a desire to advance freely and more rapidly in the socio-economic and political life of the country. This does not mean Czechoslovakia is following the same road we have taken. It has become evident there, too, that life brings in its wake many things that have to be changed and that one has to adopt a flexible attitude toward questions affecting the development of a country. For what is good today is not necessarily good tomorrow; nor what is indispensable tomorrow necessarily indispensable today.

President Tito demonstrated his reaction to Czech reforms by paying a demonstrative visit to Prague, where he received a most cordial welcome. Prague became the front-page story in Rumania, too. The press provided detailed accounts of party conclaves, of the implementation of the reforms, and of the population's mood.

Rumania's "double top man," Nicolae Ceausescu, General Secretary of the Communist Party and Chairman of the State Council, also hurried to Prague to express his solidarity with the new man and the new regime. His reception was also uncommonly cordial.

Hungarian reaction was expressed in *Népszabadság*, the government organ, under the signature of János Gosztonyi, its editor-in-chief, who was also a member of the Central Committee of the Hungarian Socialist Workers' Party (Communists): "A renaissance has begun in Czechoslovakia, full of political hope and Socialist in content." He pointed out that current party activities in Prague aimed also at establishing new relations between the two "nations" constituting Czechoslovakia. For the first time a Communist country spokesman mentioned Slovakia as a "nation."

Equally warm were the reactions of the leaders of the Communist parties of France and Italy, the largest ones in the West. To them, too, Czechoslovakia seemed to have embarked on a notable and laudable experiement. They wished her luck and assured her of their moral support.

Not all Communist parties exulted in the "Czechoslovak Dawn." The leading organ of the D.D.R., East Germany, mouthpiece of the S.E.D., pseudonym of the Communist Party, reached the conclusion that the Czechs were about to abandon the fraternal Socialist policy, ready to make common cause with Bonn. The daily complained that it was conceivable that Prague might establish diplomatic relations with Bonn, "headquarters of the German revanchists." It admonished Prague: "The victims of German Fascism in the Buchenwald, Majdanek, and Mauthausen concentration camps, as well as those of Lidice [the Czech mining town destroyed by the Nazis during the war] are warning signals that should keep us from entertaining illusions about the profits of cooperation with German imperialism." East Germany was evidently concerned with the facts of geography, being flanked by two ideologically alien forces—Prague and Bonn. Also, she was apprehensive about the role of the Wall separating it from the West. East Germans would be able to enter Czechoslovakia at one point and leave it at another point, adjacent to the non-Communist world.

Stark imperialist plots hatched in Prague were seen by Polish press organs, headed by the *Trybuna Ludu*. It asked several leading questions, such as this: Was Czechoslovakia about to be the staging area of the foes of communism in their long-contemplated project of launching frontal attacks on the fraternal countries? The Czechs had better shed their political innocence and beware of Western wiles.

Meanwhile, the Czechoslovaks were groping for the new way, a communist regime that was democratic, too. Party-head Dubček made a basic policy statement in the city of Kladno, in which he disowned infallibility for the party. It was not an end in itself, he said, and its authority depended on the extent to which people assigned it a leadership role. He further said that such leadership required a mechanism to insure political change in an orderly way. Political change? Did it mean changing the tempo or the tune? Did he envisage the possibility of a non-Communist, and possibly an anti-Communist, regime? He provided no answer, not as yet. But party theoretician V. Pachner did indicate a reply: "There can be no democracy in which society is divided into 'whites' and 'blacks'—the former carrying CPCS [Communist Part of CS] membership cards and all the rest of them 'blacks.'"

AND THE SOVIETS?

The Institute of Political Science of the Central Committee of the Communist Party of Czechoslovakia prepared a questionnaire, distributed to readers of the *Rude Pravo,* the party daily. These were some of the questions:

Does the internal democratization of the Communist Party provide a sufficient guarantee for democracy? Can one speak of democracy when the leading role is held by the Communist Party? Should the Communist Party carry out its leadership role by devotedly promoting free progressive socialist development or by ruling over society? Will the new political system have to provide free and democratic platforms for the wide-ranging requirements of the various strata of the people in a socialist society in order to form political decisions? Are there classes in our society opposed to one another? Is the Czechoslovak way of constructing and developing socialism our own internal matter, to be decided by the peoples' sovereign will?

These were straightforward questions that could have been asked in any democratic country. That was just the point—any *democratic* country. The questions were read in the Kremlin too, as were the speeches of the Czech leaders about future free elections, political parties, all the facets of what we call the free world. All of these sent chills down the spines of the Kremlin leaders. Czechoslovakia was not a world unto itself. She was a small country, and if she got away with this, why should the others not copy the model? And what about the people of the Soviet Union itself? Counterrevolution was the name the Kremlin had for what the Czechs thought was free inquiry. What were the Soviets to do? Then there was also the possibility adumbrated in the *Slovak Writers' Union Weekly* by Milan Simecka:

Europe's intellectual elite will watch with curiosity our experiment with Socialist democracy as a possible alternative to the traditional bourgeois society built on capitalist foundations. The new radical left, the skeptical European liberals, and also the progressive currents in the Christian movements will be curious. There will be sympathetic observers all over Europe, to which we are linked by a common bond. Our return to Europe is our great opportunity.

A great opportunity, indeed, and the same also for the other satellite countries. Geographically they were in Europe, and culturally, too. The Soviet Union, on the other hand . . . well, the Czechs evidently thought that Russia was not Europe, and that bonds with her did not represent an opportunity.

To top this all off, the West German weekly *Der Spiegel* had this to say:

The most civilized nation of Eastern Europe, politically-minded Czechoslovakia, is groping for a new and enlightened communism. . . . It may not be absurd to postulate a communism harking back to its idealistic and humane origins, fitted into the conditions of the nuclear age. It could be a left-oriented breakthrough toward a visionary goal which a heretic Marxist, Milovan Djilas, sketched in these words: "We live in an age which is moving toward unity. The diverse ideologies and systems are shifting closer together. Socialism is getting more liberal and capitalism more socialistic. This is one of the most momentous developments of our time."

It may have been the most momentous development for Milovan Djilas and *Der Spiegel*, but not for the Kremlin, the Vatican of the ecumenical church, with doctrines, dogmas, and visions of its own, which were not those of the other visionaries. The more the Czechs, the Slovaks, and their well-wishers spoke about the common meeting ground for communism and socialism, the more the Kremlin had apocalyptic visions of *dies irae*. If there was to be a meeting ground, it should not be Czechoslovakia. But there was, evidently, no such intermediary point.

Early in the summer, maneuvers of Warsaw Pact countries took place. Authoritative sources said that Soviet, Hungarian, and Polish troops streamed across Czechoslovak frontiers in June, in numbers never fully communicated to Prague. Their number was estimated at 16,000 soldiers, and they took with them, according to the sources, 4,500 vehicles, 70 tanks, and 40 airplanes. They were under the command of Marshal Ivan I. Yakubovsky, Soviet chief of Warsaw Pact forces. Prague announced that these were routine maneuvers and they were so accepted by the population. The new Prague team had public opinion under control. No disturbing incidents were reported, and by the middle of July the troops were reported to have left the country.

About the same time, the delegates of five Communist countries—the Soviet Union, Bulgaria, East Germany, Poland, and Hungary—met in Warsaw, and they signed a

declaration. Couched in the Kremlin jargon, it reiterated
the usual clichés—strengthening the bonds among the
Socialist countries and the cause of socialism itself on the
basis of proletarian internationalism. The declaration admonished Czechoslovakia to fight determinedly for the
cause of socialism. "Pacts and treaties link our nations.
The mutual obligations of the countries and their people
are based on the common endeavour to protect socialism
and to guarantee the collective security of the Socialist
nations. Our parties and people are invested with the
responsibility not to let the revolutionary achievements go
by default."

Significantly, Czechoslovakia and Rumania were not
signatories of the declaration. Because of the proliferation
of the clichés, insufficient attention was given to the tone
of the declaration. In short order, it was followed by another one, this time on Czechoslovak soil, in the lovely
city of Bratislava, a few miles from Vienna, down the
Danube.

ON MALOSTRANSKE NAMESTI

Happy is the country in the chanceries of which the
lights are not burning at midnight. Lights were not burning in the Waldstein Palace, a stone's throw from Malo-
stranske Square at the foot of the Hradcany Hill. The
Czech government offices were, evidently, relaxed. Yet the
historic meeting in Bratislava took place during these days
and nights.

Happy also is the country whose president is protected
as lightly as Ludvik Svoboda was during these days. Only
one leisurely policeman was in evidence. During the day
of the Bratislava negotiations, as on all days, tourists from
all over the world were streaming through the gates of the

presidential palace, looking at the Old Castle, at St. Vitus' Cathedral, at St. George's Church, at the Archepiscopal Palace, at all the many religious landmarks, kept in perfect condition even under the Neanderthal regime of Novotny.

Prague is never so enchanting as when the summer twilight replaces the late-afternoon glow. Then the soft breezes descend from the mountains in the north. Having sated themselves with photographing one of the most photogenic places of Europe, the tourists are still standing around the Old Town Hall, to see the sight about which many of them had heard since childhood—the procession of the apostles in the tower of the town hall when the hour strikes, and the climax of it all, the crow of the cock.

So it was during these days, too, the days of the Warsaw declaration, the Warsaw Pact maneuvers, and the Bratislava meetings. The Czechs are a remarkably relaxed breed of people, as gentle as people can be, apparently easygoing, and courteous to strangers to a fault. They appeared to be even more relaxed during these days than usual, walking resiliently. Many people had come from all over the world to look them over. Their fame had spread because of their many achievements, their pavilion at Expo 67, their far-famed films, and now their historic role, the great experiment, which looked to many like a turning point in the history of the world. Would they be able to reconcile communism with democracy? Would they be the instrument of destiny to put an end to the fatal fear of the two worlds?

Most of the tourists were gone in these late hours of an early August day. The Old Town Square, with its Tyn Church, Old Town Hall, and Carolinum (the oldest university in that part of the world) is an enchanted place in the midst of history. Suddenly, it became crowded. There were thousands of people, young and attractive, laughing, joking, in a bantering mood. The rest of the world was in anguish about the people of Prague, but they were not. The meeting in Bratislava was still going on. All was going very well. Suddenly, there was a commotion at the corner of the square closest to the old Jewish ghetto. Surrounded by happy youngsters there was a man whom they all helped to get on the landmark monument of Prague, that of John Huss, erect in the midst of recumbent figures. The man was one of the cabinet members whom some of the young people had called by telephone, to come and tell them about the great events going on. And he came, as good-natured as only a Czech cabinet member could be. He spoke into an amplifier so that all the thousands could hear him well on the large square. What he said was very much to the point, and short.

You want to know what is going on in Bratislava. I can tell you that. Everything there is going fine and there is no need for concern. We have very able spokesmen who understand you and, I am sure, you understand them. No doubt, there will be a communiqué in the press and on the radio tomorrow. I was just about to retire when you called, and I did not want to disappoint you. It is rather late now and I am going home to sleep. I wish you a good night and pleasant dreams.

There was applause enough to wake the dead, and there was the happy laughter of youth all around. The minister left, but many of the young people stayed. They went in groups, and occasionally stopped to settle a point or two. They did this very articulately, with a maximum of relish. There was a lot of laughter at these impromptu meetings and a lot of pleasant banter. It was very late when the streets of Prague were relinquished to the nocturnal street cleaners. It had been a good day.

Then there was the communiqué the following day, as the cabinet member at the Huss monument had said there would be. It summarized the meetings held in two places, both in Czechoslovakia: the first in Cierna, in the extreme east, and the other in Bratislava. *The Sunday Times* of London summarized the substance of the two meetings in one sentence: "Summit says 'Carry on reforms but be wary of links with the West.'" This was distilled from a ten-page document. *The International Herald Tribune* of Paris did just as well in one long headline: "Russians and Allies Concede Inability to Make Czechs Stop Liberalization." *The Times* of London entitled its leading editorial on the subject: "The Sledgehammer and the Strong Nut." The editorial summed up the reaction of public opinion. Premier Dubček said: "I declare sincerely that our sovereignty is not menaced." He, his cabinet, and his country were showered with congratulations from nearly everywhere, including endorsements and best wishes from the two largest Communist parties of the non-Communist world, Italy and France.

"The encounter between Moscow and Prague remains one of the most extraordinary episodes in modern European history." This from the editorial of *The Times*, London, addicted to understatements rather than strong words. "After building the whole affair up to the level of a major crisis by staging heavy troop maneuvres," the editorial said, "calling up reservists and furiously denouncing the heretics, the Soviet leaders have apparently come round to see the Czechoslovak movement as nothing terrible after all. They have come to see it as most sensible people regarded it before all the uproar began."

THEN. . . .

The Czechoslovak radio broadcast on August 21:

Yesterday, on 20 August, around 2300 [11 P.M.], troops of the Soviet Union, Polish Peoples' Republic, the D.D.R. [East

Germany], the Hungarian Peoples' Republic, and the Bulgarian Peoples' Republic crossed the frontiers of the Czechoslovak Socialist Republic. This happened without the knowledge of the President of the Republic, of the Chairman of the National Assembly, the Premier, or the First Secretary of the Czechoslovak Communist Party Central Committee.

All citizens were asked to maintain calm and not to offer resistance to the troops on the march.

About the same time the official Soviet news agency made an announcement in Moscow: "Tass is authorized to state that party and government leaders of the Czechoslovak Socialist Republic have asked the Soviet Union and other allies to render the fraternal Czechoslovak people urgent assistance, including assistance with armed forces. . . ."

Who were these party and government leaders? No names were provided then, or ever. Urgent assistance was provided against what? "Counterrevolutionary forces." Again, no names or units were provided, nor was the nature of these forces. Within hours the Soviet troops and their allies completed their occupation of Czechoslovakia, tens of thousands at first, and hundreds of thousands at the peak. The estimates of the strength of the "fraternal forces" ran as high as six hundred thousand. However, neither the Russians nor their allies divulged authentic figures.

THE OCCUPATION AND ITS AFTERMATH

The Russians rounded up the key men of the Czechoslovak Communist Party: First Secretary Alexander Dubček; Premier Oldrich Cernik; National Assembly President Josef Smrkovsky; and Party Secretary Cestmir Cisar. Although they seem to have offered no resistance, they were manhandled and transported to Moscow. Meanwhile, President Svoboda had flown to the Soviet capital of his own accord, to seek a resolution of the crisis, and there he met the other leaders. "In the shadow of tanks and planes," the Czechs negotiated with the Russians, in the words of Assembly President Smrkovsky. The pressure was intense.

The choice facing the Prague leaders was, evidently, this: either they signed an agreement thrust upon them by the Kremlin or else the Soviets would physically occupy their nation, operating through puppets. On August 26, President Svoboda and his fellow leaders signed the agreement. Under it the Russians consented to a gradual troop withdrawal, with this exception: two Soviet divisions were to be stationed along the border of West Germany. The Czechs agreed to forego their liberalized communism, to disband the non-Marxist political parties, renew the press censorship, remove certain people from public office, and to permit a measure of Soviet control over the administration in Prague.

Returning to Prague, President Svoboda said: "In the spirit of the January, April, and May plenums of the Central Committee, we want to continue to develop the socialist social order and strengthen its humanist democratic nature . . ." and First Secretary Dubcek echoed: "We are convinced that we will find ways and means of developing with you all a policy that will eventually lead to the normalization of the situation."

These were brave words, following the Soviets' brutal deeds. They had been basking in their new respectability, reputed to be a force of stability. And now they were compared to Hitler, as a result of the treatment they meted out to the Czechs. Some of the most prestigious Communist parties spoke up against this new evidence of

Kremlin brutality. Without a doubt, the Soviet leadership
lost a propaganda battle. What was the explanation?

There were many of these, in the Soviet leaders' eyes.
There was danger in creating a precedent. The monopoly
of the Prague Communist party gone, what was to pre-
vent its being replaced, first, by non-Communist and,
possibly, anti-Communist groups? Then, the "domino theory" would come into play. Prague gone, would Budapest,
Bucharest, and Warsaw be far behind? Next door to the
Czechs were the restive Ukrainians, who might topple
next. These events might influence the other non-Russian
nationals in the Soviets. This turmoil would weaken the
Kremlin at the time it needed its strength most in its
"fraternal cold war" with the Chinese. Then there were
the Soviet intellectuals getting more restless, with such
tempting examples before them. The intellectuals were
the triggering forces of all movements of change.

"He who controls Bohemia," Chancellor Bismarck had
said, "also controls Europe." The Soviets saw Bohemia in
historic perspective, as the pivot of the continent. Next
door to her was Germany, the most successful country of
post-World War II, always the victor, even in defeat.
Because of her enormous dynamism, she was bound to
exert a fatal gravitational pull on the land of the Czechs,
unless Czechoslovakia were firmly imbedded in the Soviet
bloc. Within this problem, there was also the special case
of the German Democratic Republic, Communist-con-
trolled East Germany, the undemocratic fief of Walter
Ulbricht. His famous Wall was preventing East Germany's fatal hemorrhage, the loss of irreplaceable man-
power to the West. Once the Czechs opened their doors to
the world, what was to keep individual East Germans from
performing two related frontier crossings, from Communist Germany into Czechoslovakia and from there to West

Germany or Austria? Another East German Wall was out
of the question, because of the cost, the time, and the
terrain.

Now all the "shooting" appeared to be over in Prague. A
few people had been killed, victims more of fear than of
intent. Frightened Bulgarian and Soviet soldiers, scared
out of their wits when surrounded by Czechs, had discharged their guns. There was no blood bath comparable
to that of the Hungarian uprising twelve years before,
when thousands fell. The Czechs appear to have done no
shooting, as had the Hungarians. Magyars and Czechs are
next-door neighbors, their places of settlement overlapping in parts, and yet what a difference this tragic episode
in human history revealed in their national traits. The
Czechs did not shoot; the Hungarians had shot. Both of
them must have known that resistance was useless—the
resistance of a tiny country against a global empire, two
small specks on the frontier of a nation of continental
dimension. Perhaps the Czechs learned from the Hungarian tragedy. Or else they knew that shooting would
solve no problems. They lost their gambit—for the moment. They were going to lie low for a time in the manner
of the good soldier Schweik. In the long run they were
going to win, as they had in the past. They had better
nerves than the Soviets, and that was the evidence of their
greater strength. They showed up the weakness of the
Soviets, which was demonstrated by the tremendous concentration of manpower and armor to shake off an idea
that, at the most, was a humane communism, a democratic way. The Soviets may have shown the Czechs that
they were dreamers. In the past, however, their dreams
had come true.

Their reaction to the Soviet "friends" was expressed in
their underground poetry, plastered on Prague store
fronts:

Welcome friends—
You have come as brothers
And now our blood lies on the ground.

Welcome friends—
Thank you for the roses
On our children's graves.

Welcome friends—
We welcome you
With salt in our eyes.

Then, what seemed to be the Epilogue. The crew of the "spring," headed by Dubček, was replaced on the top. In came the new First Secretary of the Communist Party, Gustav Husak, acceptable to the Kremlin. While not a reformist, he was not an extremist either. But, then, he was a Czech. He had to subscribe to the ominous new Kremlin doctrine, though: "If 'socialist achievements' are imperiled in any bloc nation, the others have the right to intervene."

A chapter seemed to be closed, and it bore the hallmark of the Czechs. It was in their national tradition that they —the people of John Huss and Thomas Masaryk—should have voiced their protest against the Kremlin-controlled Ecumene. Perhaps this was not the last chapter, or the Epilogue. It was significant that it should have been tried at all. Perhaps it was the first word of a new Prologue.

Meanwhile, the Czechs will follow the national tradition exemplified by the "good soldier" Schweik, who said *"ja, ja"* to the Habsburgs, while acting in the spirit of *"nein, nein."* This time it may be *"da, da"* and *"nyet, nyet."*

10

Rumania—
Which Way the Wind?

To understand Rumania one has to be a meteorologist, not a political scientist. Her policy is determined by the prevailing winds of diplomacy. Nor is it enough to observe the wind. It has to be anticipated, a faculty for which the Rumanians have developed a special sense. This aptitude has enabled them to master an environment in which the craftiest has the best chance to survive.

Rumania's location between the hammer and the anvil has predetermined her national life. In the past the hammer was the Russia of the Czars, the anvil the Ottoman Empire—the devil and the Black Sea. How the Rumanians have managed to survive is one of the beguiling chapters of history.

There is therefore historic import in the fact that in recent years Rumania has chosen to go her own way within the Communist bloc. It indicates Rumania's fine sense of fathoming the fog. A look at the country's past may reveal the springs of the Rumanians' anticipatory sense, this in spite of large gaps in the history of the region, which are explained by a geography that shows invasion routes of aggressive forces and the defensive sanctuaries of the Balkan mountains in the background. The goals were, depending upon the epoch, the protective

shields of the Roman empires, East and West, and the
southern warm-water approaches of defensive strength
and trade.

This region entered history as the easternmost outpost
of the Roman Empire, under Trajan. Therefore its Roman
name, and therefore also its language—Rumanian, Ro-
manian, Roman—Latin, representing the farthermost advance of the ecumenical tongue, too.

Since this was the staging area of swarms of invaders,
its history is so troubled that it can be indicated only in
vignettes.

AFTER THE ROMANS

Chaos was so complete in this region after the downfall
of the Western Roman empire that the records of Rumania's early history got lost. That history begins to take
shape only in the thirteenth century. For the ensuing five
centuries the area was divided into Wallachia in the south
and Moldavia in the north, each carrying on in a semi-
organized, semi-chaotic way.

During this age the native population had sought
shelter in the tangled mountain ranges of the Transylvanian Alps. At the end of the thirteenth century the main
thrust of the barbarians was blunted, and the mountains
began to disgorge their refugees. They descended on the
lowlands in the valley of the Danube, the land of the black
soil. Tradition says that *Negru Voda, the Black Prince*,
was the founder of Wallachia, while the founder of
Moldavia was Dragos, the son of Bogdan, who led his
followers from the Carpathian Mountains to the Lower
Danubian promised land.

Then came the Turks in the fifteenth century, and that
was a major trauma. They reduced the two principalities

to the positions of vassals, and introduced an indirect regime, ruling through native satraps. They collected their tithe from them and let the local princes retain the rest. The mortality rate among the native princes was great because of disagreements as to what constituted the leftovers. When the native lines became extinct, the Turks turned to the *phanariots* to serve them as their henchmen.

These were Greek residents of the Ottoman capital, Constantinople, so named after the *phanar,* the lighthouse, on a small peninsula of the Golden Horn, near which they had their settlements.

Appointing Christians to rule over Christians was the Turks' way of deflecting hatred from themselves. "Let the accursed *giaour* kill the *phanariot* dog," the Turkish master said. The substance of the *phanariot* rule was summed up by an Austrian consul of the time: "All posts from the highest to the lowest not only bring in good income, but carry with them the right to plunder the people." "Plucking the hen without making it cluck" became a Rumanian proverb.

At the end of the eighteenth century, the Rumanians, ruled by fellow-Christians, were worse off than the Serbians and Bulgarians, who were governed directly by the Turks. "When the people murmur," the subjects complained, "the Prince makes a bonfire of their petitions and calls out his Albanian guard." When despairing appeals were made to the Prince, he rejoined: "Pay your taxes and your life will be spared."

THEN CAME THE BEAR

The life forces of Turkey were ebbing away, due to maladministration and the withering of her *élan vitale*. The life forces of the Russians, to the north of the Da-

nubian principalities of Wallachia and Moldavia, on the
other hand, approached full tide. The Muscovites had a
country of continental dimensions but lacked a warm-
water outlet. The natural highway to that outlet was by
way of the two Danubian principalities. "On to Byzantium" was written on the triumphal arch of Catherine the
Great, announcing the new Muscovite policy. Peter the
Great began to style himself the "Monarch of Russo-
Greeks." Again, the road to the land of the Greeks, which
was warmed by the waters of the south, traversed the twin
principalities.

The two Danubian regions were united at the end of the
eighteenth century. They shared a common fate, anyway.
The Russians became more insistent on "aiding" their
Christian brethren, and the Turks were on the defensive
everywhere. Their hold on the Danubian principalities
became increasingly more feeble. It was only the opposition of leading Western powers that kept the Russian bear
from pushing down to the warm waters of the south. The
West wanted to keep Russia from that strategic spot. But,
because of the weakness of the Turks, the Russians exercised protective authority over the Danubian principalities, extorting concessions from the Sultans. It was then
that the Rumanians, as the more sophisticated upper
classes of the two principalities began to call themselves,
were forced into the practice of diplomatic meteorology:
which way was the wind blowing, from the north or from
the south? It was mostly from the north, from the Russian steppes. Early in the nineteenth century, the Russians worked their way to still greater influence in the
Danubian principalities. They did this informally, with
the aid of influential people in what was to become the
capital of the united country, Bucharest.

For the majority of the people in those days the concept
of Rumanian nationality was still a hazy notion. What

counted in their eyes was their religion, the Greek Orthodox creed. Unsophisticated people, therefore, considered
themselves Greek, the nationality of their historic rulers,
the *phanariots*. There was even a plan afoot to establish a
greater Greece, from the Carpathians to Constantinople.
The headquarters of the planners was in the Russian
Black Sea port, Odessa, and this greater Greece was to be
a Russian satellite. In this way, it was hoped, the warm-
water thirst of the Czars would be slaked.

Religion was the social framework in the Lower Danube region; Christianity confronted Islam. But not even
this remote reign could resist nationalism, which began its
triumphant march on the Paris barricades in 1789. It took
half a century for this idea to reach this area of the
Danube, there to be turned into a quasi-creed. It was a
curious amalgam of nationalism and religion, a Christian
revolution. A manifesto was read from church altars in
the light of tapers illumined in honor of the country:
"Have no fear, save the fear of the Lord, and then you can
chant without blushing: 'Christ is with us.' Rise in His
name, and then the angels of heaven will smite the foe,
will crush the rider and his horse; his arms and chariots
will be scattered into dust, his projects dissolved like
smoke. To arms, Rumanians, to the arms of salvation!"

The revolutionists, inspired by the equalitarian principles of the French, demanded a free country with an
elected prince and parliament, equal rights, the emancipation of Jews and Gypsies, the abolition of the death penalty, and a free press. The opposition was strong; it came
from the landed magnates, *boyars*, who held much of the
countryside under their thumbs. "If the *boyar* could have
laid his hand on the sun," a peasant spokesman said, "he
would have seized it and sold to the countryman for
money, the light and heat of God."

This time the Russians and Turks agreed on a common

policy—that the revolution must be crushed—and the
Turks denounced the movement as "inspired by the spirit
of socialism." Both neighbors were to control the country
until it was fully pacified. While the Czar's soldiers evacu-
ated the principalities, after a time St. Petersburg demanded indemnity for the costs of the occupation, which
the Rumanians considered an affront.

THE WEST WIND

Turkey was sick, and, but for the administration of
strong stimulants, would have succumbed. The stimulants
were administered by Western powers bent on keeping the
"sick man" alive. Should he die, the closest great power,
Russia, would have been the heir, as the offspring of
Byzantine culture, and prime beneficiary of the "three-in-
one" lifeline: the Bosporous, the Sea of Marmara, and the
Dardanelles, the Straits. The Ottoman Empire weak and
Russia not strong enough to pursue an autonomous foreign policy in the region, the Danubian principalities
became the tools of the Western nations in their balance-
of-power policy in Europe's East. The local leaders of the
twin principalities had had their schooling in how to play
out one neighbor against the other in their own balance-of-
power game. Step by step the two principalities became
almost one country—Rumania—with limited independence.

Now the Rumanian meteorologists had a larger horizon
to survey and for the politicians to trim their sails on.
Russia was no longer the preponderant influence in the
Lower Danube region after her defeat in the Crimean
War. In 1859 one Prince was elected to the headship of
the two principalities, and the head of state was no longer

an alien but a native son, Alexandru Juan Cuza. Gradually
the separate institutions of the principalities were merged,
and two years after Cuza's election Rumania was one.
Although he was a top *boyar* and the guardian of the
established institutions, he could not help moving with the
times, and so he instituted free education and freed the
serfs, two basic moves. But he was a gradualist, moving
too slowly in a revolutionary age. "Gentlemen," he had
said at his election, "I fear you will not be satisfied with
me." He was right. He was too indolent (an Oriental
ailment), and under his reign public office meant private
plunder. The regime of the first native Prince of united
Rumania was no pathway to Eldorado, as expected. With
the Rumanian flair, acquired throughout the centuries,
officials in the palace noticed the change in the wind.
Geographically Rumania was in the east, but her language and ideology originated in the west, with the Latin
tongue and the political influence of Paris. The center of
the cultural life of the better classes was France. Also, it
was to the West that Rumania owed her life. Because of
these factors, the dominant court clique deposed Cuza and
went in search of a Western prince. It finally found him in
the person of Prince Carol Charles, of Hohenzollern-
Sigmaringen, who, even though German, appeared to be
the incarnation of the West. He was a member of the
southern branch of the ruling Prussian family. He had his
links to France as a cousin of Napoleon III, Emperor of
the French, and through his paternal grandmother he was
even related to Napoleon the Great. These were all factors
that indicated a Western orientation in an eastern land.
The political meteorologists of the new country foresaw
fair weather in the Occident and a barometric depression
in the Orient.

The late eighties of the last century witnessed the
Russians' boldest attempt to wrest a warm-water outlet

from the Turks, and their route to victory led across
Rumania. That meant Russian troops traversing the country on the way to the straits. How was Rumania to react?
She knew the Turks were weak, but she also knew that
the outcome would be determined, as often in the past, by
diplomatic maneuvers, not the feat of arms. The Rumanians' historic traditions counseled caution, and
Carol's government acted in the accepted way. It had an
agreement with the Russians, which was secret, placing
army stores at their disposal, against payment in gold. At
the same time, the Rumanian armed forces feigned resistance to the Russians' crossing the country on their way
to the Turkish Straits. The Russians won the war but lost
the peace because of Western jealousy. The Rumanians,
on the other hand, won the peace without entering the
war. The Berlin Congress recognized Rumania's full independence, and on May 22, 1881, Carol became the sovereign King. Characteristically, his royal crown was made of
steel from captured Turkish arms.

A DIPLOMATIC PATTERN

For chanceries in Europe "Rumania-watching" was a
profitable occupation. Bucharest seemed to have an intuitive perception of who was going to win the diplomatic
games. Two years before the outbreak of the first World
War, she was on the sidelines, observing the outcome of
the war between the Balkan nations and the Turks. The
Ottoman Empire lost, and promptly the victors fell out
among themselves. This time it was safe for Rumania to
enter the arena. Again she was on the winning side.

In the early years of the first World War, it looked as if
the Germans were going to win. They were on enemy
territory on all fronts. The Rumanians disdained to look at

the map—they anticipated a change in the direction of wind, and they knew that it did not favor the Reich. They joined its foes, and the Germans wiped out Rumania. No matter, since their victory was short-lived. In the end, the Rumanians found themselves on the winning side. As a reward, Rumania's territory was more than doubled. Transylvania the beautiful, with her subterranean mineral treasures, became hers, and its millions of Rumanians, who had been under alien rule for centuries, were united with the "old kingdom." It received the fattest farmland of the Banat from Hungary, Bessarabia from Russia, and Bucovina from Austria. This time, too, it had paid to be a good political meteorologist.

Rumania became the postwar pivot of the "Little Entente," of which the sponsor was France. Rumania made common cause also with Poland, and thus formed a chain in the link of the *cordon sanitaire* against Communist "contamination" and the shield of the West. As the easternmost outpost of the West in Europe, Rumania presented herself in the role of the champion of Occidental cultural values against the onslaughts of a new barbarism.

These were her roles for most of the inter-bellum period. Her hope for calm was crushed by the aggressive successes of the Third Reich. "New German" ideology was hailed as the "wave of the future" in many parts, the synthesis of proven economic processes with new insights leading to desirable change. It was inconceivable that Germany should not prevail, and Rumania concluded a trade treaty with her in March 1939. Two months later she concluded a similar treaty with Great Britain, just in case. . . . When all continental Europe stood in awe before the muscle-flexing performance of new Germany, the Rumanians, being master political meteorologists, had their doubts.

They shed their doubts however, on June 22, 1941, when the German armies launched "Operation Barbarossa" to knock out the Soviet Union in a gigantic nation-wrecking operation. Rumania had seen what the *Reichswehr* could do; Germany had knocked out her ideal and model, *la grande nation*, in a week, and smaller countries in days. This time, there could be no doubt as to who would win.

The Rumanian army joined the Germans in attacking the Soviet Union, and within a short time Bessarabia and Bucovina, snatched by the Russians a short time before, were reincorporated in the kingdom. The Rumanians proudly marched into an anticipated global conquest. The vital section of the Ukraine between the Bug and Dniester rivers was placed under Rumanian military rule. Had the Rumanian meteorologists been right again? They were certainly right at the time. Only the demons in Hitler's mind might have known Rumania's fate had she failed to toe the Nazi line. There was the tragic example of Poland, the northern neighbor. At Stalingrad, the tide turned, and the Rumanian meterologists made their prognostication promptly. While the Germans still entertained the hope of victory, born of their invention of a brood of secret weapons, the trained Bucharest weather prophets predicted a new wave of the future. This time they foresaw Hitler's eventual defeat. Changing sides with awe-inspiring rapidity, the Rumanians signed an armistice agreement with the Soviet Union in September, 1944, under which they were to change sides and join the war against Germany by supplying twelve infantry divisions to the Russians, their foes of yesterday. They were also to detain the German occupation forces. While the war was still being fought ferociously and some doubt prevailed about its end, the Rumanian political meteorologists had completed new weather reports.

THEN CAME THE SOVIETS

The events that followed were similar in most details to those in the other bloc countries. The opposition parties, National Peasants and Liberals, were sliced up in the classical "salami-cutting" method, incorporated, first, in the National Democratic Front and, later, in the Peoples' Democratic Front, both of them Communist controlled. The first of these was under the leadership of Petru Groza, leader of the Ploughman's Front. Gradually power slid into the hands of a team led by Ana Pauker and Gheorghe Gheorghiu-Dej. Interparty bickering eliminated Pauker and left Gheorghiu-Dej on top for a dozen years, until his death in 1965.

For most of these years, no country was a more loyal satellite of the Soviets than Rumania. Her government mirrored nearly all the domestic and foreign twists and twirls adopted by the Soviets. Dutifully, Bucharest ranted against Western "imperialists and warmongers," in spite of Rumania's historic orientation to the West. Rumania, the model pupil in Uncle Ivan's kindergarten, received all she had lost to the Hungarians as a result of an Axis territorial award. This in spite of the fact that the regained territory contained a couple of million Hungarians.

After Yugoslavia's expulsion from the Cominform, relations with her became strained, in spite of the fact that the conflict placed heavy burdens on Rumania through the suspension of economic and diplomatic relations. Rumanians went further than any other country in forming an anti-Tito committee and making Bucharest the seat of the Cominform. Purges of pro-Tito and other Communists of doubtful loyalty continued. With the elimination of

some of the early leaders, such as Ana Pauker, in 1952,
party leadership became the shadow of its Soviet prototype. Former Justice Minister, and one of the founders of
the Rumanian Communist party, Lucretiu Patrascanu
was convicted of espionage and executed in 1954. Following the example of the Soviets' twentieth party congress,
Rumania read Stalin out of its hall of fame.

THEN NATIONAL COMMUNISM

The last undisputed old-line Communist ruler in Eastern Europe to serve as party chief and premier was
Gheorghiu-Dej. He was followed in 1965 by Nicolae Ceausescu, holding the same posts. It was under him that
Rumania astounded the world with an increasingly independent stand. This abrupt change appeared to deserve
special attention because of Rumania's reputation as the
international weathervane. From internationalism, Rumania made a swift turn to nationalism.

THE POET AND THE PATRIOT

The poet and the patriot are akin in Rumania. Writers
have shaped her language, formulated her political aspirations, and guided action. They helped the twin principalities, Moldavia and Wallachia, to become one nation, Rumania, and to become a cultural offspring of Rome. What
Rumanian child does not know the name of Andrei Mure-
sianu, a national poet, and what Rumanian heart fails to
beat faster at the melodic sounds of his "Blaring Echoes,"
a national poem? Writers like Dimitri Bolintineanu

helped to create the mystique of Rumanianism with poetry such as the "Breeze from the East" (to be mixed with the whirlwind from the West). Writers fathomed the spirit of the people in the folk tales they themselves shaped into collections expressing the unique qualities of the country folk—dreams woven out of reality.

The West came directly to the East in the writings of poets like Vasile Alecsandri, whose "Song of the Latin Race" is a declaration of love for the Occident. It was with their aid that Bucharest became the Paris of the East, and France the cultural home of the Rumanian. The poets' admiration for Western culture infused the country's politics also. The new Roman Empire, a cultural realm, expressed a policy aspiration in diplomacy, too. The magnetic pole of Bucharest had been Paris, never Moscow.

Because of his role in the national renaissance and in the articulation of political dreams, the Rumanian writer has acquired a special status as a seer, a prophet, and, within the Rumanian context, a meteorologist. No more could a popular Rumanian writer walk in the streets of Bucharest unrecognized than could Elizabeth Taylor remain incognito on New York's Fifth Avenue. The launching of a major work of a major author in the capital of Rumania is still a cultural event, with all the excitement surrounding fame—autographing sessions, interviews on radio and television, long reviews in the press.

The signs of the nationalist revolution in Communist Rumania first flared up in literature. Before the politicians, the writers were set for the change. Even in the jungle of politics, the writer was shielded by traditional immunity. A typical example of this is the story of a family, Marin Preda's *Morometic*.

The family of the Morometes was rent by political partisanship in their ancestral home of Salistea. In an atavistic gesture of self-defense, some of them sought the

protective influence of the Muscovites. The ancestors had
survived the Scythians, Dacians, Visigoths, Gepidae, Avars
and Lombards, and above all, the Tatars and Turks. They
would survive the Muscovites, too; this, compared with
the eternity of the Morometes, was to be only a passing
phase of life.

Some of them had greeted the "dawn from the east"
that ushered out the darkness of the *boyar* rule of large
estates. In spite of that, the Morometes had become a
leading peasant family; but at what cost? The harder they
toiled the more they had to fill corrupt officials' coffers.
And what chance did even a well-to-do peasant have in
bureaucratic antechambers? He was looked upon as an
inferior breed.

Nicolae's eyes were bulging with stars when the Communists came. The *boyars* went, the corrupt bureaucrats
were marched off to jail. Many of the farms were collectivized promptly, to be sure, but the people were assured
that theirs was the opportunity to make their way in life,
with the *boyars* and corrupt officials gone.

Nicolae became a party worker. But the patriarchal
head of the family remained in opposition to the new
regime. Suspicion of authority was in his old bones. The
Morometes fell victim to the generation gap.

The trouble began when the government agents descended upon the farmstead to collect a share of the grain
quota imposed upon the district. Nicolae knew that it was
too high and that its collection would cause trouble. This
meant that they had toiled endlessly for scraps of food.
Where was the new era, the better life, for the toiler? Still
a believer, Nicolae attributed the high quota to an error,
and decided to present the facts of what the farmstead
produced and what it could afford to spare. He had the
self-confidence of the believer talking to like-minded comrades. He did talk to the tax collectors, but they were
people with "no ears," and so they could not listen.

Nicolae learned that they had been members of the Iron Guard, a fascist organization under the old regime. Now they were Communists, the type of people always in the saddle—Fascist yesterday, Communist today—so filled with self-interest that their minds were immune to argument.

Nicolae's disenchantment followed, unadmitted at first because of pride. He found himself in the midst of nowhere—no faith, no friends, no future. No longer the village spokesman, he turned inward. Luckily, he found understanding among the flowers, became a horticulturist, a new Candide, ready to cultivate his own garden. There was no more opposition to the old patriarch in the ancestral house. The spirit of the nation lived on in the old man's heart—the old frustration and the instinct to live and work and work, to live and live.

"There were a lot of people in the Morometes' house again today," Ciulca said, "while *Mister* Ilie Moromete was cursing us [the Communists] again, and people on the road could hear him far and wide."

"What did he say?" a cousin asked.

"We will see," he said, "what it will be like when the Communists are gone."

"What will it be like?"

"When they are gone, the Americans will be here, and it will be his sacred duty to skin ten Communists alive."

This was printed by a publishing house of the Rumanian Communist regime. Can one read this as a sign in the direction of the prevailing wind, from East to West? The bureaucratic publishers may have followed the national tradition of meteorology.

If this were an isolated incident it would not be significant. But it was not. There were numerous other indications of the changing direction of the wind, such as Ion Lancranjan's *Solar Eclipse,* the work of another literary seer, a meteorologist.

He too spoke of the eclipse of the cause disloyally
served by men who could serve no cause except their own.
"I am the public, and my interests are those of the community," keynoters of the regime say. They are committed
to promoting foreign interests to stay on top, and the
dedication they profess is to the service of the creed of
which they are the idols. That is what the main character
of this novel asserts. He is a traditionalist, grass-roots
Rumanian. All his life he had bent his back to serve the
soil. He was not going to bend his back to serve other men.
Proudly he avows that he is a self-made man, one of the
few remaining *kulaks*, affluent peasants, in the region. For
how long he did not know. The winds of doctrine could
not shake his confidence in himself. A non-Communist,
perhaps anti-Communist, he was presented to the public
as a hero in Communist Rumania.

THE HERALD OF CHANGE

Few people outside the country read Rumanian novels,
indicating a basic change. Tourists were not welcome, and
Rumania produced no more news than Tibet. Meanwhile,
changes were taking place after the death of Gheorghiu-
Dej. Rumania had nostalgia for the West, and gradually
the barriers to Occidental tourists were removed. What
they saw surprised them. The West had penetrated the
country in urban development, industrial plants, and—
most obvious to tourists—in holiday resorts, mainly on
the Black Sea. The resort area, centering around Mamaja,
was the French Riviera of the East, modern, attractive,
and available to those of limited means. The rest of the
land became accessible, too. Bucharest surprised the
Westerners with its well-planned new sections, large pub-

lic housing projects, massive school-building program, and, above all, its intense nationalism, revealed in official announcements and private talks. Even a fleeting impression suggested a change in the direction of the winds.

But Rumania was not one of the countries, as yet, to which Western newspaper correspondents flocked. It was not seen as a storm center. Embedded in the core land of the Communist bloc, it seemed to go its satellite way. In the United Nations, the Rumanian delegate watched the prevailing wind in Moscow. He voted the Kremlin route.

Because Rumania was not near any storm center, the Western world took barely any notice of the weather forecasts of political meteorologists. One of these was the First Deputy Prime Minister, Emil Bodnaras, who told the ninth congress of the party in July 1965: "The independent development of the nations encompassed within the world socialist system cannot be considered as one outside of the range of possibilities. Only through the independent actions of the socialist nations can the proletarian fraternalism acquire real substance and effectiveness." A similar thought was expressed in the same month, in the official party organ, by Alexandrus Draghici: "Only by achieving signal successes in the construction of socialism at home, by firmly guiding the toilers in the struggle for a high rate of industrial and agricultural production, can our party fulfill its international duty, thus contributing to the strengthening of socialism throughout the world."

Such cryptic hints indicated a change in the prevailing winds long before they occurred. The change assumed importance mainly in connection with the two international bodies within the bloc—Comecon, the Council for Mutual Economic Assistance, and the Warsaw Pact of mutal defense assistance.

Comecon, the Soviet's answer to the Marshall Plan, had

remained dormant for years. Then Nikita Khrushchev
revived it in the late fifties, this time as the bloc's answer
to the European Common Market. As we know, the Soviet
chief's plan called for intensified integration and specialization of the member countries' economies. The plan was
favorably received by the industrially more advanced
peoples' republics, especially Czechoslovakia and East
Germany. The Rumanian reaction was an implicit indication of Bucharest's national policy. Rumania opposed the
Comecon plan under which each member would participate in the body in accordance with its comparative advantages in production. Rumania was a larger producer
than the others of industrial raw materials such as petroleum, several minerals, lumber, and food. She did not
want to be mainly a purveyor of raw materials to other
members. On the contrary, she wanted to enlarge her
sphere of industrialization. The comparative advantage of
the Czechs and East Germans was their broad spectrum of
industries; they were able to fill foreign orders, too, including those of Rumania. Under the Khrushchev plan,
Rumania would have been encouraged to concentrate on
the production of raw materials, of petro-chemicals, lumber, food, and light consumer industrial goods. For the
record, the Rumanians agreed at the Moscow summit
Comecon conference of June 1962 to abide by the "principles of international socialist division of labor." They
interpreted it as an assurance of "complete equality, respect for territorial integrity, national independence,
sovereignty and noninterference in each other's internal
affairs." It was this nationalist stand that led to the shelv-
ing of the grandiose Kremlin plan.

With the Comecon battle won, the Rumanians proceeded even more boldly to assert their full national sovereignty. Going beyond their opposition to the Kremlin's
plan for the Comecon, they took the offensive in asserting

their right to protect their interests even against the Kremlin. They insisted on the equality of the Communist parties of all the fraternal nations, and declared categorically: "No one can decide what is and what is not correct for other parties and countries. . . . There cannot be a 'parent' party and a 'son' party. . . . None is 'superior' and none 'subordinate.' "

In line with this categorical policy, Rumania stood up against the Soviets' monopoly in the Warsaw Treaty Organization, established in answer to the West's N.A.T.O. on May 14, 1955, as a "Treaty of Friendship, Cooperation and Mutual Assistance." The W.T.O. remained a Soviet-controlled body, staffed and led largely by Russian officers. Obviously it served as a cover for the stationing of Soviet troops in East Germany, Poland, and Hungary, and thus for the effective limitation of the sovereignties of those countries. At the twenty-third party congress of the Communist Party of the Soviet Union in March 1966 the Kremlin spokesman called for the further strengthening of the Warsaw Pact. The secretary general of the Rumanian Communist Party, Nicolae Ceausescu (also the head of its ruling standing committee), gave his country's answer to First Party Secretary Leonid Brezhnev of the Soviet Union.

Ceausescu was the spokesman of a nationalist Communist Rumania. Who was this man whose name the West now had to learn? The village of his birth, Scornicesti, was so small that a magnifying glass was needed to find it on the map. Strangely, nationalism had driven fifteen-year-old Nicolae into the embrace of international communism. A peasant youth, such as he, had had no nation and therefore no support in Rumania. The country was the feudal domain of the estate owners and their bureaucratic liege. The peasant youth could find his nationalist identity in those days only in an opposition party. Only

the Communists represented the genuine opposition. In
their ranks he was found, hauled above ground, and
clapped in jail. He was still in his teens when the second
World War ended, and the Soviets enabled him to exchange places with his jailers.

Fame did not beckon to him at first in the Communist
Party (then the Workers' Party). He seems to have been
tainted with the nationalist heresy from the outset; yet he
was not important enough to be closely watched, so that
his views went undetected, and that is how he politically
survived the Stalin years. After the usual time of troubles,
the routine inparty combat ensued. He proved to be a
skilled man with the dialectic sword. In the interparty
jungle fight he got the upper hand. Personable, intelligent,
a good organizer, he employed the right clichés, mastered
the language of the rank and file, had the required small-
village background, and was robust in an unassuming
way. Above all, he had Rumania in his bones, and thus
expressed the feelings of the new age. Also, he was a good
political meteorologist. He knew that it was time for his
country to adjust itself to the prevailing wind. The Kremlin was not to remain for long the weather-kitchen of the
Marxist world.

The new secretary general spoke in the spirit of this
nationalism when he declared: "The existence of blocs
and the sending of troops to other countries is an anachronism which is incompatible with the independence and
national sovereignty of the peoples." He had the Warsaw
Pact in mind when he said: "The Soviet policy of integration is tantamount to domination."

A few years before, he would have been struck down by
the Kremlin's lightning. Speaking for a new Communist
Rumania, he attacked the Soviets' policy directly. In a
survey of recent history, he charged that it was the Soviets
who had forced his country into the Third Reich camp

during the war. The Kremlin had wrested Bessarabia and Bucovina from Rumania. The Soviet leadership had appointed non-Rumanians to key positions in Bucharest. Then, in an unprecedented outburst of heresy, he declared that the Soviet leaders, including Lenin, had been responsible for the "blackest periods of Rumanian history in this century." Could anything have been more heretical than to question the superhuman qualities of Lenin?

Then he ventured further into the hitherto uncharted sphere of dissidence:

"The nation will undoubtedly continue for a long time to come to be the basis of our society's development during the entire period of building socialism and communism." Denouncing attempts to declare the fatherland incompatible with socialist internationalism, he further declared: "The steady strengthening of each socialist nation not only does not conflict with the interests of socialist internationalism, but, on the contrary, corresponds fully to the interests of the cause of the workers' class and the toiling people throughout the world."

This unequivocal assertion that the interests of the international proletariat were not necessarily interlinked with those of the Soviets was an explicit challenge to the traditional identification of Soviet interests with the entire socialist cause. It indicated, on the contrary, that the building of communism had to be undertaken in each "socialist fatherland."

Regarding Moscow's efforts to tighten the Warsaw Pact, making the members' armies a more cohesive force under Soviet command, he launched a counteroffensive. He asked for a basic change, so that the command of the military alliance be rotated among its members—Bulgaria, Czechoslovakia, East Germany, Hungary, Poland, Rumania, and the U.S.S.R.—and the use of nuclear arms on a member's territory be subject to its consent. Did the

Kremlin's thunder strike dead the Rumanian miscreant?

Far from that. The Rumanians' pressure tactics were rewarded at the pact nations' Bucharest meeting in July 1966. In spite of Kremlin pressure, the Warsaw Treaty Organization was left unchanged. Besides, it was decided that with the dissolution of N.A.T.O., the Warsaw Pact should also end. That year, Rumania decided to sit out the military maneuvers under the pact.

THE WINDS OF CHANGE

The Kremlin had envisioned the Socialist bloc as a homogeneous unit, a confraternity of countries dedicated to a common cause. The Soviet Union had been the only one in a position to direct the destinies of the fraternal countries because of its strength and experience. "What is good for the Soviets is also good for Rumania . . . and Bulgaria . . . and . . ."

By 1960 Yugoslavia had been going her own way for a dozen years, Hungary had been slapped back into the rank and file, and the bloc countries were toeing the line as members of the Comecon, of the Warsaw Pact, and of the pro-Kremlin cheering section. The interests of the Soviets took precedence over their own welfares.

Then Rumania moved across the line, first with diffidence and then boldly. Her dissidence can be traced to the third congress of the party in June 1960. Already then, the keynote speaker said that national conditions of the Socialist countries determined the "correct line," leading to ultimate solutions. Adhering to the national character of the country, it was set forth, the process of social transformation would enable Rumania to make the maximum contribution to the realization of communism, the supreme goal. Its attainment would be aided by collaboration with other socialist countries. As Rumania's independent role took shape, Bucharest insisted on noninterference in her internal affairs. As a *quid pro quo* and an equal partner she pledged her support of Russia's positions in the diplomatic field. But the people of the country were told to give precedence to the execution of their own party's program, and that in the spirit of devotion to their fatherland, the Communist Party was heir of the "most glorious fighting traditions of the people for their national and social liberation." It was at that congress that details were worked out about the withdrawal of the Soviet troops from Rumania.

While the punches were exchanged between Bucharest and Moscow, the split between the Soviets and the Chinese had become a deep abyss. The Rumanians saw that the conflict between Moscow and Peking weakened the Soviets, who could not afford to wage a two-front war. Correspondingly, Bucharest became bolder, intensifying its resistance to the Soviets. This time the leaders harangued the people themselves, so as to create a national consensus. The radio airways resounded with harsh words against the Kremlin. The Rumanians were told to rally in an effort to strengthen the "socialist patriotic sentiments," their ancestral heritage.

The breeze of change now had become the winds of change. Until now there had been only talk, but now the time came for positive action. It took the shape of an official statement on the "Stand of the Rumanian Workers' Party (Communists) Concerning the Problems of the International Communist and Working Class Movement." It was adopted by the enlarged plenum of the Central Committee in April 1964, and it made explicit what had been implicit heretofore.

The statement made it clear that "Rumania is for the

Rumanians" and not for the Soviets. It subscribed to the
aspirations of all countries, whether members of the
Socialist camp or not, small or large, to follow their
national destinies on the basis of their specific conditions.
The right of all countries to achieve this aim was to be
internationally guaranteed.

This was a warning of stronger winds of change. Significantly, no distinction was made between members and
nonmembers of the Socialist camp. The issue was
nationalism, not ideology. They were all nations and entitled to live their lives according to their historic destinies,
and to "international guarantees of independence."

In the ensuing turmoil the Rumanians took the offensive, and Bucharest turned to the "grand strategist" for
support. In 1965 it published the *Notes of Karl Marx on
the Rumanians,* shot through with anti-Russian views. It
made little difference, in the context, that the target had
been Czarist Russia. Marx condemned Russian imperialism and argued for a Rumanian Bessarabia, the area now
part of the Soviet Union: the Moldavian Soviet Socialist
Republic. Thus Communist Rumania fought Communist
Russia on a national territorial issue. The Kremlin riposted with a flanking movement on another territorial
issue—Transylvania. That sylvan area of forested hills
covering land well stocked with mineral deposits had been
returned, bargained back to the Rumanians by the Soviets,
after the second World War. The Magyars claimed part of
the region on the ground that it was the dwelling place of
two million of their ilk. By effecting the transfer the
Soviets made the Hungarians pay for the Kremlin's acqui-
sition of Rumania. This time the Kremlin hinted that the
fate of the "Land Beyond the Woods" was not a closed
issue. Moscow even suggested that the fate of Transylvania might be determined by a plebiscite. For the sake of
parity, let there be a plebiscite also in Bessarabia, it added,

certain that it had the means to control the "peoples' will."
The Rumanians called a halt to their propaganda attack.

At the party congress in July 1965 Rumania promoted
herself from the status of a "people's republic" to that of a
"socialist republic"—the same rank as that of the Soviet
Socialist Republics. At the same congress, Secretary General Nicolae Ceausescu turned to other issues to oppose
the Soviets. The Kremlin wanted a slower rate of the
development of heavy industries. It questioned the sense
of making heavy investments in costly projects as long as
the Rumanians' needs could be covered by imports from
the more highly tooled countries, the Soviets, Czechoslovakia, and East Germany. Again, this was the Russians'
Comecon hobby-horse. But the Rumanians wanted heavy
industries, irrespective of cost. Thus they were to safe-
guard their economic freedom, national sovereignty,
equal rights among the bloc nations, and noninterference
by others in their internal affairs.

To show the Kremlin that she had not lost her skill in
"weather forecasting" Rumania turned to America as a
trading partner. She concluded agreements with the Fire-
stone Rubber Company and the Universal Oil Products
Corporation to construct a synthetic rubber plant and a
catalytic petroleum-cracking unit. Although the companies backed out, due to Washington's pressure, Moscow
got the message. At the same time Rumania proved the
Russians wrong in pressing for changes. She was doing
better than any of the other bloc countries, marking the
highest rate of industrial development in eastern Europe.
Bucharest lost no time in making its products. The country was well supplied with basic raw materials, a depend-
able work force, and an established industrial base. In
the midst of all the turmoil, Rumania was settling down
to some of her most profitable years.

Rumania was moving closer to independence even in

the diplomatic field. While communism and neutrality seemed to be incompatible at the time, Rumania was inching closer to a neutral stand. She demonstrated it in the conflicts of Moscow-Peking and in the Middle East. Rumania was the only satellite—not counting Albania, a freewheeler—that failed to denounce the Chinese in the accepted incantations. On the contrary, Premier Chou En-lai was given a de luxe welcome at his visit to Bucharest. Nor did Rumania participate at the 1968 conference, preparatory to another one, expected to line up the Communist parties behind the Soviet stand. It was to acknowledge the Kremlin as the official propounder of the Marxist-Leninist creed.

Another conflict area was the "two Germanies" problem. The Eastern bloc countries—the Soviets excepted—maintained diplomatic relations only with the D.D.R., and not with the Federal Republic. Bucharest took the unprecedented step of establishing diplomatic relations with Bonn. Here was proof that even in a matter of such overriding importance the Kremlin was unable to keep its flock under control. The unity of the Eastern bloc was rent, and again national interests prevailed.

Even greater surprises were in store for intra-bloc relations in June 1967. After a six-day lightning war the Israelis scored instant victory over the Arabs. The Soviets promptly sided with the Arabs, denounced "Israeli aggression," and severed relations with Jerusalem. All the satellites fell into line with a single exception—Rumania. That country's press, too, took a restrained position, reporting developments from the Israeli and Arab sides. The Rumanian government signed an accord for expanded economic and scientific cooperation with Israel. The Bucharest diplomatic meteorological station may have developed greater sensitivity in forecasting the direction of the prevailing winds in the Middle East.

Rumania pursued an independent policy in other matters too. The United Nations delegate from Rumania no longer took the Soviets' action as his cue. Rumania voted at the U.N. political committee in favor of a study of a nuclear-free zone in Latin America, while all the other Eastern-bloc countries abstained. To make the point stick even more, the Rumanian spokesman, Gheorghe Diaconescu, welcomed the agreement with particularly warm words, hailing it as the first instance in history of the establishment of such a zone in an inhabited area. Also, Rumania purchased a nuclear research reactor from Britain, not Russia. Without Kremlin prompting, she established consular and trade relations with Spain and signed commercial agreements with Austria, Denmark, Iran, Italy, Turkey, and Greece. The Rumanians pursued their traditional national and not fraternal policy in their dealings with the "Magyar Autonomous Region" in Transylvania. The fraternal Hungarian government in Budapest complained that the special status of the region was constantly being impaired. The Rumanians acted again as nationalists first, and as Communists not at all.

The world began to take notice of this unique independent foreign policy line of Rumania. Appreciation of the Rumanian stand assumed numerous forms. A Rumanian, Corneliu Manescu, had the distinction of becoming the first Communist elected president of the U.N. General Assembly. This was in the autumn of 1967. Manescu could not have reached his prestige position without Western backing. Also, the Rumanian Prime Minister, Ion Gherghe Maurer, was the first Communist government head to be a White House guest. He visited Washington in the summer of the same year. In his speech before the U.N. assembly, President Lyndon Johnson lauded Manescu for his skill in conducting deliberations, adding that he gained honor for his country. Also, President

Johnson's special scientific and technical adviser, Donald
Hornig, played host to Rumania's Vice Premier, Alex-
andru Barladeanu, chairman of Rumania's National
Council of Scientific Research.

Rumania's independent foreign policy earned her high
praise from countries as far apart in ideology as Yugoslavia and France. Bucharest became the "little Mecca" of
statesmen from underdeveloped countries, who came
from Kabul to Timbuctu. Among many visitors were the
Iranian Minister of Land Reform, Abdulazim Valian, and
Abdul Malik Ismail, the newly created South Yemen's
Minister of Economy.

While relations with the West were warming up, rap-
port with the Kremlin was getting chilled. The Soviet-
Rumanian Treaty of Friendship, Co-operation, and
Mutual Assistance reached the end of its twenty-year term
early in 1968, and normally it would have been renewed
with ritualistic pompous solemnity. It was not so renewed,
merely allowed to continue automatically for another five
years. Rumania expressed herself against the agreement
to end nuclear proliferation, which Russia sponsored.
Diplomatic documents in the bloc countries usually incorporated condemnations of Federal Germany. Now Rumania let it be known that anti-Bonn clauses no longer
reflected political needs. Still more important, Rumania's
trade with the Soviets dropped from 54 percent in 1955 to
less than 34 percent a decade later, while trade with the
West bounded from 18 to 40 percent over the same span.

Bucharest criticism of the Kremlin became routine, and
not even the prestigious names were spared. In a
paroxysm of heresy, Chief of State Ceausescu characterized Communist international bodies, such as the Comintern and Cominform, "completely dated" and "better to
be left buried." He added that they would be out of bounds
for his country, should an attempt be made to revive
them.

The party and government chief challenged the Kremlin to leave Bucharest alone, intimating that it was engaged in plots to replace the Rumanian party leadership. He also warned members of his own party not to incur the risk of contacting foreign Communist parties—meaning Moscow—outside of the regular chain of command.

In cultural matters, too, Rumania shed the rigid molds. Artists were encouraged to create works in styles suiting their individualities. Quick to react to such encouragement, Rumanian artists proceeded promptly to break new ground. Nonfigurative paintings were displayed in public exhibitions, drawing sophisticated crowds. "Positive" social content—propaganda—was no longer a must for plays. Eugene Ionescu's way-out dramas of the absurd were produced. "As long as you can cite an argument—any argument" a playwright said "that does not sound negative politically—the chances are good that a challenging play will be produced." Under the guise of criticizing bureaucracy, although not the political system itself, many bold truths about the regime could be said on the stage. Rumanians have never been known as being short of rationalizations, and now these were available in abundance, too.

This was a new way of life, unshaded by fear of jail. Whereas in the past a Rumanian might tell a foreign friend midway through a restaurant dinner: "I wonder where I will spend the rest of the night," now he knew that it was either in his bed or in a nightclub.

The Chief of State announced the basic policy in matters of self-expression: "It is not the citizens who are at the service of the state and the public officials, but it is the state, the public servants—and they should be really servants—as well as the party apparatus, that are at the citizens' beck and call, and it is their bounden duty to comply with their demands." And in another context: "Within the broad debate of problems affecting the peoples' lives different views may pop up. We must not consider them harmful to the interests of the development of our society."

As in other satellite countries, the secret police had played a nefarious role in Rumanian life. Party Chief Ceausescu was the first to disclose past police misdeeds. The drastic abridgment of police powers was one of the reasons for the relaxed atmosphere. Like their French prototypes, Rumanian sophisticates like to gibe, they are *moqueurs*. So, not afraid of "long ears," they made the Soviet Union the butt of many jokes. This was the Rumanian tradition, anyway, the tradition of the country between the hammer and the anvil. Party Chief Ceausescu's sturdy stand toward the Soviets was a plus in his popularity. Knowingly the people nodded: "He is a real Rumanian."

One of Rumanians' traditions was—alas—widespread corruption, also an historic heritage. Under the Ottoman rule their badge of survival was craftiness. That type of national tradition did not appeal to the new regime, and a great housecleaning was initiated to put an end to it. "No member of the government or the party has the right to flout the law." It was no longer permissible to bestow several jobs on kin and kith. Lifelong financial benefits were no longer the corollary of honorific titles in arts, science, sports, academic life, and other occupations. State funds were not to be squandered on the junkets of bureaucracy. Public officials were not to indulge in luxury at public cost.

Thus the Rumanians sought to follow honorable traditions and to break with undesirable ones. Collectivism was to remain their way of life. *Boyars* were no longer to run the land. The bulk of the population was not to sink back into abject poverty. The few were not to become nabobs again, and the many beggars. People were to think their own thoughts and utter words that were on their minds. The party line became more elastic. This was national communism of the Rumanian variety.

The Kremlin left the country alone. When Czechoslovakia tried to follow the new model, the Kremlin stepped in. We saw the reason for this differential treatment—the reason was geography. Rumania was not adjacent to Germany, East and West, as was Czechoslovakia. Rumania was in the backwoods, in a dead-end street, in a blind alley in the world of diplomacy. Czechoslovakia, on the other hand, was a "staging area" for the Germans—what they would call *Aufmarschgrund*—and a shield, or a staging area, for the Soviets, too.

The Rumanians' way of knowing which way the wind is blowing is an historical fact. They knew it when they joined the Entente in the Great War, at the time when its sky was dark. They knew that the sky was dark before the breaking of the dawn. When the Axis swept across the world the Rumanians could not resist it. They were lifted out of their element. But they knew the jig was up for the Third Reich, proclaimed to be eternal. They helped to sweep that eternal realm into limbo. Overnight, they, the vanquished of yesterday, became the victors of today, their own strength unimpaired.

There seems to be great significance in the fact that Bucharest has dared to defy Moscow. The lesson may be drawn from it that orthodox communism is retreating into history, a wave of the past. Throughout their history the Rumanians have been able to anticipate, gauge, and act upon their knowledge of basic trends. They are tuned in on the *Zeitgeist,* the time and tide. The spirit of independence Rumania has been displaying toward the Soviets may be a meteorological forecast, and the indication of a world-wide trend.

11

Poland Is Not Lost Yet

J eszcze *Polska nie zginela*—Poland is not lost yet,
Poles used to intone; it was a prayer, more than an
anthem. She is one of the curiosities of the world—now
she is there, and again she is not. She was not there
for over a century, dismembered, the wisp of a prayer,
not a reality. Then she was there again, and not there
again, incorporated in the German Third Reich, a colony—Africa in Europe. Then she was there again. Or
was she? Is she there? That is the question.

The prayer, in lieu of the anthem, provides us with a
clue—Poland is more than a nation: Poland is a religion,
even under the Communists. Situated in Europe's eastern
marches, back to back with Russia, she still claims to be a
part of the West. She considers herself a crusader for
Western values, against the obscurantism of the East—
which is Russia, as the Poles see it. Out of the East
darkness, and out of the West light. Poland is a radiant
country (again, as the Poles see it). In the heart of every
Pole there is a compact that is the fusion of two creeds—
the Church and State, the Catholic Church and Catholic
state, even when it is under an atheist regime. There is a
compact between the two even now.

Nationalism in Poland being a creed and religion being

part of patriotism, this question emerges: Why this unprecedented condition? Why is Poland unique? History
provides the answer instantly; the past is more intensely
and persistently a portion of the present in Poland than in
other countries. The next question is this: What does this
past-present tell us?

First, it tells us to pay heed to Poland's name—*Polanie*
—dwellers of the fields. That fact is significant. Poland is
an "open field country" without east-west natural boundaries, and thus subject to invasions, abrasions, erosions.
She is situated on the highway of perennial conflicts, in
the core land of the Eurasian plains, which present a
standing threat of invasion. Few European countries—
perhaps none—have been invaded more often than Poland; twice within a single generation she was invaded by
Germany in this century.

Today, she is an anchored "flat-top" for the Soviets,
whose engines of war are always primed there. Poland's
northern frontier, the Baltic Sea, is Russia's *mare
nostrum*, which, in turn, is the northern terminal of the
historic Amber Road, leading to the south, to the Adriatic,
to warm waters, the Muscovite goal. Poland's present
anchor in the south is the Carpathian range, and danger
does not lurk on that flank alone.

A country in that location is likely to fall victim to the
prowling beasts, hungry wolves, and famished neighbors.
And neighbors are always famished on open land without
frontiers. Occasionally, in her stormy history, Poland
gained the upper hand, when the neighbors had over-
extended themselves. Then the Poles turned against the
Germans—Teutonic Knights—and the Muscovites. Few
nations have experienced more extreme changes in their
fortunes, spasmodic ups and downs. There was a time, in
the seventeenth century—and this seems incredible today
—when the Moscow Kremlin echoed the sharp commands
of Polish men of arms.

IN SIMILARITY THERE IS NO HOPE

The Poles are Slavs, as are the Russians, and thus they are akin. But kinship has made no difference in the two peoples' homicidal relations throughout history. Though both nations professed to be Christians, the difference was provided by their creeds. . . . They were Christians of different rites, and to each the other was "infidel," "blasphemer," and "heathen." It appeared to be of small portent that to both of them the Lord was Christ. Important were other facts. Important was that the Pope reigned over the Poles as the Pontiff. To the Russians, the Messenger of Trinity was the Ecumenical Patriarch on the Golden Horn. With the loss of second Rome, the religious head became the Patriarch in the third Rome, Moscow, and still later, the Holy Synod, headed by the Czar. Because of these divergences the Christian spirit was not revealed in the two nations' dealings.

The problem of the Poles was their neighbor, the Borussian (who was to be called Prussian in later centuries). The Borussians were pagans until the crusading Teutonic knights converted them to the love of Christ by subjecting them to genocide. The conquering Christian knights adopted the name of their surviving victims and became known as Prussians. They were Roman Catholics, as were the Poles, and not Greek Orthodox, as were the Muscovites. This, however, did not make the Poles and Prussians brethren in the Christian fold. There were other lines of separation, their different tongues, German and Slav. A more important line of separation was their greed for the fruits of the plains. Neighbors, they had to be foes. The Germans were the first to enter into the aggressive spirit of the West.

The West attempted to copy the Roman Empire, the memory of which had lingered as the Golden Age. The European core-land sought to lay the foundations of a new global realm, the Holy Roman Empire, enwrapped in the peace of *Pax Romana*. The Germans were the pivots of the global realm of the Holy Roman Empire of the German Nations. In this empire the Deputy of God was the Protector of Virtue and Punishing Hand of Sin, the Holy Roman Emperor Otto I. Because of his bold initiative history was to know him as the "Great." He moved against the recreant world of darkness inhabited by the Poles in the tenth century. It was in self-defense against the ruthless missionaries that the "dwellers of the open fields," the Poles, under their chief, Mieszko I, embraced the creed of Christ. Thus the Poles became Catholics and shared the Teuton's faith. This should have been a protection to the Poles. It was not. There was always the greed for the fat, life-giving land.

To the east of the Poles was the Kievan state, later absorbed by Moscow, which, in turn, became the Russian core. The Kievans and Muscovites followed the Christian rites of "Eastern Rome" on the Golden Horn. There was now this new line of division between the Slav neighbors. The Poles had joined the West, its ideology and way of life. The ways of Russia, on the other, became rooted in the East. And there were the open fields, rich with wheat, the object of greed for both.

In the rivalry that ensued many steps were taken. Poland and Baltic Lithuania became united through a diplomatic marriage in an indissoluble bond. Greater Poland, bulging with strength, undertook a crusade against the Russian brothers in Christ. The rites of the Russians were different, and hence they were heretics. To the Russians, the Poles were an abomination and blasphemy. Meanwhile the rains of spring fattened the soil out of which life burst forth, wheat and livelihood. Dynastic troubles had weakened Moscow, and a series of awesome events occurred early in the seventeenth century. The Polish hosts were sweeping into Moscow's Kremlin. History knows this period as Russia's Time of Troubles, indeed, the time of disintegration.

THE RINGING GROOVES OF CHANGE

The mortal danger of Russia became her means of redemption in the war for life with the Poles. The Muscovites learned to rally round the crown of thorns of their rulers, whether they were great or puny, sound or mad. The Czars were revered as the incarnations of sainted symbols, Holy Russia, centers of national unity, superhuman, semidivine. On the other hand, the Poles were veering toward disunity, the price they paid for pride. Members of the higher nobility acquired the perquisites of kings. Within this royal autocracy there was a divisive democracy of aristocrats. Central authority became a farce, and the King a figurehead.

Having had their traumatic experience with the Poles, the Muscovites learned their lesson. Never again was the country to fall heir to the mortal danger of a Time of Troubles. Thus monolithic Russia was in the making. There was no place for two strong countries on those endless Eurasian plains. Russia began to design Poland's end. She had two partners, Prussia and Austria. In a unique development, an erstwhile great power was dismembered. Russia took the choicest portions, while Prussia and Austria grabbed the rest. As a political unit, the land of the Poles ceased to exist. Thus the eighteenth century ended.

How did the Poles take this traumatic event? "Poland is

not lost yet," they proclaimed. From the map, Poland was
transferred to their hearts. There it was, an invisible
kingdom, but real to them. Now a new history of Poland
began. That history consisted of two antipodes. One of
them was the idealized concept of their sanctified Christian land, the radiant city of God. And the other one was a
religious crusade against the archenemy, the Russian, the
arch-fiend. Freedom was the lodestar of conceptualized
Poland—liberty all over the world. That is how Pulaski,
Kosciuszko, and others entered American history.

The name of the "indomitable Pole," Casimir Pulaski,
became engraved in American memories. He was the
noble Pole whom Congress commissioned to organize an
independent cavalry corps in a crucial moment. At the
siege of Savannah he died for the American cause, which
he linked to that of human freedom. His name became
enshrined in Fort Pulaski, in Georgia, and in the spectacular Pulaski Skyway, in New York.

History knows few more romantic names than that of
Thaddeus Kosciuszko, the Polish patriot, who set his foot
on the first rung of immortality as colonel of engineers in
the American Continental Army. With the construction of
the West Point fortifications, he moved higher, advancing
to the rank of brigadier general. After America's victory,
he returned to Poland, there to fight the Russians whom
he—a Pole to the marrow—saw as the incarnation of
unfreedom. He was honored in many parts of the world.
Australia gave his name to its highest mountain peak.

Poles fought tyranny on the barricades of many other
lands. They fought it in the streets of Paris, in Austria,
and the German lands. Joseph Bem was another one of
the indomitable Poles, who fought Louis Philippe in
France, the Habsburgs in Hungary, and the Russians in
the Ottoman empire. Still another notable Polish freedom
fighter was Count Henryk Dembinski, who fought the
Russians as commander in chief of Polish insurgent

forces, fought them in the service of Mohammed Ali of
Egypt, and as supreme commander of the Magyar forces
against Austria in the mid-nineteenth-century war of independence.

Nor was Poland lost in the realms of science and art.
New luster was added to the eyes of many generations
through the stirring polonaise of the most romantic of all
romantics, Frederic Chopin, half French and all Pole. To
the very end and beyond he remained a Polish romantic.
His last will provided that, as soldiers were interred in
their uniforms, so he should be buried in his concert
clothes.

The spirit of Poland was throbbing in the music of
another man of genius, Ignace Paderewski, composer and
piano virtuoso, who enthralled music-lovers with his Polish strains. They became acquainted with his peoples'
spirited folk dances, the krakowiak, the headlong tune.
"Poland is not lost."

Warsaw-born Marie Sklodowska opened the gates to a
new age in the field of science with her work in radio-
active elements. When she discovered the new element
she named polonium, her native land was on her mind.
The world knows her better under her immortal married
name, Madame Curie. Twice she was recipient of the
Nobel Prize. Hers was a family of creative gifts, as her
daughter Irene received the same coveted prize. Another
daughter, Eva, made her name as a writer.

JOINING THE DISJOINTED

Poland was not lost yet, indeed. After the first World
War she was resurrected by a thankful world, repentant
of the injustice done to a gallant people, and practical-
minded in creating a balancing force in diplomacy. Not

only in millions of hearts, but on the map, too, there was a
Poland again, extending to the Baltic Sea.

After generations of oppression, mankind expected
Poland to become a model of humanism. The country's
Premier was Paderewski, and could there have been a
more romantic beginning?

The beginning was auspicious, indeed, but the sequel
was not. Difficulties were compounded as new Poland
swept into herself a farrago of nationalities: Ukrainians,
Byelorussians, Lithuanians, Germans, and Jews. Now the
oppressed of the past became the oppressor of today, and
the nationalities were treated as low-caste minorities.
Soon the world resounded with their complaints.

Re-established Poland displayed few signs of human
charity. Again the *szlachta*, the large estate owners, and
their hangers-on, at home and abroad, had the final say,
as their ancestors had before the partition. *Szlachta* puppets followed Paderewski, who tarried at the top briefly.
Turmoil was again to engulf the land, turmoil generated
by the discontent of the minorities and of the lowly. To
put an end to it, the helm was seized by the leading
freedom fighter of the past, Jozef Pilsudski, ex-Socialist
and dedicated Pole. At his new command post, he led a
fight against freedom, the pivot of a government that
equated charity for the lowly with an act of subversion.
His was a regime in which the little people received
comforting words, while the big people got the benefit of
deeds. Under his leadership, as the head of the armed
forces, the country fell under the rule of a semi-military
regime. It was hard under this regime to reconstruct the
image of the ethereal vision of the land about which the
people had been humming: "Poland is not lost yet." This
time many people held the view that Poland—the real
Poland of their dreams—*was* lost.

During the inter-bellum era two antagonistic world

forces were face to face—the Communist Soviet Union and the anti-Communist world. Poland served as the pivot of what came to be known as *cordon sanitaire*, that shield against the Soviet "contagion." Slavs were again pitted against one another—Communists against the aggressively anti-Communist Poles. The Catholic Church in Poland, again strongly entrenched, was the spiritual leader of the feud.

Pilsudski died in 1935, but his era did not die with him. It was continued by a "colonels' clique," so named because of its military tincture, headed by Colonel Jozef Beck, who earned the Communists' ire as a Fascist. They saw him making common cause with the Third Reich's Hitler against the Soviets, but they were totally wrong. It was the Soviets that made common cause with Hitler, with Poland as the victim. On September 1, 1939, the Fuehrer's hosts blitzed into Russia, and the second World War began. In a few days Poland's resistance was broken; the Germans took Warsaw, and established a government-general puppet regime. As a penalty for the Poles' resistance, some 80 percent of the capital was destroyed. The Carthaginian peace was to begin with a Genghis-Khan-like war. Because of Russia's role as an accomplice, again the Poles had cause to see Russia as their hereditary foe. Again Poland seemed to be lost.

Again Poland went underground. The armed forces of this "catacomb country" comprised at first some twenty thousand fighters, each of whom deserved his nation's fervent thanks. If caught by the Nazis, they were not merely strung up on the nearest tree, but first they were tortured in a way that recalled the early Christians' martyrdom. Around their fields of activities all human dwellings were wrecked, and, indeed, whole communities were rooted out. The Poles appeared to the Nazis as *oestliche Untermenschen,* eastern subhumans, that dared

to resist those who were the best breed, *Uebermenschen,*
Aryan supermen.

Again, as in the past, there was another fighting Poland, a country in exile, with about two hundred thousand
men under arms. . . . Again the Poles were engaged in
crusades against oppressors, this time the Fascist countries, Germany, Italy, and their acolytes. The Third Reich
had meanwhile launched a gigantic campaign against the
Soviets, who were now fighting for their lives. Under
General Wladyslaw Anders, the Polish army distinguished
itself in many theaters of war. Polish airmen were reported to have destroyed every seventh Nazi plane in the
crucial Battle of Britain. Polish land, sea, and air forces
fought in the historic battles of Ancona and Monte Cas-
sino, in North Africa, at the Normandy invasion, in Nor-
way, the Netherlands, Belgium, and France. The Allies
responded to Polish gallantry, helping to establish a government in exile, rooted in historic tradition. Its president
was Wladyslaw Raczkiewicz, former head of the Senate,
and its premier the indomitable Sikorski. Was Poland not
lost yet?

Meanwhile the impossible began to take shape. It had
appeared to be impossible to blunt the edge of Nazi armor.
As fighters, the Germans seemed to be supermen, indeed,
perfect machines of murder and genocide. But on the
Volga, Russia's River of Sorrow, the tide of war turned;
the Germans had been defeated at Stalingrad. The un-
beatable Hitler's armed forces were now being steam-
rolled west. It was still feared that they might swing
around when the retreating hosts reached former Poland.
But the spunk had left them; the old magic failed. Fatally
struck, the "superarmy" caved in.

At the Soviets' approach, an anti-German uprising
erupted in Warsaw on August 1, 1944. It seems to have
heeded the signal of the London-based Polish government

in exile, and the Soviet army did not extend a helping hand. Now, in the Polish city of Lublin, a rival cabinet was being formed in which the Communists played the leading role. That was, obviously, the government favored by the Kremlin. Should liberation materialize, Poland was to be in the Soviets' camp.

The ring around the Germans was now closed. The war was approaching its culmination. An old-line Socialist, Edward Osubka-Morawski, became the premier of the Lublin government. Real power seemed to rest in the hands of two Kremlin trainees, Boleslaw Bierut and Jakub Berman, the former the president of the National Council and the latter the undersecretary of state. Moscow promptly recognized this Polish government of national liberation. Now the Poles had two governments, one in Britain and the other one in Poland. Eventually the one in Lublin prevailed, moving to Warsaw. In the year of victory, 1945, Wladyslaw Gomulka, who was to give his name to an era, became the general secretary of the Communist Party, camouflaged under the name of Polish United Workers' Party. Once more there was a Poland, but she was the satellite of Russia, against which the Poles had fought for centuries.

In the rest of eastern Europe, too, the Soviets established Communist governments, joined together in "fraternal unity." Promptly, the Soviets set out to turn this swath of nations from the Baltic to the Adriatic into a field of their operations. It was a shield, perhaps, against possible Western attacks or proving ground for imperialism, camouflaged in communism. The Soviets had to reckon with the peoples' bias against their ideology, a bias based on traditions and the Christian creed. In the eyes of many people of the region, the Kremlin creed was Satan's handiwork. Therefore the aliases, such as the Polish Workers' Party, representing coalitions of Communists and fol-

lowers, but never anti-Communists. Producers of the
political show were the Communists, tightly organized
and unburdened by scruples. The Soviets controlled the
region through the weight of their authority, enhanced by
their stunning victory, through their superior armed
forces and "interlocking directorates" in basic economic
ventures.

ENTER WLADYSLAW GOMULKA

The secretary general of the Polish United Workers'
Party and number-one politician was Wladyslaw Gomulka,
minister for the recovered territories. Born in the part of
dismembered Poland under Austrian rule, a worker in the
oil fields at Borislav in Galicia, he had lived under a more
relaxed regime than fellow Poles in Russia. In his early
youth he was attracted to Marxism. After the first World
War he turned to communism. In "free" Poland the party
was outlawed; its members were hounded, even though
they were idealistic, as he was. Gomulka fell victim to the
ruthless treatment accorded to the presumed foes of the
Pilsudski regime. He was held in several places of detention, and was a prisoner in the notorious Bereza Kartuska
"reformation camp." There his resentment at the brutal
treatment made him an even more dedicated Communist.

After his release he managed to sneak across the frontier into the Soviet Union, where he saw only what he
wanted to see, his vision blurred by his idealism. This is
what he saw: there was no *szlachta* in Russia, no landed
gentry, no foreign capitalists, to make much money and to
pay little in wages. There was not the gaping abyss between the many—the poor—and the few—the rich. What
was black in Poland was white in the Soviets, and to
Gomulka it was pristine white. The means of production

in the Soviets belonged to the community, and that Gomulka liked. Russia, too, had labor camps, which, however, were acceptable to the young Pole, since, he was told, they contained the toilers' foes.

Back in Poland, Gomulka continued to ply his dangerous trade, an official of the "catacomb party," relishing its dangers, always skirting jail. The sacrifice was worth making, since, as he saw it, it was for a noble cause. He saw himself a religious man, his religion being that of Marx and Lenin, the common cause of humanity.

He was not among those who retreated from Poland when the Germans moved into the country. He remained a member of the Communist catacomb behind the German lines. Had he been caught, his fate would have been torture and lingering death. In the midst of the war, he became the secretary of the Warsaw group of the Polish Workers' Party, Communists. A year later, in 1943, he stepped up to the still higher post of secretary of the Central Committee. Then came the Russian victory, and Gomulka was elevated to the highest party post.

He was not a spectacular figure, nor a good speaker, and he did not radiate the aura of charisma. His voice was subdued, and he played his part in a low key. But he had the traits leadership needed. He was a competent organizer, well aware of priorities in administrative values. Also, he was a "true believer," convinced of the justice of his cause. In Poland true believers were in short supply. The country was a Catholic stronghold, and, as it had been the hinge of the interbellum *cordon sanitaire*, the people were saturated with anticommunism. Besides, Gomulka was not a member of the nationalities, the communism of which was the result of revolt against discrimination. He was an authentic Pole, from the lower depths of life.

The Kremlin trusted him, and in those early postwar

years the "Man of Steel," Stalin, was the Kremlin. His trust in Gomulka was so great that he commissioned him to call a meeting of great portent in Warsaw in 1947 to launch a new international Communist body. The year was that of the Marshall Plan of economic reconstruction in the West. The new organization Gomulka helped launch was the Cominform, to advance the international Communist movement through the close coordination of national policies and party tactics, insuring a more complete control of the satellites by the Kremlin. Stalin, "father of victory," was then at the crest of his fame; total victory over the Axis, credited to him, was to be followed by triumph over the satellite countries' traditional anticommunism. They were to become the shield behind which the Soviets were to find security, and Poland was to be the center of the plate.

Then the reformers' heresy in Yugoslavia erupted, followed by the Kremlin's thunder: the Titoist regime was following a hateful course, the Kremlin declared, lining up behind the imperialists, treating Russia as a helot. This event, traumatic in the Communist world, was followed by the well-known heresy hunt.

Gomulka shied away from Tito. Warsaw and Moscow were too close, but there must have been an edge in his voice, revealing that he was not completely in the Kremlin's fist. He was a Communist, to be sure, but an indigenous Pole withal, and, as such, a dreamer, and idealist, one who saw his people's martyrdom under Russian rule. While communism was Gomulka's line of political thought, it was colored by his people's historic recollection. Gomulka held that the coexistence with the capitalist world that the Kremlin had begun to preach should be applied also to the relations of the Communist nations among themselves. While he was ready to concede that the Soviets, being the first in line, had accumulated a unique stockpile of experience, it was adjusted to their own needs. The other fraternal countries, Gomulka thought, would have to apply their own methods of using the party ideology to serve their practical aims.

Stalin must have had the intuition that enabled him to feel, rather than to know, that Gomulka was straying from the Kremlin path. "Gomulka is building a wall of mistrust between Poland and the Soviet Union," wrote *Nowe Drogi*, "New Ways," of Warsaw, a Kremlin organ. Some of Gomulka's close associates faded away, tried for the crime of being Polish nationalists while professing to be international Communists. Jozef Dubiel, former deputy minister of the recovered areas, was made to confess to having been a Gestapo agent. The former deputy minister of national defense, Marion Spychalski, and the former chairman of the parliamentary group of the party, Z. Kliszko, were taken into custody under top-secret charges. An anonymous Lodz textile worker's letter to the French Socialist newspaper *Le Populaire*, smuggled out of Poland, provided a graphic picture of conditions in the land:

We live like miserable wretches, driven by the Communist party to produce ever greater norms for ever lower pay. . . . Our trade unions fail to protect us. On the contrary, they are against the workers. Strikes are prohibited as acts of sabotage and people advocating them are subject to penalties meted out for common crimes. Informers, picking up rash words, uttered in fits of anger, are all around us. One indiscreet word and a poor wretch is yanked into a forced labor camp.

Gomulka was also spirited out of sight, and people thought that this was his end. It was later people learned that he was alive, kept in enforced residence in a Warsaw suburb, Miedzieszyn. That enforced residence lasted for many years.

A DEAD MAN AND THE LIVING TOMB

He had gone insane, we know that about Stalin today. His mind beclouded, he died in 1953, but the Stalin age was not yet over. A slow thaw followed, a transition period. Some three years after the tyrant's death the top Communist, Nikita Khrushchev delivered a historic denunciation of the late leader (*Vozhd*) to the party congress. The "secret" leaked out to a stunned world. The Soviet Union, one-sixth of the land surface of the globe, had been for years under the thumb of a madman.

The first country to react to the change in the Kremlin was Poland. A rebellion erupted in the industrial city of Poznan. That was a national tradition. Some fifty thousand industrial workers assembled on June 28, 1956, demanding the departure of the Russians, free elections, and living wages. Riots followed, a security officer was lynched, fifty-two people were killed and about two hundred wounded, the official reports admitted. The Polish Communist party was split three ways—pro, contra, in between. Soviet divisions stationed in southwestern Poland were moving toward Warsaw, while a Soviet naval squadron appeared before Danzig. Meanwhile, Polish workers and university students, aroused by the Soviet intervention, demonstrated at meetings and processions, demanding the return of Gomulka to leadership. An emergency top-level meeting of Polish and Soviet leaders followed, at which the former explained to the latter that Poland must become an equal, independent, and sovereign state, bringing its own creative contribution to the camp of socialism. There was not much time to spare when the Soviet tanks halted on Warsaw's outskirts.

THE RETURN OF THE ENTOMBED

Wladyslaw Gomulka, whom many people thought dead, was the political leader the Poles wanted, him and nobody else. There was no way to blunt the public will. Quickly, he was reinstated as Poland's number-one man, first secretary of the Polish United Workers' Party.

At the time, Polish armed forces were under the command of a Soviet wartime hero, Konstantin K. Rokossowski, who had been given the post on the ground that he was Polish-born. That region of Poland had been a part of imperial Russia. Now he was divested of his role, his command entrusted to an "authentic Pole," Marion Spychalski, Gomulka's associate. In response to public demand, Soviet troops were withdrawn from the Polish capital; their numbers, locations, and movements in the country contractually circumscribed. Thenceforth, Moscow, not Warsaw, was to bear the cost of maintaining these troops. The Polish government was free to accept economic aid from the West. The United States thus became a contributor to the Warsaw government funds, making Poland the first country after the defection of Yugoslavia to receive such aid. The Poles were free to arrange their internal affairs without fear of Kremlin intervention. Farm collectivization was ended, and nearly all the peasants now elected to stick to cultivating their own small parcels of land. This was a particularly notable concession.

This was a Polish reformation movement, the first one after that of Tito in Yugoslavia. It was not that thoroughgoing, though. Between Yugoslavia and Russia there were buffers, other satellite countries, while Poland and the

Soviets were adjacent. Further, the south Slav land of
Tito, a rugged land of tangled peaks, was protected by
topography. The Yugoslavs had shown the world in their
wartime stand against the Axis how they could use the
maze of ranges. Poland, on the other hand, in the center
of the Eurasian plains, continues across the Soviets.

Parliamentary election took place in Poland the year
after the Poznan uprising. It went as far in self-expression
as it could under its type of regime. Other parties contended besides the Communists', designated as the Polish
United Workers' Party. In this Catholic land, the Catholic
Parliamentary Club had its own slate. The United Peasants' Party also had its candidates, since even under her
accelerated industrial program, Poland was a land of
farms. The voters retained the right to cross off names.
But . . . the candidates of all parties had to be approved
at Communist headquarters. Gomulka knew how important it was for his country that the rebellion should not be
extended to the polls: the Soviet troops were stationed in
his country. He saw what had happened to Hungary when
she wanted to turn away from the Soviets. He addressed
his country both as a Communist and as a patriotic Pole:
"If you cross the Communist candidates' names off the
election lists, you may be crossing Poland off Europe's
map." The Poles heeded his words, and his party received
a majority of the votes. This was achieved only as a result
of a compromise.

THE LIVING CHURCH AND THE
COMMUNISTS

With the exception of a fraction of 1 percent, the
Poles were born in Christian faiths, and about three

fourths of them were offsprings of Roman Catholic families. In Poland the Catholic faith had reached its easternmost frontiers. Beyond them, in the East, was the domain of the Orthodox Church, which appeared to be an abomination to the Catholics. The Poles considered themselves crusaders in the service of the Roman faith, against the negation of the creed in the East, the Orthodox Catholics and Islam. In the name of their creed, they fought the Russians for centuries. They helped the Habsburgs at the ramparts of Vienna in the seventeenth century to free the Christian world from the incubus of the Moslem Turk. In Poland, Catholicism and nationalism have always been closely linked.

When the Communists first swept into Poland under the Stalinist Muscovites, they tried to make loyalty to the Church equivalent to treason. The main representative of the Church was an effective spokesman of Catholicism, Cardinal Stefan Wyszynski, Primate of Poland and Archbishop of Warsaw and Gniezno. The Cardinal waged his crusade against the "tendentious, malicious, and untruthful" accusations of the Stalinists. The Communists accused the Cardinal of double-dealing, and of being a "Roman tool."

As the Stalinists' reign of terror had increased, the Cardinal was detained simultaneously with Gomulka, and Warsaw forbade Church nominees to occupy their sees. For alleged wartime collaboration with the Nazis, the Bishop of Kielce had been sentenced to twelve years in jail. A priest had been condemned to death and others to long prison terms for "acting as agents of the American intelligence service." Witnesses had been produced to testify that Poland's former Cardinal Hlond had been a "man without a nationality" and that Popes Pius XI and XII had been pro-German. Religious instruction in the schools had been dropped. The Communists had set up a pro-regime Committee of Patriotic Priests to fight the Church. Another front set up by Warsaw was the Committee of Catholic Intellectuals.

Poland's national reformation, with Gomulka again at the helm, reversed the trend. The Cardinal was released from his enforced residence. Both the commissar and the Cardinal knew where they stood. Gomulka knew the meaning of the Church to the Poles and Wyszynski knew the Russians' stake in Poland. If he had to accept a commissar, it might as well be Gomulka, his fellow-detainee. Religious instruction was reintroduced in state schools as an optional subject. Agreement was reached about the installation of the bishops who had been prevented from occupying their sees. The state undertook to make financial contributions to "catechism centers" for the religious education of youth. While church income for the payment of priests and other ecclesiastical employees remained subject to taxation, church institutions were freed from the payment of income tax. Even under the Communists, the Church had to be recognized as an historic national force.

It was with the history of their country in mind that the Cardinal and the commissar, both Polish patriots, established a *modus vivendi* at the crucial election. Tacitly, the Church did not attack Gomulka, and Gomulka refrained from attacking the Church too bluntly.

After the election, however, with the nation's life no longer at stake, the controversy between the Church and the state was resumed. The basic discrepancies were paramount. Each looked at the problem from its own angle, and this is what the state saw: "There is no conflict about religious matters between the Church and the state. The trouble is this: the battle waged by the clergy does not concern episcopal matters alone. It is fighting for the privileged position of the hierarchy, and privilege is out of place in socialism. Having its roots in the Middle Ages, the episcopate wants to subordinate the lay activities of the people to Church management. . . . The Church leaders are aiming far beyond the teaching of the Gospels and the cult of God."

It was in line with Polish nationalism and out of line with international communism that Gomulka spoke in an interview with Hubert Beuve-Méry, editor of the representative Paris daily *Le Monde:*

> Religion is deeply anchored in the majority of our population. . . . We are not for trampling anyone's convictions underfoot. Atheistic propaganda in Poland is often weaker than it is in the West. . . . Whoever wants to go to church may, indeed, do so, and the only thing we object to is the church being used to oppose socialism. . . .

Some churches, particularly in Warsaw, employ loudspeakers that sound their messages in the streets. Religious processions continue to be characteristic features of the Polish countryside.

In turn, the Bishops spoke of the "sufferings and hardships they had to endure for the sake of justice and of the need of defending the faith against the encroachments of the state." In pastoral bulletins read at Sunday masses they criticized the attempts of state organizations to subordinate the teaching of the faith to government organs, not only in the government-financed catechism centers, but also in chapel and church.

A PERIOD OF CHANGE

In the inter-Gomulka period, grumbling had been considered an antiparty offense, and paeons had to be intoned in honor of the Kremlin. The official line had been simplicity itself: there could be no better place in the

world than the Polish plains. This in spite of the fact that
they were short of many amenities.

Basically, the Poles are grumblers, as are most people
in the eastern European countries. The sophisticated
people in Poland are super-grumblers, and to please them
is beyond man's ken. Under the new Gomulka regime the
country was doing better than before, and yet the Poles
began to taunt their masters. Without number were the
quips they directed at people on lofty perches. They did
this, not only in the intimacy of their homes, but also in
public places, in irreverent political-minded cabarets, and
organs of the press. The nature of this teasing was indicated by the very name of the best-known organ, *Po-
Prostu*, Off the Cuff. Often it was *Off with the Gloves*.

This took place in spite of the fact that economically
the country was not doing badly during the decade following "Polish October," the great change. The overall growth
of industry was high, the annual growth of GNP (gross
national product) a respectable 8 percent, and an increase
of exports to about two and a half billion dollars. Among
the world's largest producers of steel, Poland moved to the
tenth place. Her industries were varied and reasonably
well run. The great controversy in the Communist world
for decades had been this: which branch of the industry
should have the higher priority, production for immediate
use, such as footwear, or for delayed use, such as the
building of machines. Poland hit upon a compromise:
priority was accorded to both sectors. The remarkable
reconstruction of Warsaw after its second World War
devastation was called the "Eighth Wonder of the World."

Being Poles, they were grumbling just the same. Also,
they had cause for grumbling. With the rise in living
standards, more people could afford to buy more goods;
but goods were unavailable, and so they grumbled. House-
wives were grumbling against standing in line at the

butchers' shops. Farmers were grumbling, although they
had the least cause for it. Poland is the only bloc country
in which they are owners of the land. They were fretting
because the principle of collectivization had never been
denounced, and the peasant suspected that the toleration
of individual landholding was only a temporary device.
Although the censorship was less insidious than in other
bloc countries, the intellectuals found it vexing.

Ten years after Gomulka's return to power, Poland was
seized by a familiar malaise. It was due to several factors,
revealing an historic pattern of Polish ways. Mainly it was
factionalism. Communism is supposed to be monolithic,
fashioned of one solid *Weltanschauung*. Yes, everywhere,
but not in Poland, the land of the *liberum veto* in its pre-
partition past. Not even communism could make the Poles
toe the party line. Ten years after the reform, the political
unity of the country was rent.

Loud in their claims for recognition were the Partisans,
wartime freedom fighters, headed by sour-faced Major
General Mieczyslaw Moczar, Minister of the Interior. He
became the spokesman of Polish nationalists who felt
cheated when the Soviet army put into office Muscovites,
men who had fled to Russia during the war.

The Technocrats formed the other group, an assem-
blage of technicians and industrial administrators, headed
by Edward Gierek, the party boss of Silesia, member of the
Political Bureau, top party organization, and the first
secretary of the party organization in Katowice, an important industrial base. The Technocrats spoke in apocalyptic
terms of the German threat, asserting that Poland's interests were best served by the Kremlin.

Again, as so many times before, the voice of the "anti-
Zionists" (anti-Semites in reality) was heard in the land.
Out of Poland's population of some thirty-two million, the
Jewish population amounted to less than thirty thousand,

less than one tenth of 1 percent. The real target of this group was not so much the tiny Jewish community as the Muscovites, many of whom were Jews. Also, the anti-Zionists may have been against Gomulka, whom they sought to identify, at first, with Zionist influence, although he spent the war years in Poland. The opponents felt that Gomulka had been in power too long, getting aged and losing his grip. Younger people felt they had the right to try their hands at the helm.

Two specific factors contributed to the dissatisfaction. There was, to begin with, the disposition for the shift, people craving excitement, a change, getting bored with Gomulka. And there was the "triggering effect," which in this instance was a classical stage play.

FOREFATHERS' EVE

Its author was Adam Mickiewicz, a Polish immortal, whose genius was unfolded in the first half of the last century. One of his most notable creations was the classic *Dziady* (*Forefathers' Eve*), a long romantic drama in four parts. It was abridged by P. Dejmek, and presented on the Warsaw stage early in 1968. In the play, the author grieves over the Polish patriots' sufferings in Czarist jails. At one point, this is what a leading character says on the stage: "The people they send us from Moscow are jackasses and fools." Although the reference was to Czarist times, the Polish audience interpreted it as a contemporary event; the words elicited thunderous applause in the National Theatre in Gomulka's Warsaw, followed by more tumultuous applause in response to this line: "For a few silver rubles we have sold our souls to Moscow." Promptly the classic was withdrawn as "unfit for public view." The university youth protested and trouble flared up.

As street demonstrations followed, the police moved in, and groups of students withdrew to the university grounds, traditionally out of bounds for the police. The Warsaw gendarmes transgressed upon the college grounds. Thereupon, more disturbances followed. This time the student community was thoroughly aroused.

These events coincided with the reform movement in Czechoslovakia. Was Prague to become the Belgrade of the north? Why leave the initiative to the Czechs, a placid people, and not to the Poles, who were filled with "revolutionary blood?" Restlessness spread to other strata of society, and was reflected in news organs. Among these, *Polityka* sounded a particularly critical note: "The present moment encourages a revaluation of attitudes and programs of action, and we trust that a better life will emerge as a result of this. We shall defend the principles and achievements resulting from the changes that took place after October 1956."

What was wrong?, the critics asked. The bureaucrats were on the rampage again, was the answer. They were watering down the reforms of the Polish October, forgetful of the passage of time and of the profound changes in all the world. Those bureaucrats had reached the safe haven of middle age and were no longer able to grasp the concern of the new generation, which wanted to be heard. What did it want to say? It wanted to say that this was no longer the age when people wore armor. The tired bureaucrats lived in a world that was past. They were inaccessible and ignorant of life. Shielded by armor, they were manipulating machines instead of dealing with people. The younger people were not content with "machine socialism." They wanted a humane regime.

Poland had become an important industrial country with many technically competent people, the *manadzers* (a Polish corruption of manager), a word the politicians had turned into a derogatory term. The opposition as-

serted that there was no justification for this, since they
were the ones who kept the wheels of the economy moving and accounted for the impressive increase in the GNP.
Hence their subordination to the political bureaucrat was
not to be excused. And what about the *manadzers* themselves? Did they advocate changes in the economic system? They did. They wanted to change the system under
the "Plan."

PARTIAL DECENTRALIZATION

"Partial decentralization" is a most undramatic term.
Yet how much promise it contained when the plenum of
the party adopted it in 1965! It was the beginning of the
economic thaw. No longer were the bureaucrats of the
Planning Commission in Warsaw to determine every
move the *manadzers* of, for instance, that big machine
plant in the Wroclaw vaivodeship were to take it. It was
recognized that the local managers were in a better position to size up their producing potentialities. So they and
many other producing enterprises were authorized to
make their own major decisions. They were invested with
the authority, too, to finance their investments out of
profits—all of this, of course, within the framework of the
overall plan. They acquired the right to carry out profit-
sharing projects, too, in connection with the plans' own
workers' councils.

Carried out fully, this might have led to the erosion of
the major features of the planned economy. But it was not
carried out fully. In Poland, nothing is. The Pole, especially the city-bred type, is intensely individualistic. So
attitudes toward the partial decentralization crystalized
into the policies of antagonistic groups. One of these

wanted to go the limit. At that limit there was the promised land of free economic choice—free private enterprise with a social-minded objective. At the other end were the conservatives, concerned with the dominant position of the party. They were apprehensive that a *manadzerial* take-over would diminish their stature.

Polish bureaucracy is different from all others within the Socialist bloc. Its roots are in three different soils, because Poles were the subjects of three empires during the crucial developmental process of European industrialization: the subjects of Russia, Prussia, and Austria. Most pervasive was the influence of imperial Russia, with its intensely autocratic bureaucracy. During the generations when Poland was merely an ethnic concept, not a nation, the Poles fought it more strenuously than they fought the easy-going Austrians and the efficient Germans. In fighting Russian bureaucracy, they assimilated many of its traits. Today, too, bureaucracy in Poland is far more than a peripheral phenomenon.

At its worst, it is *the worst*. The Germans used to have a disparaging term to describe it, the more devastating because so innocuously tailor-made: *Polnische Wirtschaft*—"Polish mess," literally, "Polish management." It can be utterly perverse. In normal bureaucracy, the occupant of one office chair does not know what the occupant of the chair next to his is doing. The super-bureaucrat in Poland knows it very well, and he does the reverse.

Luckily, the breed is on the defensive. Poland is a country blessed with a large assortment of human skills and natural resources. Without the bane of bureaucracy, it could have astounded the world. Even so, it has achieved much, as attested by the miracle of Warsaw's rebirth from "made in Nazi-land" ashes. The leveling process typical of the countries of the bloc has done away with the *szlachta* and the financial oligarchy. Business

concerns financed from the West in the interbellum spell
are properties of the nation. As in the other bloc countries
a new higher middle-class is in the making, composed of
people endowed with special gifts, not the least of which
is their skill to make money in a supposedly un-money-
minded society. The jungle of TV antennas on rooftops is
one indication of the new wealth. The possession of wash-
ing machines and refrigerators is the norm. Any kind of
motorcar will no longer do. It has to be Mercedes-Benz.
The hallmark of an incipient affluent society—including
purchases on installment plans—is all over the land. The
trademark of Poland before the second World War was
the thatched-roofed hut in the midst of brooding plains.
The plains are still there, but the thatched roofs are gone.
Equalization has devoured picturial romance and has
nudged living standards upwards. So the Polish Everyman
asks: When the tile roof is here, can the garage lag far
behind? And after the car, the costly interior decoration?
Is there such a creature as capitalistic socialism? One can
see some of Europe's best-dressed people on Warsaw's
streets. Capitalist affluence is written all over them.

A HERITAGE OF ANTI-SEMITISM

For a country of her size, Poland had the largest concentration of Jews up to the second World War. Polish
rulers of the Middle Ages—Boleslaus the Pious of the
thirteenth century and Casimir the Great in the fourteenth century—invited groups of skilled people from the
West: French artisans, Dutch shipwrights, Germans, and,
above all, Jews (who had the reputation of being good at
trade and finances) to help build up an urban civilization
in a backward peasant land. The ancestors of the Jews

thus invited formed part of the Central European Dias-
pora (dispersal) after the loss of their Mediterranean
base in Spain. Many Jewish immigrants spoke the German of those days, the foundation of Yiddish, which
many of them cultivated in their new Polish homes.

In their new environment, the Jews adopted many
Slavic customs, too, including that of garb, and one of
these was the "typically Jewish" caftan. The Warsaw
burghers of the time wore visored round caps, which the
Jews adopted too. Polish noblemen wore decorative fur
caps, costly and serviceable in the harsh northern climate.
Wearing such furred headgear was a class privilege withheld from the Jews. After the demise of Poland such
restrictions were lifted, and Jews took to wearing the caps
as status symbols. In the course of time the wearing of the
fur caps became a tradition associated with their creed—a
religious duty. Today such fur caps are worn on blazing
summer days in the subtropical climate of Israel by religious Jews, who would go to death rather than being
separated from the decorative headpiece adopted by their
ancestors in imitation of gentile Poles.

When Poland was dismembered at the end of the eighteenth century, her most productive parts fell to the Russians. The Czars set up the discriminatory "Pale of Settlement" for the Jews, in the Polish regions, and there the
opportunities of the Jews were limited to petty trading and
money-lending. Money-lenders were unpopular, and the
Czarist governments were disposed to let the cantanker-
ous Poles discharge their venom on the heads of the Jews,
leaving less of it for "Fatherkin Czar." Anti-Semitism thus
became a problem of the Polish Pale.

Shut up in their crowded ghettoes, surrounded by
sullen resentment, articulate young Jews became forebod-
ingly apprehensive of their plight. Was there an escape
hatch? Many of them saw one in the writings of the latter-

day prophets of social reform, and mainly in those of Karl
Marx. His apocalyptic picture of the age shook their
resentment into action. In Poland the revolt had a nationalist tinge.

Although alienated from their non-Jewish neighbors by
St. Petersburg's policy, many Jews sided with the gentiles
in fighting the Czars, and so they responded promptly to
Kosciusko's appeal. In the ranks of his forces a Jew,
Joselovich Berek, once a private, now a colonel, commanded a cavalry brigade, and he died for Poland on the
battlefield. In the most famous classic of the age, *Pan
Tadeusz*, the Jew Jankiel cuts an heroic figure. When
Napoleon held out the promise of resurrecting Poland,
representative Jews beseeched him to mete out justice to
the "most tragic nation on earth."

In the periodical revolutions that erupted in the Russian Poland, the Jews continued to play important roles.
This was particularly the case in the 1861 revolt for
independence, in the course of which Jews had a hand in
the establishment of a "catacomb cabinet." The revolt was
crushed, and life became more intolerable in the Pale.

Then came the resurrection of the martyred land, the
hope of new Jerusalem on the Polish plains. It was not
that for the Jews, though. Restrictions not only continued,
but grew worse. A new generation of gentile Poles now
contended for the Jews' places in the professions,
finances, and trade. Professional rivalry intensified the
deeply rooted bias. Many Jews reacted by joining causes of
revolt.

Across the eastern frontiers of Poland there was now
the Soviet Union, in the construction of which young
people with Jewish backgrounds played important parts.
To Polish Jews life across the ideological fence looked
better than it was in real life. Thus the Jewish protest in
Poland acquired a left-wing tinge. The Warsaw authori-

tarian regime, strongly rightist, now claimed to have additional reason to fight the Jews. Then came the second World War and Auschwitz.

THE FIVE CHIMNEYS OF OSWIECIM

About forty miles west of Poland's old coronation town, Cracow, there is a unique museum. It is in a small town that witnessed the extermination of more people than any other single place, not only in our days, but in all time. In comparison with the record of this town the mass assassinations of Attila, "The Scourge of God," and of the unspeakable Genghis Khan were puny. The town is Oswiecim—Auschwitz—and the museum was erected in the shadow of the five chimneys that saw the exermination of some four million people, mostly Jews, during World War II.

In this museum there are exhibited hundreds of thousands of broken, down-at-the-heels shoes of men, women, children, and small babies. In other rooms the visitor sees mountains of decaying toothbrushes, and still others are piled high with eyeglass frames, collected by "conscientious" Germans. They had removed the good shoes and toothbrushes, and extracted the glasses from the frames. This is what was left of some four million people.

No less macabre is the museum's filing cabinet. It contains the documents the Nazis prepared about their victims with German thoroughness. With the incredible cynicism that became the Nazis' hallmark, they never used the term "gas chambers" but coined an unusual word for their genocidal act, *Entwesungskammer*—Desubstantiation Chamber.

It was as a memento to the horrors of Nazism that

Poles constructed the museum after the war. Nazis considered the gentile Poles, too, an inferior race, because they are Slavs; and they exterminated many of them too. It was not only the ghetto but most of the country that fell victim to Teutonic wrath.

After the second World War there were many Jews in the top echelons of the Polish Communists. This was the continued legacy of the past from the time of the Czarist regime, when the revolt of the oppressed assumed an ideological frame. Many of the top Polish Communists with a Jewish background were Stalinists. As the Poles reacted to Stalinism, a chain reaction of political intrigues represented the people's atavistic anti-Semitism, reinforced by the power play in the leadership.

Three major waves of anti-Semitism struck the country up to the year of reform, 1956. The first one was launched in 1951–1952, when many leaders of Jewish descent were ousted from the top echelons. The second wave struck two years later, lasting for three years, when numerous people of Jewish origin were ejected from the armed forces. The third wave, up to the reform, removed additional Jews from the Polish United Workers' Party. The actual work of purification was undertaken by activists instructed to poke into their comrades' background. The Jews who fell under the axe were denounced as "cosmopolitans."

During this time, the surviving Jewish community, about thirty thousand people, felt the purifiers' heavy hand. (Before the war Poland had some four million Jews.) The Central Committee of Polish Jews was liquidated, and its successor, the Cultural and Social Union of Polish Jews, was placed under stricter party control. The Union of Jewish Writers and Journalists was dissolved, and its activities were transferred to the All-Polish Union of Writers, while Warsaw's Jewish Historical Institute was forced to follow the Stalin line. A Communist newspaper, *Folksztyme*, was the only one, and *Yidische Szriften*, described as a literary and art monthly, appeared under the imprimatur of the Cultural and Social Union.

Jewish schools of traditional learning faded away as religious education was denounced as the hotbed of Zionism. Parents had to send their children to the national schools, where they were impregnated with local communism wrapped in a residue of anti-Semitism. Press campaigns were conducted to encourage Jewish workers not to stay away from work on their holidays.

Toward the end of his life, we know today, Stalin became rabidly anti-Semitic, and his creatures in Poland followed his ways. Official anti-Semitism in Poland, however, did not end with his death. At the seventh plenum of the party, in July 1956, serious thought was given to the radical solution of the "Jewish problem." The question was asked whether people professing to be Jews should not be restricted by a *numerus clausus* in selected walks of life. As Poland entered its reform age, "the Gomulka era," the debate remained suspended.

Gomulka himself always worked closely with party members of Jewish backgrounds, and he had a Jewish wife. But he, too, ran into snags on that score, even though he became the pivotal political force. Combating him in devious ways, Stalinists sought to retain a toe hold. They formed the "Natolin group," so named after their meeting place in a villa reserved for visiting bigwigs. Members of this group formed a hard core in the party's Central Committee. A reformed Stalinist, J. Putrament, recorded: "Natolin planned to solve the problem of responsibility for past mistakes through the classic method of finding a scapegoat, and that was the Jew."

Some of the top-echelon Communists with Jewish background had left the country on government missions and turned up in the United States, where organs of the Polish press reported that the C.I.A. welcomed them warmly. Was that welcome warm because the Poles arrived with a heavy baggage of secrets they had collected in their responsible posts?

The Polish top leadership was not anti-Semitic, it may be assumed. Both the head of the party, Wladislaw Gomulka, and the Chief of State, Marshal Marion Spychalski, had wives of the Jewish faith. All their lives these men had fought alongside their Jewish comrades. The Warsaw monument in memory of the anti-Nazi uprising of the Jewish ghetto is the most impressive memorial in all Poland. Yet it was the top party echelon that touched off the latent anti-Jewish feeling.

THE SIX-DAY WAR

This anti-Semitic feeling gushed forth in a paradoxical way. In one of the most decisive, and, certainly, one of the shortest wars in recent times, Israel defeated her Arab enemies, who were about forty times more populous than she. It was a stunning victory in June, 1967.

Although anti-Semitism is in the blood of many Poles, the people of the country stood up cheering Israel wildly. And that was the paradox. This time, the Poles saw the Israelis, not as Jews, but as victors in a fight against overwhelming odds. They saw only the odds that the Israelis faced, then substituted the Arabs for the Russians and themselves for the Israelis. The Jews dared to do what the Poles would have liked to do.

The official policy of Poland toward the six-day war followed that of the Soviet Union. To the Kremlin, the Israelis were the aggressors and the Arabs the innocent victims of a sneak attack. Official Poland said "amen" to Moscow's incantation. There were exceptions, though, in the reaction of some of the party leaders to the official line. Carried away by the popular sympathy for Israel, they took their stand behind Jerusalem. That was too much for Gomulka, the low-key party chief. He could not put up with this digression from the path laid down by the Kremlin. In a huff, he denounced the Kremlin critics as "Zionists." The anti-Semitic innuendoes followed.

Gomulka promptly realized his mistake. What was he to do now? There had been already too many disruptive influences at work in the country, and now he added one more to the collection. He decided to explain his statement, and that complicated matters even more.

His *ex-cathedra* commentary on his unfortunate reference to Zionism addressed itself to anti-Semitism. He opposed it, he said, without any reservation. The party, he added, was going to oppose all manifestations bearing the traces of anti-Semitism "with full determination." All the trouble had been caused, he said, by the group of people who under the old regime were addressed as *Jasnie Oswiecony*—Brightly Enlightened Ones. They were feudal-minded people, a tiny group, making a lot of noise. They were anti-Soviet, and, in this instance, pro-Israeli.

As to the Jews of Poland, he said, they could belong in three categories. The largest one contained "our citizens of the Jewish faith who are rooted in the soil on which they were born and whose fatherland is Poland." The second group contained the "cosmopolitans," neither fully Polish nor fully Zionist. He advised them to turn to fields of activity in which "national affirmation was not a *must*." Finally, there were the dedicated Zionists, and for them the door was open to leave, if they so wished.

ETERNAL POLAND

Anti-Semitism is a fellow-traveler of anti-liberalism, and of authoritarianism. Anti-liberalism and authoritarianism had been the hallmarks of the interbellum Polish regimes. Naturally, they had been anti-Communist, too. The party had been outlawed, its members hounded. Landmarks of Polish political life had been the places of detention for political offenders. Most notorious of those was the Bereza Kartuska camp in the insalubrious vicinity of the Pripet Marshes.

Many of the Polish Communist leaders had been detained in this and its companion camps in Bialystok, Kowel, and Kobryn. The victims were today's "partisans," who had stayed behind during the war, and not the Muscovites. (In the end, some of the Muscovites fared worse, as victims of Stalin's blood purges.) Wladislaw Gomulka had been one of these. The most hated foe of the Polish Communists was Jozef Pilsudski, denounced as the "enemy of the working class" and "arch-Fascist." That was before the second World War.

On the fiftieth anniversary of Poland's reemergence as an independent nation—in the fall of 1968—Marshal Pilsudski's crypt in the Wavel Castle in the city of Cracow had become a place of pilgrimage. The National Unity Front, the Communist-dominated organization that groups small political parties and social institutions, announced the government's decision to celebrate the anniversary around the personality of Pilsudski.

In the past, credit for the liberation of Poland had been given to the Bolshevik revolution of 1917, which "destroyed the Czarist empire, erased the Polish partitions, and recognized Poland's right to independent existence." Now credit was also given to Marshal Pilsudski, the erstwhile "arch-Fascist enemy of the working class." Again nationalism proved to be stronger than party ideology.

The intense nationalism of Poland has its boundaries traced by geography. From the Soviet point of view Poland is *espace vitale,* a strategically retractable space. Twice within a quarter of a century it was used to inflict grievous, almost fatal harm on Russia. Even if they wanted to, the Soviets could never loosen their grip on it. And the Poles knew it. They also knew that it was not Russia alone that had their fate in her hands, but also the United States, the other major star of the international constellation. They knew that as long as American troops were stationed in West Germany, Soviet troops had to remain in East Germany, backed by other Soviet troops in Poland. They did not like that, but they had not liked many things in their tragic life. They knew that their geographic location itself was a tragedy. But they learned to be patient. They learned that in their geographic location patience was the price of survival. Without it, there would be no Poland.

Poland's destiny is prescribed by her location on the plains, between Germany and Russia. Those plains extend deep into Central Asia, on the one side, and Western Europe, on the other. In this ambiance, schizophrenia is made to order. Should the Poles opt to join the East or the West? At the time national traits were formed, historic ideologies were expressed in church loyalties. Poland became Catholic, flanked by Orthodox Russia and Protestant Prussia.

There should be a technical term for "triple personality," since the Poles were bound to have it after their country's vivisection—chunks to Russia, Prussia-Germany, and Austria. No psychoanalyst is needed to point out that love for one's neighbors did not become a Polish trait.

The Poles' portion of those endless plains became a continental drilling ground on which their despoilers eventually fought one another. And the Poles were in between. The Germans, affected by the overheated dynamism of the West, were more aggressive, and they sought to create an eastern *Lebensraum* for themselves—*Drang*

nach Osten. This went on and on, from the days of the
Teutonic Knights to the era of the Third Reich.

Restored to the map, Poland became a victim of the
fatal space, a satrapy of the Germans or the Russians,
depending upon the outcome of the latest war. Now it is
a Soviet satrapy, and the Poles (including the Communists, as far as they dare to be) are in patriotic revolt.
The Soviets created a mutual assistance pact—set up, of
all places, in Warsaw—for the Kremlin knows where its
bulwarks must be strengthened. And this situation is
bound to continue until the lion and the lamb (two lions,
perhaps) learn how to coexist in amity.

12

Bulgaria, in the
Heart of the Balkans

Happy is the country that makes no newspaper headlines. Hardly ever does the name of Bulgaria emerge on the front pages. Yet she is in the depth of the Balkans, known to history as the bloody peninsula and the powder keg. Plenty of blood flowed in the Bulgaria of the past, and the powder was always kept dry. Today Bulgaria appears to be quiet. But there are signs of change, revealed by a higher awareness of nationalism.

She is surrounded by countries with which she has conflict areas. This is as true of her Communist neighbors as of the anti-Communist ones. Turkey and Greece became anti-Communist crusaders in the post-World War II age, under the Truman Doctrine, which extended the defense perimeter of the United States to this area. Greece, particularly, has become an anti-Communist redoubt, at the front door of Communist Bulgaria.

Yugoslavia—Bulgaria's western neighbor—was, of course, the launching pad of the reformation movement in the Communist world. And Rumania, the other neighbor, launched the second stage of reform. Surrounded by antagonistic regimes, Bulgaria has remained steadfast to the orthodox Communist creed and loyal to the Soviets—a unique case of consistency. This unspectacular consistency has produced no newspaper headlines. Bulgaria has remained quiescent, and in this very placidness a national trait is revealed. To see its causes, we have to survey the historical background.

IN THE BEGINNING. . .

It was a strange case of the victim conquering his victor. That is how the Bulgarians became the Slavs they are today. They had sallied forth from the pallid north in the seventh century, a Turkish-speaking people, Turanians. Their very name was Turanian—*Bol-Agalar*, plowman. Or was it derived from the Volga, the river of their ancestral home? They pushed into the luminous land south of the Danube, in the Balkans inhabited by Slavs, whom they conquered. That was conquest by physical force, which, however, was nullified by the cultural victory of the defeated Slavs over their victors. The Turanian Bulgars became Slavic Bulgars, as they are today.

"Bulgaria assumed a rank among the civilized powers of the earth as early as the tenth century," Edward Gibbon wrote. The title of her Simeon the Great was "Emperor and Autocrat of all the Bulgars and Greeks." After having challenged the Byzantine Empire, he exacted tribute from it. From the Aegean to the Adriatic, the Bulgarians ruled over the Balkans.

In their new location, they embraced Greek Orthodox Christianity, as did their neighbors all around. Also, they evolved one of the most unusual deviations from the Christian norm—Bogumilism. That was in the tenth century. Their Greek neighbors called their creed *Bulgarorum haeresis* and its followers *Bulgari*, whatever their ethnic roots.

THE BULGARIAN HERESY

"Beloved of God" is the translation of the Slavic word Bogumil. Beloved of God, and hated by Orthodox Christians. Bogomile appears to have been the name of a Bulgarian priest, after whom the sect was named, according to another interpretation. The Bogumils believed that Satanael and Jesus were the two sons of God; that pride was the cause of the damnation of Satanael, God's firstborn, who was cast out of heaven; that he created a new heaven and the earth; that he also made man, whom God invested with his soul; that Satanael rebelled again, and this time God created Jesus to counteract him; that Christ overthrew Satanael and ascended to heaven, the throne of power.

The Bogumils refused to pay homage to the cross and decried the practice of the Lord's Supper. They protested against the worship of the Virgin Mary and against the veneration of images and saints. Save for the Psalms and the Prophets they rejected the Old Testament teachings, and even in the New Testament accepted only those passages that dealt directly with instructions by Christ. They had no churches and uttered their prayers in private huts; they had no professional clergy, and their "teachers," elected by them, were their spiritual guides, since each member of the consecrated community could obtain the perfection of Christ. Indeed, each member could become Christ himself. Baptism was considered a spiritual force to be embraced by adults when mature enough to grasp its sublime significance. Marriage was not a holy sacrament. The Bogumils maintained that the bread and wine of the eucharist were not transformed into the flesh and blood of Christ. The last judgment, they held, was not executed by Christ, but by God.

All the Bogumils considered themselves members of mendicant orders and wore their garb. They were keen missionaries, traveling far and wide to propagate their creed, and while traversing many frontiers, they sought to exorcise evil spirits and heal the lame. They sowed the seeds of a deviant religious literature, including legends about Adam and the cross, and produced tracts bearing such titles as *Letters from Heaven,* and *Wanderings through Heaven and Hell.*

From their Bulgarian homeland the Bogumils' creed spread in all directions: into the land of Russ, where it formed the roots of such later creeds as Dukhobortsi, Strigolniki, and Molokani. Spreading westward across the Balkans the creed took roots in the rugged mountains of the Bosnians. Being persecuted, the sect took refuge in many nearly inaccessible areas, the crest of the Carpathians, the Dinaric and the Swiss Alps, and the Provence of France, where it assumed the shape of the Albigensian and Waldensian creeds. It moved into Germanic lands, where it became known as Anabaptism. It spread to Spain, finally crossing the channel into the British Isles.

The Church execrated the Bogumil creed. Its first martyr was a physician by the name of Basilius, who lived in the twelfth century. In all parts of the world crusades were waged against the followers of the faith, who were slaughtered mercilessly wherever found. The sect ceased to exist in the fourteenth century, officially. This was the beginning of another tragic history.

AN UN-NATION

Then came the Turks from Asia across the Straits, and Bulgaria was extinguished in 1330. Many members of the higher classes converted to the victorious creed of Islam;

the persecuted became the persecutor, and others were lost. Bulgaria's indigenous aristocracy was wiped out. Because their religion was Greek Orthodox, many people thought that they were Greeks. Yet under their Moslem rulers the Bulgarians maintained an old Slavic institution, a form of patriarchal communism, traceable to ancient times, *zadruga*, the house-community. Under this system, family groups, sometimes scores of members, dwelt together on communally owned farms. The house-father, *domakin*, and the house-mother, *domakinia*, ruled over the group, assigning specific tasks to members, who practiced a variety of trades. Their earnings were paid into the common treasury. The fees of the priests for weddings, baptisms, and funerals augmented the common fund. This, too, was a sort of primitive religious communism.

Later, much later, the Bulgarians' aptitude for communal associations was displayed in the *gradinarski druzhini*, organizations of market gardeners. They were members of pre-Communist collectives who left their huts in the spring for the purpose of cultivating gardens on the outskirts of Bulgarian towns and abroad. Returning home in the fall, they divided the profits among all the members. In other ways, too, the Bulgarians' aptitude to form communal organizations was revealed. They established associations not only for farming (for instance, in their far-famed attar-of-rose fields), but also in mining and simple industrial pursuits. They founded mutual-aid provident societies and many of their handicraftsmen organized themselves in *esnafs*, guilds. Communism was not new to Bulgaria when the Soviets came.

Before that, for centuries, Bulgarians were not aware even of their nationality. While Bulgarians were under Ottoman rule, not many students of Slavic literature knew much about these strange people, with their exotic history, from the peak to the abyss, their uncommon deviation from the church norm in the past, and their esoteric social ways. They lived deep down in the inscrutable Balkans, in a world apart.

The simple countryman of what we call Bulgaria today knew only that his hated oppressor, the Turk, was a "pagan," and that he himself was a true believer, Orthodox, a Christian. He also detested his own Greek priests, who did not speak his language, whom he did not understand, and who were rapaciously greedy for their tithes.

As usual it was in the wake of Western nationalism that Bulgarian nationalism too began to stir, and, again, as usual, it was among the few literate people. This was at the end of the eighteenth century. On Mount Athos, sequestered from the world but keeping in communion with its spirit, Father Paissy was among the first to appeal to Bulgarians, recalling the radiant history of their country centuries before. Religion and nationalism formed an inextricable whole, even in his thoughts, as demonstrated in his basic *History of the Slavic-Bulgarian People, Czars and Saints*. Only after the middle of the last century was the appeal to literate people enlarged through an embryonic press. The thought of a country of their own did not occur to the countrymen. They suffered from what Father Paissy called his people's "Christian resignation," and against this misinterpretation of their creed he took a stand. As one of his admirers pointed out: "He stepped in just in time to save his nation from extinction."

Poets and other writers were the first nationalists of Bulgaria, and they looked to the fellow-Slav, Russia, for aid. They were a small country; Russia was huge. The noted lyrical poet of the age, singer of Bulgarian liberty, Christo Botev, launched the first Bulgarian Revolutionary Committee in the Russian seaport Odessa. Russia's famous anti-Czarist writers, such as Alexander Herzen and Nikolai Chernyshevski, were mentors of Bulgaria's Luben Karavelov, who spent nine years in Moscow and published newspapers outside of the Turks' reach under such "subversive" titles as *Independence* and *Liberty*.

Inadvertently, the Turks aided the cause of Bulgarian resurrection by giving their approval to the establishment of an independent church organization, the Bulgarian Exarchate, which freed them from the Greeks. Now even the simple peasants learned that they were not Greeks or Serbs. They were Bulgarians.

THE SICK MAN OF EUROPE

"We have a sick man on our hands," Czar Nicholas I of all the Russias was quoted to have said to Britain's Sir George Hamilton Seymour in the middle of the last century. "It will be a great misfortune if his estate slips through our hands one of these days, especially before the necessary arrangements are made."

The "sick man" was the Ottoman Empire, once a world power, and now in rapid decline. Russia was vitally interested in the sick man's anticipated demise, because Turkey was the keeper of the Straits, Russia's door to the world. The Czar's Empire had a surplus of land, and a shortage of sea. The Straits in Russian lands would have opened the world of the open seas to the Muscovites. Czar Nicholas suggested diplomatic arrangement with the British, but the only scheme the British wanted was to keep the Straits out of Russia's grip. With the Narrows in their possession, the British saw the Russians adding to their huge land surface also a vast sea surface, and thus upsetting the power balance.

Instead of an arrangement with the British, there was a war with them in Crimea. The Russians were defeated. A score of years later, they tried their luck again, this time by way of the part of the Ottoman Empire in which the Bulgarians dwelt. The Turks were massacring the Bulgarians in an explosion of wanton fury that characterized the deeds of a regime in rapid decline. The Russians went to the Bulgarians' aid against the Turks and scored a quick victory. It was within sight of the minarets of Constantinople that they dictated their truce terms to the Turks, at San Stefano. The Sultan was to lose much of his extensive Balkan possessions. For the Turks this was a Carthaginian peace. For the Bulgarians, on the other hand, this was a dream come true, because they were to fall heir to most of the Turks's holdings in the Balkans, from the Aegean almost to the Adriatic. The beneficiaries of this arrangement were to be the Russians, the power behind the throne in a country with a still-undeveloped sense of nationality.

At that point the other great powers intervened to save the power balance from Russia. The Berlin Congress of 1878 put the Russians in their place. Bulgaria was defeated by diplomacy, to become a small Balkan principality. The key of the Straits was not to be in the Czar's hands, and he was not to have free access to the warm waters of the south. Still, for the first time in more than half a millennium, there was a new country by the name of Bulgaria.

AN AGITATED HISTORY

Briefly, Bulgaria did make the front pages in those days. For her, it was a turbulent age. Once nationalism hit the land, many of its literati—followed eventually by less literate people—became fanatically nationalist. Related linguistically to the Bulgarians are the Macedonians, fellow-Slavs, whom the Bulgarians now claimed. They were also claimed by the Serbians, the Turks, and the Greeks. The Macedonian issue became a fuse of the Balkan powder keg. Besides the Macedonian question there was also the problem of how the Bulgarians could turn their country into a viable nation, and viability meant mainly the people's livelihood.

Bulgaria was then a typically peasant country. Through itinerant Bulgarian gardeners, Europe became acquainted with the industrious, thrifty habits of the people. Because of the migratory habits of Bulgarians and the political links with Russia, some contradictory ideologies penetrated into the land. One of these was that of the Socialists.

At the time when the rest of Europe knew next to nothing about the Bolsheviks, a Bulgarian radical group, strangely named "Narrow Socialist," adopted a Communist platform. It advocated class warfare, voiced opposition to nationalistic wars, and expressed the need for an international organization of like-minded parties. The "Narrows" opposed the "Broad Socialists," who subscribed to a patriotic, gradualist policy. The first leader of the Narrow Socialists, Dimitar Blagoev, had received his training in the Russia of the Czars, working together with the ultra-left *Narodnaia Volia* group, which anticipated the Communists with its highly developed party hierarchy. This quasi-Bolshevik group prepared the ground for future developments.

First, however, Bulgaria had her period of "time of troubles" in another form, the Balkan Wars to free the peninsula of the Turkish incubus. This was the prelude to the great war. Among all the small Balkan countries pushing the Turks out of Europe the Bulgarians gave the best account of themselves. That was to their disadvantage, because appearing to be the strongest they offered a perfect target for jealous foes. Their "allies" ganged up on them and thrust them back within their cramped boundaries. Their fellow-Slavs and neighbors, the Serbs, were their most jealous foes. From that point on, the Bulgarians were in the coalition camps opposed to the Serbs. They were so opposed in both world wars of the century.

The Bulgarians were at odds among themselves too. A democratic peasant party was opposed by a more authoritarian representation of the urban classes of "better people." The social and economic reforms that Aleksandr Stamboliski, head of the Peasant Party, introduced after World War I were to help the underprivileged peasant. His end by assassination introduced the reign of Aleksandr Tsankov, spokesman of the higher classes. An age of turmoil ensued, in which Bulgarian governments appeared to be more interested in getting chunks of Serb Macedonia than in the problems of their peasantry.

In the second World War, the Bulgarians again faced their Serb kinsmen as their foes. Even though the "better" people lined up Bulgarians with the Fascist Axis powers, the basic decency of the peasants kept them from playing a killer's game. Officially, the country subscribed to the insane racial policy of the German Third Reich, of which Bulgaria was the ally. Unofficially, Bulgaria was the only Eastern European country in which racial minorities were not threatened by extermination. While all around the country, in German-occupied Europe, the gruesome policy of genocide was carried out, the Bulgarian peasants offered sanctuary to the threatened minorities. This was paradoxical, because in large parts of Yugoslavia, the Axis enemy, large-scale massacres of dissidents took place.

THEN CAME THE COMMUNISTS

"Standard procedure" is the apt description of the events that ensued with the arrival of the Soviets. The wartime coalition of anti-Fascist parties, *Otechestven Front*—Fatherland Front—handed the power to the Communists under Kimon Georgiev, and Bulgaria, a kingdom until then, became a republic. A year after the end of the war, Georgi Dimitrov became the Prime Minister. He was the only Bulgarian, probably, about whom the world had known. Accused of having set fire to the Berlin Reichstag in the early days of Nazi rule, he dared to hold up the Third Reich to ridicule in its own star chamber. He had to be acquitted of the charge.

The roots of the new regime reached deep into the native soil. Communism, which Arnold J. Toynbee called a Christian heresy, had been anticipated by the Bogumil heresy in Bulgaria. The Soviet-type *kolkhoz* had its predecessor in the ancient system of *zadruga,* the household-community. The Narrow Socialists of the Bulgarian past had not been any narrower than the dogmatists of the narrow interpretation of the teachings of Marx and Lenin in Bulgaria. The absence of a native aristocracy had helped the leveling process of the new regime. The Communists' investment policy in forming an industrial base did not run counter to the principles of private enterprise in a country that lacked even the minimal means for the creation of a sophisticated infrastructure. More than any other country within the Eastern bloc, the Bulgarians were ready for the grand experiment.

It began in an ominously negative way. When Tito broke with the Soviet Union, the Kremlin flashed the signal to Sofia to stir up incidents along the Yugoslav frontier. Thus was the unspeakable heresy to be exorcised. The south Slavs were not scared.

The Bulgarian top echelon toed the Stalin line. More than that, it launched the classic witch hunt against the "untrue-believers," "nationalists," and "splittists"—the suspected local brand of Titoists. The usual trumped-up charges were hurled at Traicho Kostov, a top bureaucrat,

whose name as a "traitor" had been drawn out of a hat.
Espionage was the charge, and the outcome of the trial
could not be questioned. The accused was hanged as a
deterrent to Titoist heresy.

As in other countries of the bloc, the death of Stalin had
set off the thaw. But while the other countries of the region were slowly moving away from the Soviet Union, the
Bulgarians were inching closer. That was surprising, however, only to those who were unaware of the Bulgarians'
history. Poles and Hungarians hate the Russian because
of their national heritage; the Rumanian shies away from
him; the Czech considers him not quite grown up; but the
average Bulgarian feels affinity for him. His neighbors—
Rumanians, Turks, Greeks, and Serbs, are not his friends.
The Bulgarian is constantly reminded of his country's
close contact with Moscow. His ancestors had come from
the Volga region, the Russian core land. Both countries
had the same cultural heritage by way of Byzantine Constantinople. Bulgarians and Russians had earned their
spurs in fighting a common foe, the Turk. A common
Slavic heritage had kept the Bulgarian national spirit
alive. The concept of greater Bulgaria in the seventies of
the last century was a Russian diplomatic device.

Even though there was an upsurge of Bulgarian nationalism, it was not directed against the Kremlin. It was
directed against Yugoslavia, and the centennial celebration in 1968 of the Treaty of San Stefano provided the
occasion. That treaty, which, it will be recalled, liberated
Bulgaria from Turkish rule, assigned to her all of what is
Yugoslav Macedonia today, a region inhabited by a Slavic-
speaking people whom the Bulgarians consider their kin.
We have seen that the San Stefano version of greater
Bulgaria was never put into effect. After World War II the
Yugoslav portion of Macedonia became a component re-
public within the Federation headed by Tito. By develop-

ing the Macedonian language and culture, Belgrade sought to give the local residents a distinctive national identity.

A Bulgarian press campaign related to the San Stefano celebrations was stressing the theme that the ineffectiveness of nineteenth-century Bulgarian diplomacy had frustrated the realization of a greater Bulgaria with what were described as just ethnic frontiers. The press campaign denied the existence of a Macedonian nation and raised the specter of Bulgarian irredentism. Bulgarians claimed the Macedonians as their own, and not as a separate nationality. And that was good old-fashioned nationalism.

THE NEW WAVE

How does a peasant country become an industrial one? No country in the Eastern bloc had been so rural as Bulgaria. Russia had launched the process of industrialization in Bulgaria, but she gradually established her own priorities. Boldly, she moved closer to the Western world. She reached an agreement in the late sixties with the French Renault Company to set up an assembly plant at Kazanluk. A new trade protocol was concluded with Great Britain for a sizable increase in trade between the two countries. Also, an agreement was reached with a West German firm to produce typewriters in Plovdiv and to train Bulgarian workers.

Reporting on the fourth five-year plan (1961–1965), Todor Zhivkov, the Premier, said that the GNP had risen by 51 percent and the national income by 38 percent, and that Bulgaria now ranked among the countries with the most rapidly rising rates of economic growth. The fifth five-year plan (1966–1970) aimed to make Bulgaria an industrialized country. Industrial output was to increase from 74 to 79 percent of the total national output, and by 1970 Bulgaria would produce sufficient steel for two thirds of her needs. Marked priority was given to the development of heavy industry.

Behind these gray figures of production there was drama, and a national purpose. The smoke of the new industries in what used to be the economically most backward region of the peninsula gave new meaning to the hackneyed term, the "darkest Balkans." This time the darkness was caused by factory chimneys.

In another field, spectacularly successful was Bulgaria's policy to lure Western tourists to her lovely beaches on the Black Sea. The Golden Sand Beach north of the seaport city of Varna had just about everything tourists used to have in the halycon pre-World War II days on French and Italian beaches—a beautiful setting, attractive hotels, meals on spacious restaurant terraces to spirited tunes, entertainment galore, and popular prices. The English were the first to discover Bulgaria as a tourist paradise; they were followed by others, including Americans. The tourists had a good time beyond the financial abilities of most of them in the West, while the Bulgarian acquired foreign currency.

THUS SPAKE CANDIDE

The Bulgarians, on the fringes of Christianity, have been holding their own against the dynamism of the Moslem Ecumene. Their latter-day nationalism was rekindled by this dramatic contrast. The Kremlin version of communism, imposed upon them, made them reject the ancestors' creed—for a time. It re-emerged in recent years, again as the reassertion of their nationalism. It is as Communist national leaders that party priests now attend St. Cyril's festival on May 24, the day of the inventor of the Cyrillic alphabet.

The same national-communism has prompted the "ex-cathedra" statement of first party secretary Zhivkov: "Admiration for everything foreign must be eradicated with red-hot irons." And the same party pontiff employed the authority of his office in speaking out against the "misinterpretation" of communism as a negation of patriotism; he denounced this attitude as "national nihilism." *On revient toujours*, or should one say: *Plus ça change, plus c'est la même chose?*

In their tragic history, the Bulgarians had witnessed more than their share of plague, pestilence, cruelty, war, disease, famine, injustice, and greed. Longer than any other people, the Bulgarians were the victims of the Turks at their most unspeakable. During the interludes of the historic nightmare, the Bulgarians were industriously and quietly working, happiest when they were forgotten, providing little grist for the historians' mills and providing few front-page headlines. When Voltaire's immortal Candide had tried his hands on humanitarian deeds, convinced at first, trusting his teacher's words that this was the best of all possible worlds, and finding that this was the worst of all possible worlds, he finally reached the end of civilization on the site of Bulgaria. "To work without philosophizing," he found, "is the only way of making life bearable." From this negative philosophy he moved to a positive one, summarizing the wisdom of all ages, encompassing the solution of man's problems: *Il faut cultiver notre jardin*. The Bulgarians, famed as a gardening folk, have been trying to do that for long. They hope to be able to stick to their predilection, to cultivate their gardens.

13

The Imperishable
Nation....China

Our empire is woven of the living, the dead, and nature," Paul Valéry's Oriental scholar said. "It exists because it sets all things in order. Here everything is part of history. . . ." He continued:

Being so, we seem asleep and are despised. Yet all things dissolve in our magnificent mass. Conquerors lose their way in our yellow water. Foreign armies are drowned in the flood of our descendants or crushed under the weight of our ancestors. The majestic cascades of our rivers of lives and the swelling succession from our fathers sweep them away.

From this the sequel:

Our politics, therefore, must be infinite, reaching to both ends of time and leading a thousand million men from their fathers to their sons, in lines neither broken nor tangled. There lies endless direction without desire. You consider us inert. We simply preserve wisdom enough to grow beyond measure, beyond all human power, and to look on while you, in spite of your raging science, dissolve in the deep and fruitful waters of the Land of Tsin. You who know so many things do not know the most ancient and potent mysteries, and you rage with desire for what is immediate and you destroy your fathers and your sons together.

THE YELLOW EARTH

There was a China long before there was classical Rome, and it is likely that there will be a China after all other empires have become dust. We bridle at this thought and call it fanciful. In this case, fancy is reality. China is hundreds of millions of human atoms, and yet it is one. It is myriads of conflicting interests, of atavistic family units, the vestiges of castes and classes, of many tongues. It is the residue of conquerors and conquered, of ages of light and eons of darkness. While the residue of the world was seared to ashes by Genghis Khan, China prospered. The rest of Asia had fallen prey to alien greed, but China survived. Her sons and daughters, millions, never leave the paternal soil even overseas, because the dust on their sandals is the extension of China. China is thus a civilization without beginning and without end. China looks like a mystery. She is a miracle, the same China under the T'angs and under Chairman Mao.

Hwang-t'u, that yellow earth of China, slips through the fingers of man, and yet it is the womb of the miracle. It is imperishable; out of it life bursts forth constantly, and to it life returns in the bodies of myriads of people whose day has come. Out of their bodies new life sprouts. Thus eternity was symbolized by Hwang-ti, the Yellow Emperor, since yellow was the symbol of eternity. He ruled the world, as all the Chinese knew, and other potentates were his slaves. *Hwang-t'u* originated in the western marches, the Gobi and the Ordos, transported by the Emperor's servant, the Western Wind. *Han-hai* was the name of the land whose horizon curved into the dusk of the infinite, the Dry Sea. To the unilluminated it was *Shamo*, Sand Desert. And so was born life, the "good earth" about which Pearl Buck wrote, soil of eternity. The yellow color was eternal rejuvenation, endless resurrection, eternal life fructified by the Hwang-Ho, Yellow River. The "Great River," Yangtse-Kiang, stood by. So the miracle continued for eons of ages, building up the loess, the miracle, eternal life, to depths of endless fathoms.

The yellow earth, the loess, was the womb, the symbol of eternal fertility, of constant rebirth. It nurtured the Chinese, sustained their homes, and became their eternal abode after their brief spells of earthly life. Billions of people throughout millennia scooped their homes out of its porous fabric, and other billions scooped small nooks into it for tired bones. Eternity was not affected even if the River of Life became the savage River of Death on a rampage. Constantly, new life sprouted from the buried bones.

China was different from any other place under the sun. The sun was different, too. It was her own. China was different from other sites of old cultures. It was different from the Land Between the Rivers (the Tigris and the Euphrates), where man had set out to lay the foundations of eternal life. There he had built the Tower of Babel and was confounded. He had tried again, building layers of civilization upon other layers, full of hope, ending in despair. The ruins of once-great cities were his memories. And so it had been with the valley of the Nile, too, where, in the words of Professor Breasted, man's dawn of conscience was the witness of his ambitions more towering than Babel. There, too, many conquerors had been conquered, but there had been no historic continuity of one race of man sustained by one elixir of life. In China there was such a continuity—everlasting life.

YIN AND YANG

The first human being was a Chinese, P'an-ku, and this the Chinese know. They smile at the arrogance of the Western man, flaunting Adam, a product of today. P'an-ku lived millions of years before; he was the ancestor of man, of the Chinese. Then came the ten periods of the existence of man (that is, of the Chinese), beginning with the Age of Terrestrial Emperors. Nature accumulated the rich soil under their rule. Other creators followed, including Sui-jon, the Fire Producer, and Yu-ch'au, the Nest Builder.

All that lived were interlinked in a community of spirits, animal and man. Fu-hi was a demigod, demon, merman with a fishtail, the incarnation of the evolutionary principle a thousand years before Darwin. Chinese mythology credits him with having turned greedy brutes into greedier men.

He it was who conceived the principles of *yin* and *yang*, the dialectical forces of life, the pendulum of history, the incarnations of change, of seasons, of frost and sunshine, the wheel of fortune, the good and bad, woman and man.

Thus the natural and the supernatural, the human and divine principles, the individual and the community were mated. Shoen-nung, the first Emperor, was such a humanly divine creature. He was toiling in the celestially human element of Chinese civilization as the "Divine Laborer." He dug into *yin*, the loess, with the *yang*, plow, which he had invented. After him came Hwang-ti, the Yellow Emperor, who took possession of his heritage, the entire earth. He became the first global Emperor. China had no frontiers.

Diverse new interests were now plowed into the soil of Chinese civilization, enough to wreck it. It was not wrecked, because the Chinese soil has the mystic capacity to assimilate and to survive, forever. That capacity has been at work ever since. Paul Valéry noted it, as quoted before, and so did others. It was noted by the perceptive Abel Hovelaque: "Everywhere, in the icy north and under the blazing sun of the tropics, one feels the same powerful influence throughout history," he said. From the outset, he continued, it has been stronger than any difference in climate, race, or destiny, inexorably molding into a unit all the ingredients of a culture, imposing an identical civilization, an absolute moral cohesion in the diversity of a country that is a world. Thus China is the same in every corner of her vast expanse, at every moment of her history, a mysterious force which, through thousands of years, has fashioned her myriads of people, "immobilizing them in their immutable habits in the supreme reality of their land. . . ."

These immutable habits were manifested under the Shang dynasty, nearly four thousand years ago. Members of that line of rulers anticipated the ways of the Communist regime of today. The gods had been organized by the Emperors in their celestial abode. Some of the rulers found that there were too many gods to be kept in line, and that their number interfered with an orderly chain of command. One of the Shangs decided to appoint a celestial supergod, "chairman of the board," of whom the mundane rulers were the sons and the executors of the divine will. Thus the Chinese Emperors became the Sons of Heaven, by fiat, and their new status made them heads of all the families in all the world. This autocratic arrangement expressed the traditional Chinese way of communication, from the higher to the lower. In a country of myriads of social units, rooted in ancestral backgrounds, individual family positions, status, interests, a more democratic solution might have caused chronic anarchy. Therefore the need for the new line of command. This way, people, the high and low, shared the divine substance of sands of loess. Thus eternal China was stabilized.

Some Emperors entered into the spirit of their civilization more than others. One of these was the fourth member of the Ch'in dynasty, Shih Huang Ti, who ascended the throne in 247 B.C. For him it was insufficient to rule the world. He was the First Principle, he announced, and before him there was the void. To prove this, he had the archives of previous regimes destroyed. He did not realize that people knew that Chinese civilization curved around the Dragon Mountain into the mysteries of infinity. It was he who had one of the wonders of the world built, snaking across 1,250 arid miles, the Chinese Wall. He was a ruler of vast imagination who wanted a shield for his realm from the dark forces beyond the confines of the earth. He had the wall built to separate *yang*, the land irradiated by the sun, from *yin*, the land of darkness.

CONFUCIUS AND TAO

The Emperor was the Son of Heaven, the High Priest, and Father of his subjects. His family comprised the people of all the ages, past, present, and future. Within the realm there were other families, the clans. And within these, there were still other groups—families as we know them. Thus was erected a system of mutual assistance in times of stress and strain. These families, too, included all the ancestors and all the progeny, a world with no end. Human life, the sage Confucius taught, was an enterprise in mutual aid. That aid made human life possible; without it life was a gaping void. Loyalty was due to kith and kin, to the superior and the neighbor, and to the ruler, above everything else. Fidelity and justice were the conditions of human survival, sustained by intelligence, benevolence, and piety. Truth and order were the building bricks of the universe. Nature itself followed simple rules of organization; it was man's duty to find those rules. "Seek your welfare through the welfare of all the others. You are he and he is you." Thus spoke Confucius.

The other illuminator, Lao-tse, taught the *Tao*—way —which he said was the cornerstone of *Te*—inherent power—which brings about the fruition. The weakest overcomes the strongest, this sage said, and happiness is born of calamity. Nature is harmony; both the seen and the unseen are its manifestations. In three stages man enters the world of knowledge. The first of these is the end of self-seeking, the process of purgation. The second stage is his union with Tao, the road to the light, the cosmic union. The third stage enables man to transcend the limitations of time and space. The Chinese concern with the eternal and transcendent was revealed in Taoism.

Confucianism and Taoism were native ways of seeking the unfindable. Added to them was a third creed, which reached the Middle Kingdom from India and which the Chinese embraced in later centuries: Buddhism. It teaches the devotee to shun desire, the source of pain. It also teaches him that there is salvation in the eightfold path, which encompasses the human spectrum all the way from right thought to right deed.

The wonders of the universe prompted philosophical thoughts in all the three religions China embraced. The childlike wonder yielded, in the course of time, to manipulation and superstitions, particularly in Buddhism and

Taoism. The Buddhist pantheon became filled with night-marish anthromorphoid figures with hideous features to scare the gullible and make them tread the path pre-scribed by authority. Taoist philosophy degenerated into *fangshui,* geomancy. The azure dragon, the white tiger, and magnetic currents, for instance, prescribed the loca-tion of the hut of the newlyweds. The landscape was filled with sacred animals, the fox and hedgehog, the weasel, and the snake; with sacred trees, the willow, the cassia, the banyan, and the pine, all of them served by greedy priests. Culture gods were set up for different occupations: the God of Letters for scholars, Tsai-Shin; the God of Wealth for tradesmen; and Kwanti the God of War for soldiers. They too had their priests with itching palms.

The Chinese were uncommonly strong, and they sur-vived even their religions and priests. They were sustained by the yellow earth and the indomitable energy of the common folk. And this in spite of the fact that they were ravaged by all manner of calamities: pestilences, droughts, floods, Emperors, and priests. Many of them died early. Since they were received into the bosom of their beloved yellow earth, they did not dread death.

Then came the "blood-sucking, carrion-eating mon-sters" who descended upon the Chinese from the hungry north. They were Tungus, Tatars, Manchus, Mongols, Turks, descending upon the country in waves of invasions for centuries. These invasions occurred during the reign of the Ch'in and Han dynasties, for about four hundred years, ending at the beginning of the third century of the Christian era. Thus the Chinese learned that theirs was not the entire world. Strong though the barbarians ap-peared to be when storming the walls, the Chinese pre-vailed. They were defending their country, their own lives, their ancestors' graves, and all their sacred sites. They were protecting the most sacred of all their possessions, their yellow earth, the loess.

CHINA'S MANIFEST DESTINY

Not only was China cleaned of the impurity of the barbarians' invasions, but she expanded her realm. From the Yunnan plateau in the south, a land of frowning peaks and angry torrents, the Chinese struck out toward the "Dragon Sea" we prosaically call the South China Sea. They became masters of the lands that history knows as Indochina, Vietnam, Laos, and Cambodia. That was a traumatic event for the people of the region, Southeast Asia's rice bowl, and they were never to forget that experience.

Moving beyond their protective shield, the Chinese swept into the horizonless spaces of the north land, crossing the Takla Makan, conquering the Tarim basin. Enduring the hardships of the arid lands, they moved into Sinkiang. They crossed the "Mountains of the Moon," the Tien Shan and the Altai range, and descended into the lowlands of the Ala-Kul and Issyk Kul. What made them go into this land of scant rain and infertile sand? Was it possible that the climate was better then? They pushed all the way to Lake Balkhash, deep in today's Soviet Central Asia, conquering the Turkic-speaking people there. Eventually, they withdrew into more hospitable areas. But they never seem to have forgotten this conquest, and centuries later they reminded their Communist Soviet adversaries of them.

There was no part of the Far Eastern world safe from Chinese intrusion. Moving northeastward they skirted the

Imperial Sea, the Yellow Sea of today, laying hands on Korea, the Hermit Kingdom. One would have thought that they would not disturb the gods on top of the august Himalayas, Karakorum and Hindu Kush, but they did. They crossed those mountains and awed the native Pushtus with their might. They had reached what today we call Afghanistan. China was camping on the frontiers of her manifest destiny—the end of the earth.

The homebody Chinese must have believed that their fighting men, having reached the rim of the earth, were now dangling their feet into the bottomless pit. They must have believed, too, that all the world was paying homage to them and that tributary caravans were thronging the imperial roads. They knew, too, that in the presence of the imperial radiance, the genealogies of the nobility paled into insignificance. Because of that, officials were selected less according to birth than through competitive tests. At the end of the second century A.D. some thirty thousand students were in attendance at the college of doctors alone. This was a high point of Chinese history, the rule of the later Han dynasty, and proudly the Chinese called themselves the Sons of Han.

Born of that national arrogance came the end of a cycle, the decline, at the beginning of the third century A.D. The designations of the regimes that followed give an indication of the nature of these troubled times: the Three Kingdoms, under which the Chinese earth was convulsed with upheavals; the Six Dynasties, under which civil wars became endemic. The dynasty of the Sui lasted only for thirty years, and then came the T'angs, weak-elbowed and weak-kneed. After their downfall, another chain of sickly reigns emerged, the names of which again tell their stories: the Five Dynasties, and then the Ten Independent States.

THE PERFECT WARRIOR

His name was Temujin, but history knows him as Genghis Khan, the leader of the Mongols. At the mention of the dreaded name the population of entire towns committed suicide. Falling into the hands of this foe was worse than death. Frightfulness was a secret of the "Perfect Warrior," the fantastic Khan. Other secrets were organization and charismatic leadership. From the home ground of the tribal federation, with its capital at Karakorum in Mongolia, the horsemen charged across thousands of miles, across drought-scourged areas, into the densely settled regions of the Eurasian plains, into the heart of Europe, to the Danube, the Adriatic, and the Elbe. That was a fabulous achievement, but not unique. Unique was their ability to vault the walls and subdue presumably impenetrable China.

For the first time in her history, China fell under alien rule. A Mongol regime, the Yuan dynasty, was established. Huge though China was, she formed only a small part of the Mongol possessions. In 1260, Kublai, the grandson of Genghis, became the Khan. Eventually, he set up his winter capital in Khanbalik, which was to be called Peking.

This was the China of whose high civilization Marco Polo wrote, the country with technical knowledge ahead of that of the West. It had invented movable type, the magnetic compass, clockwork, and the kite. It had invented gunpowder, too, and also the *huo chien*, the fire arrow, the first rocket, consisting of a hollow bamboo stick packed with chemical powder. When the country's ruler, Kublai Khan, was asked what he wanted to have

from the West, he did not ask for additional engines of
destruction. He asked for men of learning, well-versed in
the sciences and arts. The Chinese raised the Mongols to
their own high level.

All the great empires had come and gone, the Egyptian,
Babylonian, Greek, Macedonian, and Roman. China appeared to be on the verge of such a fate. She was not
conquered by the Mongols—she absorbed them. Again the
conqueror was conquered. China survived eternal and
unique. Then came Chu Yuan-chang and China's new
avatar.

THE LUMINOUS DYNASTY

Chu Yuan-chang had been given by his peasant parents
to a Buddhist monastery to save him from starvation, and
grains of rice in the friars' begging cup sustained him for
a while. Then he joined the rebels against the Yuan
regime and eventually became their leader. He was possessed of charismatic gifts, and victorious over the Mongols, he founded a dynasty, which in turn, extended its
sway to Mongolia and Manchuria. Beginning with the
middle of the fourteenth century, the ex-beggar's family
ruled for about two hundred and seventy years, under the
name of "Luminous"—Ming. Under them, China was
Tien hsia, All Under Heaven—and *Ta-t'ng*, Great Unity,
was its goal. Again the indestructibility of Chinese culture
was demonstrated by the Mings. The world of today re-
members them because of the works of art produced
under their aegis, paintings suffused "with divine im-
manence," a world of reality in man's dreams. The china-
ware in brilliant colors created in the imperial plants has
never been surpassed.

It was an age of paradox in which great creative talent was combined with monumental works of destruction. In our own age, China's Communist leader, Mao Tse-tung, gave world-wide currency to a Ming proverb: "Out of the gun barrel, power grows." Power did not grow out of it for long, however, because corruption counteracted the might of the gun, and eunuch-controlled court cabals bemused the regime. The vastness of the country caused fragmentation, and provincial satraps became "heavenly guides," battening upon a helpless peasantry and unaware of the price the future was to pay. Again China was on the verge of dissolution, and again the country's life forces were ebbing away. Again there was an invasion. The last Ming committed suicide, followed in 1644 by the Manchu dynasty, which lasted through the first decade of the twentieth century. Its name was *Ch'ing,* Pure.

The Chinese miracle occurred again; the rulers were absorbed by their subjects, and the conqueror was conquered. Again China expanded, from Hainan to Sakhalin, from Korea to the Pamirs. Also, the population increased greatly, and the works of art were in great demand. But these rulers lacked dynamism, were little concerned with their subjects. Again the country was in ferment. The imperishable quality of China was manifested again. The people still believed that theirs was the Middle Kingdom and that foreign princes were mere tribute-bearing slaves. China was alive but aslumber. "Let China be asleep," Napoleon advised. "The world will be sorry when she awakes."

These "slaves" included the European powers that had found the southern tier of Asia a power vacuum, and filled it out with their arrogant presence. The smaller the country, the more arrogant it was. The small nations of western Europe, Holland and Portugal, were the most aggressive ones. They were followed by the British and the French.

The vast expanses of southern Asia became colonies. Most of fabulous India was in British hands.

Telltale signs indicated that the Middle Kingdom was also ripe to be colonized. But China was saved again, this time by the voracity of her foes. None of them dared to tackle the monumental operation alone. They lopped off chunks of the land mass in strategic areas, concentrating on the major ports.

There were too many aspirants for the spoils. The major despoilers were joined now by the hangers-on: Germans, Japanese, Russians, and Americans. The United States proclaimed its stand in the Open Door Policy. The gates of China were not to be slammed closed in Uncle Sam's face by the charter members of colonialism. Thus China did not share the fate of India, and did not become a colony. Constantly losing face, the Manchu dynasty could no longer hang on. Its end came in 1912, with a Western-type revolution. China—the universe—was to become a nation and her subjects citizens. Western-educated Sun Yat-sen represented the ideology of the West, and his policy was to be the country's homage to the common man, as indicated by its name, *San Min Chu I*— Peoples' Three Principles. The three principles were: nationalism, socialism, and democracy. China was to leap from the Middle Ages into the twentieth century.

NEW TIME OF TROUBLES

Sun Yat-sen was an ideologue, not a man versed in practical politics. When he died in 1925 he left the outlines of a new age, but no new foundations. There was to be sure the Kuomintang, the National People's Party, but it too was a rallying cry more than a working organiza-

tion. The Chinese had to learn to handle the three principles, and do that from scratch. Chiang Kai-shek, heir to
the troubles of Sun Yat-sen, went for light to the Communist Mecca, Moscow's Kremlin.

"Democratic republicanism" was the designation of the
ten-year period 1911–1921. It had caused three nation-
wide civil wars, created a thousand war lords, and entailed huge domestic and foreign debts, but it had brought
neither political nor economic stability, let alone progress.
The system of the "Great Western Orientation" had been
proved ineffectual in solving China's problems, and the
political parties were shown to be impotent. The Great
War of 1914–1918 had helped to confirm the defects of
Western civilization and of the peace conference in particular. Three hundred thousand White Russians, many
of them in penury, flooded such cities as Harbin, Tientsin,
and Shanghai, bringing to an end the myth of European
superiority. The reactions of the Chinese people to this
changed and still changing situation were divided: some
went back to what they called "the quintessence of Chinese learning," others, unconvinced of the futility of
Western learning, continued to be its advocates; others,
again, saw a gleam of light through the Bolshevik revolution in Russia. That is why Chiang Kai-shek went to the
Kremlin for help.

The Communists taught Chiang how to organize a
modern army, and so, starting from the extreme south, he
launched his notable Northern Expedition, which was to
clean the country of the war lords, the locusts. The Expedition was singularly successful. Then Chiang decided to
shift his power base. From the many, the poor, he re-
oriented it to the few, the rich. He turned against his
former Communist allies. Nobody counted the bodies of
his victims in those days, and the estimates, usually from
Communist sources, are fantastically high. The procedure

of trial was simple. The shoulder of the accused was given a quick look, and if it revealed signs of abrasion, he was no longer of this world. The rifle strap was the death-dealing proof. Execution was on the spot, the revolver against the skull and then the fatal shot.

One of the men who had escaped the execution was a young man from Shaoshanch'ung, in Hunan province, Mao Tse-tung, of peasant origin, a graduate of the National University of Peking, organizer of the Communist Party in Shanghai, and now secretary of the party branch in Hunan.

Mao organized the First Front Army, of which he was the political director, while Chu Teh was the military chief. They were surrounded by the Kuomintang armies, and they knew what would happen to them if they were defeated. The pressure increased, and in 1934 Mao's forces broke through the opposing nationalist troops to stage its epic "Long March" to Shensi province. On the map Hunan and Shensi are close, but they were thousands of miles apart the way the escapees marched, across some of Asia's most forbidding "moonscape" mountain areas. After unbelievable hardships the Communists set eyes on their promised land in Shensi, where they set up their capital in Yenan.

Summing up the Long March, Mao said on December 27, 1935:

We say that the Long March was the first of its kind ever recorded in history. . . . For twelve months we were under daily reconnaisance and bombing from the air by scores of planes; we were encircled, pursued, obstructed, and intercepted on the ground by a big force of several hundred thousand men; we encountered untold difficulties and great obstacles on the way, but by keeping our two feet going we swept across a distance of more than twenty thousand *li* through the length and breadth of eleven provinces. Well, has there ever been in history a long march like ours? No, never.

The Chinese scholar Jerome Ch'en said about this epic event:

One may compare the Long March with Hannibal's journey across the Alps and say smugly that the Chinese did better, or with Napoleon's retreat from Moscow and say coldly that the Chinese did worse. But it must be admitted that man has never seen the equal of it before or since. In 370 days the First Front Army under Mao Tse-tung walked on and on, to cover a distance of six thousand miles.

A COUNTRY WITHIN A COUNTRY

Only in China could this happen. It could happen there because it was in the local tradition, the war-lords' way of life, and also because of the ruggedness of the country, its lack of communications, the ineffectiveness of the Kuomintang government, and the charismatic personality of Mao. Above all, it could happen because the peasantry had had enough of the ruthless landlord rule, had had enough of being treated as an inferior breed.

Under the prevailing regime the common people were considered objects, like cattle. What they were thinking about was nobody's concern. They were meant to work like draft animals. That's what counted. Work for the landlord, a feudal potentate. Not only did these peasants lead a vegetative existence, but they were considered sub-human. Then came the Communists. We have a name for what they now started doing—we call it brainwashing. From their point of view it was something more positive. They were getting the people closely involved, interested in their program. They made them believe that they were people who counted. This is what they did.

They organized the *hsueh-si*, group study, in which all had to take part; the peasant, former landlord, the city dweller, the artisan, peddler, merchant, manager, and even the "enemy of society," the political prisoner. Nobody was overlooked; nobody was considered unimportant. The group was small, consisting of six to twelve persons. The leaders were elected. Every member of the group was called upon to express opinions, and silence was not brooked. Nor was parroting the official doctrine, or the mechanical acknowledgment of the reasonableness of the party line, acceptable. The important thing was to absorb the "correct" theory so as to discredit "incorrect" conceptions. This had to be accomplished so thoroughly that the group member should be delighted to accept the correct line. The intellectual, for instance, had to admit that the source of all progress was labor, and therefore had to be eager to participate in farm work, unless he wanted to be considered filled with bourgeois prejudice. Raising of one's "political consciousness level" through group study was a lifelong process. Mao himself needed the party routine. Leadership quality was quickly recognized, and promising students became cadre members, *kanpu*, organizers. Ideologically sound, the student was expected to spread the light. He was supposed to be also a talent scout, discovering new talent and spreading membership involvement. This way a network of committed party stalwarts formed the foundation of a new regime.

Japan invaded China's Manchuria in 1931, and the Far Eastern era of wars began. It was to last more than eighteen years. In the face of the Japanese danger, former mortal enemies, the Kuomintang and the Communists, had to conclude a truce. Then the second World War erupted, in the course of which Communist armed strength increased from forty thousand to a million. Japan was now the only imperialist power in the land. She had eliminated all the foreign concessions, international settlements, free ports, and special rights. Nippon had shown that white skin is not a badge of superiority; the Communists in Shensi did not let the Chinese forget this lesson in pigmentation.

Cats have nine lives—but China proved to have 999 lives. The Japanese took possession of the vital parts of China—the river arteries and ports—and yet China survived. Her Western friends were no longer able to provide war material, and they themselves were dependent upon American lend-lease. Limited Soviet aid reached fighting China via the ancient silk route, through Sinkiang and Soviet Central Asia. Yet China survived. Corruption in high places was a fact of life, the same as droughts and locusts. China had survived that too. But now the corruption was compounded by Japanese depredations. Could China survive all these plagues? "Greed, corruption, favoritism, more taxes, a ruined currency, terrible waste of life, and callous disregard of all the rights of men" characterized the rule of Chiang Kai-shek, according to General J. W. Stilwell, in charge of all American forces in the China-Burma-India theater. The State Department in Washington described Chiang as "the hostage of the corrupt forces he manipulates."

THE COMMUNISTS ARE COMING!

Joseph Stalin did not think that the Communists could win against Chiang after World War II. That is what he told a Yugoslav delegation to his Kremlin office just before the historic decision, and he advised the Maoist delegation to make peace with Chiang. The Maoists continued the fight, and the nationalist forces fell apart. After having survived all calamities to which human flesh and soul were heirs, was Chinese history ready to close the books?

The American consular official Angus Ward was an eye-witness to subsequent events in China, and reported later at an Overseas Press Club meeting in New York. He had his tour of duty in China when the Kuomintang held the helm. At the approach of Chiang's soldiers Chinese peasants shut their huts tightly. Nothing was secure in the presence of the rampaging hordes. Then came the armies of Mao, and consul Ward had a spell of freedom before he, "an imperialist agent," was marched off to jail. "The Communists appeared to be people from another planet," the American official reported. "Property was sacred to them—the poor people's property. There was no looting, and that was unprecedented in recent Chinese history." Eventually, consul Ward was freed.

The Communists took over a classical land of D.I.P.—disease, ignorance, and poverty. The average expectation of life, 35 years at birth, demonstrated the prevalence of disease. Ignorance was fantastically high, and literacy abysmally low. Taking the price index as 100 in 1937, it was 558,900,000 eleven years later. The estimated income per head was 50 dollars a year.

China had not had a quiet moment for the last century, with wars, the presence of greedy foreigners, corruption in places high and low, revolutions, counterrevolutions, starvation, epidemics, then the "new age" inaugurated by Japan, the presumed Greater East Asia Co-Prosperity Sphere (in reality, Greater East Asia Spoliation Feast). Then the worst scourge, anarchy, with hundreds of war lords, many of them brutal beyond belief. There was the story of the woman whose husband had dared to raise his voice against the war-lord and who was taken away. The

family was starving, and she implored the lord to return
him. "Take him away," he said, "he is in the garden."
There her husband was, indeed, decapitated, his head
resting on his belly. The war-lord's soldiers brutally kept
her from taking away the head. This was one incident,
out of many, recorded by the French writer André Mal-
raux in his unconventional autobiography.

Other tragedies were to follow—the civil war, compounded with the disaster of the Japanese invasion. Could
man be as inhuman as he was in this instance, and still
remain man? And this in the land of Confucius and of the
Tao, in the land that venerated Buddha, too, one of the
most human of all humans. After thousands of years
China was to succumb. Or was she?

Then came the new revelation. It was in the Chinese
tradition, the new ethical principle, Communist Confucianism, Taoism, Buddhism, the new father figure, Mao.
As he saw himself and wanted other people to see him:

> *Dawn glows in the East, the sun is rising,*
> *Mao Tse-tung has appeared in China.*
> *He wants happiness for the people,*
> *And, indeed, he is their savior.*

Wretched poetry, this, except for the believer, for
whom it was a revelation from beyond the floating Blue
Mountains of Chinese lore. It was also an intrusion of the
outside world, the voices of the new prophets, Lenin and
Marx. But not quite that, because China was, after all, the
Middle Kingdom, the pivot of the universe. So, Maoism
was superimposed upon Marxism and Leninism.

To Marx—and to a lesser extent, to Lenin too—mankind's history was divided into two parts, B.I. and A.I.
—"Before Industrialization" and "After Industrialization."
Industrialization was the dividing line between the A.D.
and the A.L.—the "Age of Darkness" and the "Age of

Light." Socialism, communism, could thrive only in the soil fructified by factories. The proletarians were the factory workers, not the peasants—certainly not to Marx.

But China was the country of loess, of the eternally virile soil, the peasant land. To wait for industrialization to begin under the old regime was inconceivable. Industrialization under such conditions would continue to be the function of foreign capital, greedy, grasping, alien-oriented, anti-Chinese—humiliating, in one word. Contrary to what Marx and Lenin had said, the new era in China was to be based on the peasants. That was the Mao doctrine, a new article of faith. "The broad peasant masses," Mao said, "have risen to fulfill their historic mission. The democratic forces in the rural areas have risen to overthrow the rural feudal power. . . . This is a marvelous feat that has never been achieved in the last forty or even in a thousand years."

This is how the Maoists gained control of the country— through the peasants, and not by way of the urban areas. The classical strategy of civil wars had always been to gain control of the center, of the capital, the motivating agency. The Russian Communists gained eight and a half million square miles by controlling less than fifty square miles—the nerve centers of Petrograd and Moscow. The rest of the country followed. In the Chinese civil war the order was reversed. The Communists first gained control of the rural areas, with the aid of the peasants, who wanted a change of regime—any change. The cities were sucked into the whirlwind.

THE GREAT LEAP FORWARD

"The Chinese state," China-watcher Robert S. Elegant observed in the October 1967 issue of *Foreign Affairs,* "was for two thousand years aloof and self-centered as no

other great realm has been. It developed in substantial
isolation from any realms which could claim to be its
material or cultural equal, and it was, quite self-evidently,
vastly superior in power and size to all its neighbors." Now
China was ready for, probably, the most self-centered and
substantial event of her history. It was an attempt, another Western critic observed, "to overcome the gravitational pull of the human body, soaring into the ether by
sheer will-power." But, asked still another observer: "Can
one train a nation of 600 million [China's estimated
population in 1958] into Olympic Marathon-runners?
Chairman Mao thinks it can be done." In their salad days,
the Soviets had set out, in Stalin's words, "to overtake and
surpass the United States." Now China set out to overtake
and surpass the Soviets—to move from the last to the first
place, the traditional place of the country, the Middle
Kingdom, the global center, the land of light in the midst
of the cosmic penumbra. This was arrogance, but not
from the traditional Chinese point of view, which the
revolutionary Mao represented. The arrogance was in the
historic tradition. It was China's way.

First, the gigantic body had to be imparted the momentum that was to perform the great change. The classical
Communist method was employed, patterned on the Soviets' *Piatiletka,* transmuted into Peking's Five Year Plan,
with emphasis on industrialization, particularly the
"heavies," the plants producing machines to produce some
more machines . . . until the cornucopia was filled to
bursting.

Temporarily, there was a compromise with national
pride, dependence upon imported skills. Not imported,
perhaps, because those were Communist skills, those of
the Soviet Union, thousands of technicians, ready to get
the momentous innovation moving, attending to more
than two hundred major industrial projects. Communist
brothers were to share everything. They would show how

to harness the awesome energy that man discovered had
been imprisoned in the minuscule atom.

Were they brothers, indeed? They were Communists.
Was this not the answer? But the Chinese found the Russians human machines. Somebody in the center, thousands of miles away, pushed a button, and the man
reacted. It was more automatic than the "conditioned
reflex." Machines have prescribed circuits, and so did
these Soviet technicians, cogs in the mechanism. That
was not, however, the Chinese way.

The Chinese way was "autonomous spontaneity and
creativity." So Chairman Mao said, and before him so had
said Confucius. Without it the Chinese would have been
buried long before in the dun-colored loess. Every situation was different, Chinese history had taught the sons of
the Middle Kingdom, and, therefore, one had to improvise,
and, if need be, play by ear. There used to be a Chinese
tradition, active in the country's dynamic spells of history,
known as *hsia-fang,*—transferring downward. This time
it meant the exchange of skills, particularly the transfer
of managers to the front lines of production, establishing
contact between the links of the chain of command. The
Soviet officials, more rigidly regimented, were critical of
these ways.

The Chinese, in turn, were disappointed too. The Soviet
technicians were helpful, indeed, in the same way they
were in India or Ghana, aiding an underdeveloped country
to build up its potential, to create a proletarian base, upon
which a socialist system could rest. But the secret of the
"million suns," the creative and destructive force of the
atom, continued to remain a Soviet mystery. There was no
sharing of the unsharable. Gradually, the Chinese learned
that for their Soviet mentors, too, nationalism was first
and communism second . . . or third . . . or tenth.
And that was a great disappointment. They found that

they could depend upon their own resources and resourcefulness, and nothing else.

Their greatest resource was their man-power, the hundreds of millions of people. How to activate them? They could not be activated in isolation. One machine in one hour could perform more work than a million people in a year. Labor had to be compounded. With what? The combination was this: the "labor-intensive sector," provided by muscle power, was to be combined with the capital-intensive sector, motivated by the government. "Walking on two legs," was the first description of this combination. Then the walking was speeded up and became the "leap," —the Great Leap Forward.

Only the Chinese could have thought of that. Only they, because of their historic memories as the center of the universe, the pivot of the world. Was it arrogance? Looking at it from the outside, yes. Looking at it from the Chinese angle, no. They had allowed themselves to be left behind, had been kicked around, treated as pariahs. All that lost time had to be made up. And so they turned to the device that they called "The General Line of Going All Out and Aiming High to Achieve Greater, Quicker, Better, and More Economical Results in Building Socialism." That was the Great Leap Forward—every Chinese was to be a Marathon athlete. "The crux of the Great Leap was," observed *The Economist* of London," the general mobilization of underemployed rural labor, a drive unprecedented in human history, to put to work every hour of the day hundreds of millions of bare hands."

The core of the Great Leap Forward was the commune, based on the traditional administrative unit, *hsiang*. The existing collectives were fused into some twenty-six thousand communes, gigantic human ant heaps, producing units, in which men, women, and children were to toil from dawn to dusk, with a purpose, a dedication, and community involvement. The beginnings were difficult, but then, after a while, there was the reward of a better life.

The accent in the communes was on cooperation. While they supplanted the traditional system of clans, they raised it, in reality, to a higher potential. All the thousands of commune members were units of the same family. Since the most important "natural resource" of the country was the human hand, the accent was on labor-intensive projects. Members were organized in units— farming, forestry, industries, services, and the rest of the broad gamut of human occupations. One of the major problems was that of farming communities throughout the land. There was the growing season of intense work and then nature's hibernation, involving inevitable human lassitude. There were no such spells of langor in this purposeful land. Between the growing seasons, the country folk were to work in small-scale industrial plants of their own creation. In homemade backyard furnaces, close to a hundred million peasants were smelting iron; and the same number of people were collecting manure, animal and human, for the production of fertilizers. Tens of millions were moving countless tons of earth for the building of irrigation dams, and so on all the way down the line.

The communes also were to provide numerous services, including education, sanitation, communication, transportation, marketing, and other forms of trade. They ran scientific research institutes and operated as accounting units. The communes operated also the public mess halls and the nurseries, supplanting many of the functions of the individual families.

Leaps are usually of short duration. This was an unusual Great Leap, lasting for two years. It was a magnificent experiment, thoroughly Chinese, and devastatingly inefficient. The Great Leap Forward became the great flop backward. Again China had to go on short rations. The towering ambition of overtaking and surpassing the Soviets, America, all the rest of the world, failed to materialize.

Somebody or something was to be blamed. Since the accusing finger was that of Mao, he was exempt from censure. National calamities were blamed at first (and they could not talk back)—insect plagues, droughts, and floods, not the classic Ten Plagues of Egypt, but the hundred plagues of China. Then the blame was shifted to "bourgeois elements" that had penetrated the revolutionary ranks. The Soviets now raised their voice and intoned: "We told you so." The real cause of the fiasco was, of course, the impossibility of the task. China was deeply hurt, and her resentment was directed against the Soviets —neighbor and comrade, also rival and foe.

THE RELIGIOUS CONFLICT

At first, Mao too was a member of the ecumenical community of communism, as were members of the Communist establishments elsewhere. He accentuated the importance of the "solidarity of the Socialist countries under Soviet leadership," as late as the fortieth anniversary celebration of the Bolshevik revolution. Soviet leadership was an article of faith. He attacked the heresy of Yugoslavia, using the usual trite and tired words. In critical situations and in meeting everyday problems Mao's words of praise for the Kremlin were so standardized and pat that the printer's type could be left standing, with no change.

The change occurred after the failure of the Great Leap Forward. Within the Communist commonwealth the Chinese had been related to an inferior status, and that was

intolerable for the Middle Kingdom. One of the first
broadsides was discharged by the wearer of a prestigious
name, Soong Ching-ling, Vice Chairman of the People's
Republic of China, and widow of Sun Yat-sen, the central
figure of modern China's hall of fame. This is what she
said: "At the Twenty-second Congress of the Communist
Party of the Soviet Union, the revisionist Khrushchev
clique developed its revisionism into a complete system.
. . . " Revisionism in the Communist vocabulary means
heresy. It means "revising the basic tenets of Marxism," so
as to reach an accommodation with the class enemies, the
bourgeoisie and international imperialism. Now the Chinese leadership found that the Soviets were not entitled to
their privileged position at the head of the movement. The
Kremlin had abdicated its leading role because it ceased to
fight the class enemy. Instead of that it was advocating
coexistence with the capitalist world. This meant sur-
render.

Now the Chinese propaganda barrage was discharged,
and historic grievances were recalled. The Soviets were
usurping vast tracts of land in Central Asia, formerly
Chinese territory, all the way to the Caspian Sea. They
had wrested Outer Mongolia, inhabited by kinsfolk, from
China. The Soviets' far east and their maritime provinces
had belonged to the Middle Kingdom. The Kremlin had
tried to despoil Peking of Sinkiang, Chinese Turkestan,
the country's far west.

The Chinese now broached the most basic questions of
foreign policy. They went beyond accusing the Kremlin of
the supreme sin of coexistence with the foe. They charged
that the Soviets were conspiring with the Americans to
dominate the world. "So long as Moscow clings to the line
of Soviet-U.S. cooperation for world domination," said the
mayor of Peking, Peng Chen, as far back as 1964, "Moscow's gestures of Communist unity and opposition to

imperialism are mere subterfuges and camouflage. Under these circumstances, it is impossible for the Soviet Union to join the true Marxist-Leninists in any united action against the enemy." No longer did the Chinese speak about Soviet leadership within the fraternal countries. On the contrary, they called Soviet policy repeatedly (in the authoritative *Peking Review*, too) "pure national egoism, by one-sidedly demanding that other fraternal countries should submit to its needs, while opposing others' national interests. In the economic field, particularly, the Soviet High Command exerted pressure on the fraternal nations to keep them in line—the Kremlin's line—preventing them from following their own national advantages in improving their economies."

Words were followed by deeds. Mao's famous statement "Power grows out of the barrel of the gun" had to be updated: "Power grows out of the mushroom of the nuclear bomb." Making the bomb required supreme technical sophistication, which China, with her fifty-dollars-a-head annual income was not expected to possess. A Chinese proverb says: "The journey of a thousand miles must begin with a single step." In 1963 China took that step, which led to covering the proverbial thousand miles. It was after the rupture of Sino-Soviet relations that China built the Lanchow nuclear reactor, in Kansu province, on the historic Silk Road. In 1965 the "Mao I Bomb" was exploded at the Lop Nor marshy salt lake in the extreme west. With surprising rapidity the Chinese were ready to move to the production of the H-Bomb. In 1967 they detonated such a device over the black sand dunes of their Takla Makan desert.

Encouraged by these successes, the Chinese embarked upon a bolder program in the foreign field. The largest part of the world was underdeveloped, embracing more than two-thirds of the population of the globe, and the

Chinese felt that they, recently underdeveloped, were the natural leaders of the underprivileged. "Mao's revolutionary theories," said Liu Shao-Chi, Chief of State and later target of Mao's shafts, "charted a path to power not only for the Chinese people but for the billion folk in the colonial areas of southeast Asia."

Mao had experience in lining up the famished people of the world, as demonstrated by his classic strategy of taking the countryside first, and then the urban centers. The underdeveloped countries were the global equivalents of the countryside, and the developed nations were the urban centers. The Soviet Union belonged in the latter category. What was the conclusion? China was in a strategic position vis-à-vis the Soviets. The roles now appeared to be reversed. Not the Soviets but the Chinese appeared to be the natural leaders—the role reserved for the Middle Kingdom.

And so the feud continued, the words getting more bitter. By the middle sixties the split appeared to be complete. "The fight against imperialism headed by the United States and its lackeys, and the fight against revisionism, with the leading group of the Soviet Communist Party at its center, are two inseparable tasks." This was part of a joint statement by China and Albania on May 14, 1966.

The epithets were bitter, but even more so were the sentiments underlying them, which reached the outside world by way of the grapevine. The author of this book had a taste of them when standing near the Chinese frontier, in the Gobi desert of the People's Republic of Mongolia, in the summer of 1966. Standing with him were three Oxford dons who had just emerged from Red China after a visit of three months. They were objective observers who called attention to some positive factors under the Mao regime. Abject poverty, they said, so typical of the country, had been eliminated. While the food supply was not ample, it was enough to keep away hunger pangs. In spite of the great cultural revolution, then running amuck, China was no longer a victim of epidemics of starvation. Also the standards of honesty were very high. But. . .

The hatreds cultivated by the regime were beyond belief. On the surface, the concentrated venom was directed against the archfiend, the enemy of human civilization, the superimperialist—the United States. But that was only on the surface. These Englishmen had been in contact with knowledgeable diplomats, in possession of information unavailable to common clay. The real hatred in China, they unanimously agreed, was directed against the Soviets, so deep and unfathomable that they saw it as a serious cause for concern. The concern was the peace of the world.

THE COUNTERATTACK

Soviet attacks on the bourgeois and the imperialists have a common trait. They convey the impression of being undertaken not so much in anger as in sorrow. If only the attacked people could open their minds! Why can they not see reason—the reason of Marxism-Leninism? Also, Soviet attacks are never directed against an entire nation. Always they are directed against the "ruling circles." They are "impure," while the "masses" are pure.

The Soviet attacks on Communist China deviated from the usual pattern. They were—and they are—uttered in deep anger, not in sorrow. But they too are directed against the ruling clique of China, not the masses. Civil wars are known to be more bitter than wars against an outside enemy. Religious wars are even more bitter than civil wars. This was now a religious war between two sects of one faith.

Typical of this bitterness was the authoritative article
by F. Dimin in the Soviet publication *Selskaya Zhizn*. All
articles in a controlled press are authoritative, especially
when they deal with basic factors, as did this article, published in the April 12, 1968, issue of the periodical.

Because Socialist reforms were carried out at first "according to the principles of Marxism-Leninism," the
author said, China's farm program had been making
progress. The grain harvests had been successful, and
thus it had become possible to combat famines. Raw
materials had been available for industrial production,
especially for the consumer industries. But beginning with
1960 the Chinese were plunged into a series of disasters
they had not experienced before. This was the result of
the Great Leap Forward, a tragic mistake. During the
period 1960–1962, the Russian author charged, misman-
agement had caused havoc in the country. Although the
officers and men of the Liberation Army were in a privileged position in comparison with the rest of the people,
food deficiency diseases became epidemic even among
them.

"There was nothing accidental about this," the Soviet
writer continued. The forcible organization of the people's
communes, the compulsory melting of steel by all peasants, using primitive methods, the disdain shown for the
Leninist principles of agriculture, and the shortage of
seeds undermined the basis of farming. The 1961 harvest
was the lowest ever. . . . Beginning with that year
China has been importing some five to six million tons of
grain a year.

"All this was a direct consequence of Mao Tse-tung's
fallacious economic policy, which has destroyed the
peasant's interest in his farm output, exhausted his physical and moral strength, undermining his faith in the
policies of the Peking leadership."

The peasant's wretched plight was reflected not only in his inadequate income, the author continued, but also in his low cultural level, in the limited educational opportunities of his children, and in the poor medical service. About half of the population was illiterate, and thirty million out of a hundred million children were not afforded a chance to attend even primary schools. The peasant paid 250 yuans for a surgical operation, and that was almost the yearly income of his entire family.

Conditions were not better in the factories either, the Soviet author set forth. There wages have been frozen for nearly a decade. A large part of the labor force was seasonal, its pro-rata pay one quarter lower than that of the full-time staff. Both industrial goods and food products were rigidly rationed.

Not only was the government unconcerned with providing the workers with their livelihood, but it continued to reduce essential investments to the lowest levels. The production brigades—working-force units—were warned: "You must not ask for three things: grain, money, and materials." Everything was for the state, and nothing for the individual. It looked as if the individuals were not members of the state.

There was a tragic emergency in Hupeh province, according to the Soviet author. And what did Peking do? The emergency was a major earthquake. And this is what the Chinese government did. It dispatched soldiers to Hupeh; that in itself would have been to the good, if they had been prepared to extend a helping hand to the wretched people of the province. They were not so prepared. So they formed a study group to concentrate on Chairman Mao's thoughts.

Having experienced the hardships created by Mao's policies, the peasants have turned their thoughts to self-defense. In many parts of the country, they started resisting attempts to collect the grain tax due to the state. Reports started reaching the capital about the peasants' dividing up the land-holdings of the cooperatives, disposing of the farm tools and draft animals, dividing the proceeds among themselves.

Other attacks in the Soviet press were even more poisonous. In the Moscow periodical *Communist* the Russian author went all the way out in hinting at sinister events in Mao's past. In the thirties, a close collaborator of Mao, Kang Sheng, was the security officer of the Kuomintang, which, in the hands of Chiang Kai-shek, was massacring Communists. Mao survived. Were the dead victims of a foul deed to which Mao himself may have been privy? (The Soviet author does not say that Mao's wife was one of the victims.)

And another serious charge in the Russian periodical: in the early days of the war, the Comintern urged Mao to be more active in fighting the Japanese. The Soviets were apprehensive of the danger of Japan attacking them in the Far East. That would have meant a two-front war for them, with added dangers for the future, and a greater likelihood of defeat. Mao paid no attention to the Comintern's admonition. Was he so callous because he wanted to have the Soviets crushed?

"It is good to sit on a high perch and watch two tigers fight," says a Chinese proverb the Soviet author quotes. Mao was sitting on the high perch while the United States and the Soviet Union were battling the Axis. They, especially the Soviets, were in mortal danger, and that suited Mao's aims.

As early as the thirties, the Soviet author concludes, the Communist party in the province of Shensi had warned against the "monarchistic-militaristic psychology of Mao Tse-tung, who followed the line of Napoleon." He went so far as to expect the peasants to kiss his portrait in areas

controlled by his troops. He had always been a megalo-
maniac. Worse still, from the Soviet point of view: "Mao
has always been a nationalist."

THE GREAT CULTURAL REVOLUTION

Nowhere else could it have happened, said the Italian
writer Alfredo Moravia, referring to China's Great Cultural
Revolution. And had it happened anywhere else, utter
destruction would have marked its track. It was anarchy
intended to trigger the ultimate in chaos, grinding up all
the millennial-established values of an ancient culture. It
was unleashed by Mao Tse-tung, engineer of a new age,
and it appeared to be directed against that epoch. It
seemed to be the most nonsensical movement conceived
by a man's brain. So, the question arose: was that brain
demented?

The very designation of the movement, Great Cultural
Revolution, was a paradox. Anticultural—that is what it
looked to unjaundiced eyes. Young people were ordered
out of their schoolrooms, into the streets, there to shout
and disrupt life, to demonstrate against thought and logic,
humiliating learned men, their teachers, reveling in emo-
tional orgies. They were to exchange years of education
for disjointed sentences contained in minuscule booklets
in red covers, *Chairman Mao's Thoughts*. Those thoughts
were for all occasions, and, presumably, for all times.
They were supposed to be distilled from the wisdom of all
ages—thoughts and creed, the past infused into the
present, fading into the future. They were the "eternal
guidelines."

As to the meaning of the term Cultural Revolution:
"culture" is presumed to mean the sciences and arts,
distinguished from vocational, professional, and technical

skills. To the Chinese it means more, a loftier reality. It means what the Greek classics meant by *paideia*, and what *humanitas* meant to classic Rome. It means manners, and more, a way of life. Cultural revolution means an agitated movement on the level of superstructure, and not on the social level, the structure. To Mao, the cultural revolution indicated the "right path," leading to the "right goals," which are ageless, eternal. But, then, these are Buddhist terms, which the Communist leaders—atheists —must have absorbed from their country's past.

In spite of the fiasco of the Great Leap Forward, from which China had recovered, China was not doing too badly before the cultural explosion. Why did Mao, the key figure, not let the country settle down to a more even tenor of life, letting the human ant heap continue its endlessly assiduous work? The ultimate objective had been to lift the nation to a higher level of material welfare. Why was it necessary to interrupt the process? Did he do it because he had parted with reality, become irrational, living in a world of fancy?

Judging by the results, which we shall see, there seemed to be method to his exotic conduct, which was motivated by reasons that appeared to be valid to him. He saw what had happened to the Soviet Union, losing its hold, getting conservative, even "reactionary," attached to the status quo of its creation, its revolutionary life forces running out. He did not want China to become bourgeois, devoid of revolutionary sap. A new class had been created in the Soviet bloc of countries, a class of managers and bureaucrats, what Milovan Djilas called the "new ruling class." To Mao, equalitarianism was a basic factor of communism.

Then the paradox. He did not include himself in his objection to the status quo. He was the authority on the permanent revolution, the Teacher, the Guide, whose

thoughts were valid for all ages. What did the younger
people know about the new concepts of history—the
methods of guerrilla campaigns in war and peace, the
division of the world into rural areas and urban centers?
That first step he had made in Shensi was the beginning.
He knew where he was going, where China was going. He
knew it—the younger people did not. "Long and devious
will be the class struggle," he had pointed out in his discussion of "The Correct Handling of Contradictions
Among the People." "Even when all the counterrevolutionaries have been rooted out, new ones may emerge." He
knew how to handle them.

Also, he knew how to face problems of foreign affairs.
"Can the tiger be turned into a vegetarian?" China was
surrounded by "imperialists"—the Soviet Union on one
side, the United States on the other. America had forced
her way into Asia, and might be bent on global domination. To counteract these dangers, China must retain her
revolutionary *élan*, rendered physically effective by the
new unconventional weapons.

Was he too old to lead a global conflict? Was China too
old? China was eternal, and so was he. The head must be
mature and sage—his own—but the muscles must be
young, the driving force of youth. Therefore the "Red
Guards," revolutionary standard-bearers, from the
schools, and also from plants and farms.

A MILLION HEROES

The historic enemies—the ex-war-lords, the unspeakable landlords—were gone. There were now the new
enemies, the compromisers, the "flameless faggots,"
spreading the foul smell of smoke. Under the title of *How*

to Be a Good Communist?, Liu Shao-Chi had written a
book that was compulsory reading for millions of young
people. The author of the book had been Mao's close
collaborator, and was now Chief of State. To Mao he was
a fossil, his thoughts a decade old. Liu did not know that
revolutions had to "revolve" and could not sink into
apathy. The Red Guards turned against him, in possession
of "factual proofs," provided, no doubt, by Mao, that he
had taken the capitalist road, forming the core of a gang
of counterrevolutionaries, linked to the Kuomintang of
Chiang Kai-shek. That was as if Martin Luther had been
accused of having been a tool of Rome.

Many other former revolutionary leaders fell under the
ban. Public figures, in the government, the press, and
other fields were publicly pilloried, attacked on wall
newspapers, at meetings, often dumped into open trucks,
forced to wear dunce caps. They "lost face," a particularly
cruel punishment in China. Among these was the venerable chairman of the Academy of Sciences, Kuo Mo-jo,
head of the propaganda section of the Military Council,
author of seminal works, who was forced to "confess and
repent." He blabbered: "All the works I have written
should be burned."

Similar treatment was accorded to other key figures: to
the general secretary of the party, Teng Hsiao-p'ing; to the
mayor of Peking, Peng Chen; the first secretary of the
party committee of the capital, Lu Ting-yi, who was also
the chief of its propaganda department; the chief of staff
of the People's Liberation Army, Lo Jui-ching; leading
staff members of the official news organs, *The People's
Daily* and *The Red Flag*.

The reign of terror spread in widening circles, and
chaos was compounded. In Canton, capital of Kwangtung,
fighting broke out between the "true Maoist" groups, Red
Banners, and allegedly anti-Maoists, labeled "Ism Troop-

ers." In some cases fanatic Maoists engaged others in street feuds. Some of these others called themselves "Million Heroes," and they had the reputation of being less extreme. Such brawls were especially numerous in Wuhan and the surrounding province of Hupeh.

As on many previous occasions of Chinese history, xenophobia erupted into the streets. Christian churches were defaced, streets renamed; more European nuns were expelled; foreign books were frowned upon; shopkeepers were ordered to remove alien names. Western diplomats were mishandled, and crew members of a Soviet ship abused. Diplomatic protests were pouring in on Peking.

Immune to this campaign of vituperation were the "band of faithful," the co-workers of Mao, including Premier Chou En-lai and the Minister of National Defense, Lin Piao. Immunity was extended also to Li Fu-chun and Li Hsien-nien, members of the Politbureau, top policy-making group.

Meanwhile, the idolization of Mao reached paroxysmic peaks. The red book of quotations of his famous words became the script of China's hundreds of millions, not only to be read, but also recalled, and publicly professed. The following was reported as an instance of the translation of Chairman Mao to the highest "cultural" realm: scientists who had built a miraculously many-sided prototype of a machine felt impelled to express "their infinite faith, love, loyalty and admiration for Chairman Mao" in such a way that every time it started operating his portrait appeared, accompanied by the ideogram in his own hand-writing "Serve the people," and by the popular tune: "The East is Red." The machine was said to be an "all-purpose transistorized computer to be employed for the solution of problems of missile control, economics, and atomic energy."

For a while it looked as if China were on the way to

becoming again the fief of war lords. While some provinces were controlled by unruly bands of Red Guards, Red Banners, Million Heroes, and Ism Troops, others seemed to have fallen into army hands, and nobody appeared to know what had happened to such remote areas as Tibet and Sinkiang. And what happened to the schools where the Cultural Revolution had its start?

Very uncultural groups were reported to have taken control of hundreds of universities, colleges, research institutes, and other educational institutions. These were teams of workers, soldiers, and peasants which had entered institutions of higher learning in Peking, Shanghai, Wuhan, Nanchang, Sian, Taiyuan, Harbin, Urumchi, Kweiyang, and scores of other cities and towns throughout the country. They were acting on a directive of Mao, assigning a leading role to these teams. The take-over campaign was reported to have been "hailed by jubilant mass meetings and to have the enthusiastic concurrence of professors and students." Activists among the students and teachers could still have a share in the control of the schools if they were determined to carry out the proletarian revolution in education through to the end.

The immediate aim of the worker-soldier peasant teams entering the schools should be to carry out a purge, Mao said. He called this purge: "Struggle–Criticism–Transformation." It meant struggle against persons in authority taking the capitalist road; criticism of reactionary bourgeois academic authorities, and of other exploiting classes; and the transformation of education, literature, art, administrative and all kinds of office work—the entire superstructure that did not correspond to the socialist economic base.

For months the Great Cultural Revolution was being waged. It began in September 1965 and was still going on two years later. Gradually, it began to ebb away. The Red

Guards and their multi-faced substitutes were replaced by
a new type of organization, the Revolutionary Committee,
embodying a "three-way alliance—Red Guards, party
hierarchy, and the army." The Kwangsi Chuan Autonomous Region, bordering North Vietnam, was one of the
last areas to inaugurate its own Revolutionary Committee.
By the end of 1968, the Cultural Revolution was barely a
ripple. Who won? Who lost? How did China fare?

After all the noise, after all the high-pitched voices and
acrid recriminations, it was found that the victims of the
raucous commotion were not too many. Some people
lost their lives in street battles, according to Hong Kong
accounts. There were no reports of executions. Mao came
out strongly. His men commanded more peak positions in
the policy-making Politbureau and in the strategic Military Affairs Committee, of which he was ex-officio chairman, the most influential man in all China. Maoists
summed up the lessons they learned and the outcome of
the Great Cultural Revolution in these words: "It was the
most profound class struggle history has ever witnessed."

What was its effect on China? Was it followed by the
natural calamities to which the much-tried people had
become used, starvation and plagues? What has it accomplished? It has perpetuated the revolutionary fervor, preventing the people from lapsing back into their prerevolu-
tionary torpor. It stopped short of disaster.

There is a world of difference between the genial
philosopher Confucius and the prophet of perennial revolution, Mao Tse-tung. Yet the perceptive Alfredo Moravia,
in his analysis of China, has found great similarity between the two men and between the impacts of their
teachings upon their peoples. Moravia has found that
Confucianism and Maoism are closely related, in that the
individual has to be absorbed in the community envisaged
by both systems. In both systems the individual is held to

assume an attitude of respect and even of humility toward his superiors. He must consider himself the "perennial disciple, always ready to learn." That is the significance of the little red book of Chairman Mao's thoughts.

Thus spake Confucius:

Not more surely does the grass bend before the wind than the masses yield to the will of those above them.

If any ruler would submit to me as his director for twelve months, I should accomplish something considerable, and in three years I should attain the realization of my hopes.

Mao could have said this instead of Confucius, and his cultural revolution did not last the span of three years.

Maoism started with internationalism and then reverted to Confucius and nationalism.

No other country has undergone such basic changes. She had been a passive object, at the mercy of all the passers-by. She weathered a series of wars lasting a score of years, and witnessed the transformation of the modes of life for hundreds of millions, living in all types of climates, under all kinds of circumstances. She survived the catastrophic Great Leap and the calamitous Cultural Revolution, not any the worse for all these adversities. For the first time in her life, no foreigners intruded on her land, and she did not appear to be dependent on foreign aid. No country was less dependent than she—member of no alliance, nor of an international institution of any kind. She was a nuclear power, and due to that fact alone a supernation, perhaps a world force. She has been able to weather all the calamities to which countries are heirs—and even more. Truly, among all the countries of the world, history testified, there was only one that could be called eternal: her name was China, for weal or woe.

14

Outer Mongolia— Between Genghis Khan and Karl Marx

Mongolia may one day become the crossroads of the world, Bertrand Russell prophesied in the middle fifties. The British Nobel Prize winner saw Mongolia in those days far removed from great power conflicts because of her location; ready to become the focus of a new civilization; a landlocked successor of the Mediterranean culture of classic times.

Contrary to this prophecy, the People's Republic of Mongolia—Outer Mongolia—became a conflict region, and not the haven of peace. Sandwiched between China and Siberia, the former homeland of Genghis Khan was transformed into the battleground of the two Communist superpowers' own Cold War.

Mongolia shares common frontiers with the Chinese in the south—a vast border of some twenty-seven hundred miles sinuously snaking across barren mountains and arid plains, and about fifteen hundred miles in the wooded Siberian *taiga* landscape of the Soviets' Siberia. Her elongated shape conveys the impression of being crushed. Between these two neighbors, each of which claims to stand for the orthodox political creed, Mongolia is an impeccably Marxist land.

By the sixties of our century it became abundantly clear
that China had lost the game in Mongolia. It is the Soviets
that came to exercise a dominant influence over her. They
turned Outer Mongolia from a prefeudal nomadic region
into a machine-minded civilization galloping from the age
of Genghis Khan to the socialism of Karl Marx. At the
outset they had merely wanted to show Asia what they,
and not the Chinese, could do with one of the world's most
backward lands. Later, they wanted also to arouse the
interest of the new African nations. Mongolia was the
natural choice for the experiment because of her low level
of culture. This country is different from all the other
Communist countries we have encountered.

The Soviet policy in Mongolia was a deep disappointment to Mao's China. She had expected the fellow-Marx-
ists to share Peking's view that Outer Mongolia should be
returned to her, as she had been part of imperial China
for centuries. Also, the Mongols have ethnic kinship with
the Chinese. Inner Mongolia, to the south of the Outer, is
part of China today—an "autonomous area." Its six million inhabitants share their language and many folkways
with the Outer Mongolian kin.

Outer Mongolia, with six hundred thousand square
miles, twice the area of mighty Texas, and inhabited by a
million people, the population of America's Maine, is
under-populated. The Soviets have no need for this empty
land, while China needs it badly, particularly now that it
has been found to be potentially rich with sub-surface
treasures, not only coal and oil, but also a goodly assortment of such valuable minerals and metals as tungsten
and uranium. Known in the past mainly as the site of the
Gobi desert, in part, Outer Mongolia also has potential
farm land that can be developed by irrigation canals. The
Soviets manifested no inclination to return the Mongolian
Peoples' Republic to the erstwhile "motherland," and thus

China's expectations about Moscow's intentions were not fulfilled. The much-vaunted "fraternal solidarity" of the two Communist countries turned out to be an empty phrase. Not only did the Soviets fail to see the soundness of the Chinese claims, but they did even worse. They launched their Mongolian "superspectacular" after the establishment of the Marxist regime in Peking, and in reply to its anticipated claim. Soviet aid had been extended to Outer Mongolia at a leisurely pace until then. Only after the establishment of Mao's regime in China did Moscow accelerate the dramatic transformation of Mongolia.

NEON LIGHTS IN THE GOBI DESERT

The transformation was remarkable, indeed. Disbelief was often the visitor's reaction to the country, and especially to its capital, Ulan Bator. The new skyline of the capital (its name means "Red Hero" in translation) indicates a heroism of sorts, and it would be impressive not only in the depths of Asia but also in the heartland of the West. The skyline is especially dramatic against the backdrop of the traditional dwellings on the slopes of the hills surrounding the city with the suburbs of the *yurts* of a nomadic people, the ageless tents of felt.

When the fluorescent street lights of the capital blaze forth in the gathering dusk, it is hard for the visitor to recall that this was "darkest Asia," which few of the most adventurous explorers had dared to visit not many years before. Those visits had to be made on camelback, surrounded by dangers lurking in the primitive region where the quick trigger was the law.

The bold structures in the center of the capital impress

the visitor as Mongolia's national aspirations carved into marble and stone. Sukhe-Bator Square, named after the country's most famous post-World War I revolutionary hero, has been laid out on an even more majestic scale than Moscow's Red Square. Like that square, it contains the mausoleum of a revolutionary hero, with a companion, the number-two leader, Choibalsan.

The structures surrounding the square not only tell the story of the country's aspirations, but tell also of its attempts to leap across the chasm of time from the age of Genghis Khan to the socialism of Karl Marx. The center of attention is the massive government building with its ponderous Grecian columns. A nomadic nation has no native architecture, and these columns express Mongolia's identification with the farthest West. The building strives to demonstrate an old empire's newly found pride in its contemporary shape.

The large array of other public structures clustering around the square indicates the country's cultural and social goals. They include the sprawling buildings of the university with faculties that reflect the countless demands of modern times on technical skills. Young men from the remote Altai mountains and distant areas of the Gobi may be taking courses on scientific stock breeding. Graduation, they hope, will help them to fill managerial posts. A generation ago they would have remained nomads of the plains.

The central cluster of buildings includes an impressive pedagogical institute where a new generation of teachers is being trained. Then there is the large public library, with Stalin's statue in front (the only indication of dissidence from the stylish Soviet trend), the writers' union, and the national archives.

Standing near are other representative buildings, which appear to be incongruous in their setting, if one recalls that until a few years ago this land was as far removed from culture as Tibet: the opera house; dramatic theaters; cinemas; the House of Young Pioneers; and museums. These latter not only recall the country's history, but also present a unique collection of finds of its geological past aeons of years ago.

Then there are the ministries, the building of the national legislature, of the municipal government, and of the ruling Revolutionary People's Party—and all of this in one of the most tradition-bound portions of the world. There are other public buildings, too, such as the municipal hospital, with the latest equipment, and the ponderous trade union building, recalling that here nomads were being transformed into industrial hands. One of the prides of the capital is the huge Sukhe Bator Hotel, built by the Chinese, tastefully decorated by Czechs. It would be a notable landmark even in Western lands.

THE DRIVE TOWARD THE WEST

Intruding upon formerly nomad-inhabited land are rows of modern apartment houses. Some of them are high-rise structures shooting upward into the limpid Mongol sky. The flats are provided with modern comforts; and some of them are supplied even with the luxuries of opulent societies—balconies, and such sophisticated improvements as "modesty panels," to insure a measure of privacy. A special landmark is the Ih Delguur, the "Big Department Store," its five stories filled with Russian and native goods sold to the tune of piped music, both classical and jazz.

Factory chimneys discharging smoke into the pristine sky are the most surprising features of a land that pursued a nomadic existence until a few years ago. Nor is the capital the only industrial hub of the country. An even more accented production center was built in a new prefabricated factory town, Darhan, between Ulan Bator and the Soviet frontier, along the Trans-Mongolian Railway, the country's main transportation line. The new town is close to hydroelectric power stations and to the Nalaikha coal mine.

A large assortment of industries of varying sizes has mushroomed forth within a few years. Most important of these are the processing plants turning the country's basic raw materials into finished goods. At one time Mongolia was known as the "Land of the Five Animals"—camel, horse, cow (including the yak), sheep, and goat. They provide the basic raw materials and the foundations of the processing plants. Tanning is one of these industries, while other plants turn out leather goods, footwear, a broad spectrum of knitwear, and especially woolens. Having jumped from nomadism into modern industrial life, the Mongols have created "combinats" that employ their raw materials for many products under the same roof: pharmaceutical and household articles, paper, furniture, brickworks, and cement.

In the midst of this bewildering change are the stolid Mongols, who do not seem to be bewildered at all. Many of them still sport the traditional garment, *del,* the long-skirted, long-sleeved, high-collared, caftan-like robe, with double-breasted buttons on the right, which is worn by both women and men. Others wear the bland garments of the industrial West.

Fully a quarter of the population lives in the capital. Genghis Khan, the Perfect Warrior, would have been familiar with the dwellings on the Mongolian plains. In his day, as today, it is the *yurt,* a tent of trellis of latticed wood forming a cylindrical wall behind layers of felt, the ceiling consisting of wooden spokes. An iron stove in the center of the tent is topped off by a chimney reaching into the open through a small aperture. The tent-dwellers are comfortably warm in the Arctic winter and comfortably cool during the scorching summer. Evenings in arid lands are always cold.

This, then, is the look of the new civilization that has come into existence during the last generation and especially since the emergence of Mao's China. The Russians were the first in Mongolia, a peripheral land, after the fall of the Chinese imperial regime. They had no mind to settle it, nor had they the need, since they possessed more than enough vacant space of their own. But they wanted to place Mongolia out of bounds for the Japanese, who were pursuing a policy of overland expansion, a *drang nach westen,* drive toward the West.

THE SOVIET CASE

The Soviets had a perfect case in following the Czarist footsteps after World War I. They were then battling the "whites," counterrevolutionaries, some of them supported by Japan's aid. One of these was the "Bloody Baron," R. N. von Ungern-Sternberg, a Baltic Baron, who supported the whites, and was supported, in turn, by the Japanese. Fighting the Communists shortly after World War II, he used Outer Mongolia as a natural sanctuary against the "reds." The Bloody Baron had the ambition of being the Genghis Khan of the twentieth century, and he was unspeakably cruel with the foe.

Aiming at similar blood-drenched laurels was an ex-peasant, a Cossack, G. M. Semenov, who had himself addressed as the Prince. Outer Mongolia was his natural sanctuary, and he was a pathological sadist, too. Eventually, the Soviets swept into the area and the adventurers were swept out. The Russians stayed. It took several years before the Soviets succeeded in liquidating the medieval-minded Lama-Buddhistic theocracy that had ruled the country hand in glove with the "ranch princes," lording it over the nomads, who were kept in peonage. The Soviets liquidated the atavistic regime with the aid of some angry young Mongols, particularly Sukhe-Bator and Choibalsan. After a while, the ranch princes and the lama priests were run underground.

In the twenties, the Soviets combined their modernization of Outer Mongolia with their usual exploitation of the satellites, buying their raw materials cheaper, and selling them finished products dearly. They also introduced the Soviet "troika" of modernization: propagandization, education, and sanitation. Today the landmarks of the Mongol countryside are the headquarters of the Revolutionary People's Party, the hospital, and the school.

At the beginning of modernization, the Mongols were not politically minded. Today, their articulate classes are thoroughly indoctrinated with Marxism. Before the Soviets there were hundreds of lamaseries and temples. Today there are no temples and there is only one lama monastery. In those early days only about 5 percent of the people were literate; today only 5 percent are illiterate. Then the average expectation of life at birth was thirty years; today, it is close to fifty-five. Mongolia was then a classical land of "D.I.P."—disease, ignorance, and poverty. Today that description no longer fits.

The Soviet policy of modernizing Mongolia was accelerated with the emergence of Mao's China, and thus began the first phase of the fraternal countries' Cold War. It was then that the Soviet Union launched the bulk of the program that transformed the Ulan Bator skyline and began to replace the native *yurt* with modern flats. Simply, the Russians aimed to head off the Chinese comrades, in order to entrench their influence.

Since then the Kremlin has invested more money in Mongolia than in any other land. How large has been the Russians' investments in Mongolia? Because, meanwhile, the ruble has been revalued, and also because of Moscow's secrecy, the figure is a matter of conjecture. An intelligent guess hesitates around a billion dollars, equivalent to a thousand dollars per head for each man, woman, and child in Outer Mongolia.

It took the Chinese only a short time to see what was really going on in Mongolia, and to see that the fraternal nation was not so fraternal, after all. So they launched their high-pressure campaign, too. The Communist regime in China was only two years old then and still working on its own development plans. The Great Leap Forward in the homeland was anticipated by Peking's great gallop forward in Mongolia.

A ten-year agreement of economic and cultural cooperation was concluded between the two countries in 1952, when Mao's China was barely three years old. In execution of the agreement, thousands of Chinese workers were shipped to Mongolia to work on predetermined plans. Because of the color of their uniforms and their traditional working ardor, they became known as the "blue ants." It was they who started building the big apartment houses and the hotel; there were some forty thousand of them at the peak. They also launched projects to build highways, dig sewers, construct industrial plants, and fit machinery into the new textile, glass, and shoe factories they built. Including the cost of labor of the blue ants, Peking may have spent half a billion dollars on the Mongolian projects, money that could have been employed better at home. While the outside world was unfamiliar with the feud at the time, these funds were used to fight the Kremlin.

The Soviet wooing of Mongolia thus seems to have been an important factor in the Communist giants' estrangement. However, the cold war between them erupted into public view at a later time. During this period the Mongols were very unhappy people because of the feud. What were they to do, since they got help from both sides, and, besides, what was all the ruckus about? A middle-of-the-road policy would have suited them best, but they recalled that there was no more dangerous place than the middle of a busy road.

Still, a decision had to be reached, and they had little time to think. Finally, they made up their minds. For years the Soviets had been their ideological tutors, they were better entrenched, and had far more to offer to them. Also, the Kremlin appeared in better position to them to soft-pedal a conflict with the West. They recalled also generations of nightmare life under Chinese imperial rule. They accepted the Kremlin line. As a result, the pro-Peking men in Ulan Bator government posts lost their jobs.

Did the blue ants move out when the Soviets won? Most of them did, but some three thousand of them still remained. They became very unhappy blue ants, since nobody seemed to love anything they did. Yet they had to carry out commitments, and also Peking hoped Ulan Bator might have another change of heart. It did not. And thus it came about that the dominant influence in Mongolia continued to be that of the Soviets. While they remained the country's tutors, they did not rule the land. They could not afford to do so. Had they done it, they would have forsaken their propaganda gambit and would have been placed in the niche of shame of the imperialists.

LAND OF CARBON COPY

Yet basic Mongolian institutions have been inspired by the Soviets. The Mongolian People's Party is the Soviet Communist Party's carbon copy, and the government follows its directive lines. Likewise, the central legislature, the Mongolian Grand National Hural, is patterned on the Supreme Soviet of Moscow. The same as the prototype, it designates the cabinet that carries out the party's will. Also, Mongolia's economic system conforms to the Soviet pattern. Both of them have what they call a socialist planned economy, carrying out the dictum: "From each according to his ability, and to each according to his work."

In the "Land of Five Animals," the bulk of the herds has been placed in collectives, corresponding to the Soviet *kolkhoz*, under group ownership and control. The Mongol herdsman is entitled to have a portion of the herd as his private property, just as in Russia the peasant is entitled to a small portion of the land for his own personal use. The difference is this: the private possession of the Mongol *arat*, herdsman, is larger than the Russian's private land. The Mongol derives close to 20 percent of his earnings from his private stock.

Not only in the political and economic fields, but also in other matters, the Soviet influence on the Mongols is great. Russian has become Mongolia's second language; it is taught in all the schools. Lenin is represented as Mongolia's greatest hero; his likeness is in evidence everywhere. Sukhe-Bator, the native hero, is held up as Lenin's own ideological son. The similarities penetrate even into small details. The leading Mongolian daily is called *Unen*, which is a literal translation of the Russian *Pravda* (Truth).

The Mongolians have to take large doses of Russian history, too. Since their most notable figure, Genghis Khan, defeated the Russians in the thirteenth century, they are expected to be apologetic about him. This is in spite of the fact that the Great Khan's Mongols ruled over a larger realm than was the share of the greatest conquerors from the West, including Alexander the Great, Julius Caesar, and Napoleon the First. Some time ago, an unfortunate official of the Mongolian Ministry of Post, Telephone, and Telegraph committed a grievous mistake. On the occasion of a notable anniversary, he issued a Genghis Khan memorial stamp. A few days later it was withdrawn from circulation and all reference to it was expunged. In Mongol schools, too, Genghis Khan's exploits are mentioned critically. After all, a "peace-loving" Marxist country could not possibly boast of a war-lord who was an imperialist to boot.

Today Mongolia receives large doses of help not only from the Soviet Union but also from its European satellites—the East Germans, Hungarians, Rumanians, Bulgarians, Poles, and Czechs. However, these technicians cannot be expected to stay in Mongolia indefinitely. The Mongols will have gained little unless they learn to stand on their own feet. Will they be able to do it?

There is already much waste and breakage behind the impressive facade. The busiest places of the nation are its repair shops. Nor have the Mongolians seemed to have mastered the knack of government administration, which is the vitally important part of the planned Marxist economy. Their bureaucracy can be described as senseless, even fantastic, often making a fetish out of sheer senselessness.

Neither in government administration nor in industry has the past prepared Mongolia for modern life. The

warlike qualities of Genghis Khan's people were no preparations for today. Remnants of that warlike past have
been sublimated into sports—archery, wrestling, and,
above all, horsemanship. To see a man, woman, or even a
small child of the silent steppes streaking toward the
distant horizon on his small pony is a thrilling experience.
They appear to be floating into the infinite on the waves of
air.

The age of Genghis Khan was centuries ago. Can the
Mongols adjust to modern life? For many generations
they have been mainly herdsmen, a peaceful occupation,
as a rule. Their work adapted them to the tempo and ways
of their animals, leisurely creatures. In the trying climate
of these elevated northern plains, which are mostly numbing cold, with waves of summer heat for brief spells, one
cannot carry on clocklike work required by an efficient
bureaucracy and automated plants. That is why there is
so much waste and breakage behind the smooth facade.
Changing from animal husbandry to industries and government was bound to cause complications. The equivalents of "coffee breaks" taper off into infinity in Ulan Bator
plants. Because of the lack of deeply rooted work disci-
pline, absenteeism is abnormally high, and if a key person
fails to show up for work there are no substitutes. The
machinery breaks down.

The Mongols have been precipitated into the techno-
logical age largely because of the competition of their two
cold-war neighbors. Will they be able to adjust themselves
to the new age fate forced upon them in such a hurry? A
quick adjustment of habits acquired through tradition-
rooted centuries to the ways of our overheated dynamic
society is likely to hit snags. It is therefore not likely that
Bertrand Russell's peaceful doldrum-becalmed society will
take shape. It is more likely that Mongolia will continue to
be a battleground between the two antagonistic sects.

We have been discussing the relationship of communism and nationalism in these pages. The pattern in the case of all the other countries has been this: from nationalism, to internationalism, then to a more highly accentuated form of nationalism, under the Marxist-Leninist guiding star. The case of Mongolia is unique. She started with a tribal framework and was forced into a nodding acquaintance with internationalism that left no mark on her. She has reached the nationalist stage. Mongolia is the only country that communism forced directly into the national mold.

Epilogue

After nationalism in the Socialist bloc—what? In the Western world, nationalism was followed by democracy. Is that in the cards for the bloc countries too?

To provide the answer, a look should be taken at the history of democracy today. First, the contemporary democratic countries. The salient change is the relationship of the legislative and executive powers. France provides the most dramatic illustration of the change—from the supremacy of a multiparty legislature to "presidential democracy," with the accent on the *presidential*. While the shifting of the emphasis has not been quite so dramatic in other democratic countries, it has been no less significant. The presidential power in the United States has been constantly on the increase, with the diminution of the legislative influence. A Presidential heart skips a beat and American business is on the verge of a stroke. How many Congressional hearts would have to skip how many beats to bring about similar results? In Britain, members of Parliament have to watch carefully the conductor's baton of the Prime Minister under penalty of losing their seats at the next election. For the last half a century, Britain has had only one party, under the guise of two. In Germany who can tell the difference between the parties of

the Social Democrats and Christian Democrats? And so
on, down the line. What does this mean?

First, the other revealing fact, that of the underdeveloped nations. Seventy-odd new members of the U.N. were
colonies before. They launched their national careers with
brave new thoughts, steeped in the ideals of democracy.
The building of brand-new parliaments was their high-
priority task. The legislatures were buzzing with activity
. . . but no more.

All the new countries—with very few exceptions—have
turned to the executive power, neglecting their legislatures. Their multiparty systems have shrunk to one-party
predominance. The exceptions, such as India, are cliff-
hangers over the abyss of executive supremacy.

That is the world-wide trend everywhere, in the democratic countries and in the underdeveloped nations. And
why is that so? For the same reason that stockholders
cannot and do not run large corporations. They are run by
the managers—specialists in their fields, competent in
manipulating people and in production, highly centralized
professional bodies in an age of highly centralized techniques. The modern nations (such as the United States,
with an annual budget of close to 200 billion dollars) are
the world's largest corporations. The legislatures correspond to the stockholders' meetings, and the managers to
the executives.

Less-developed countries want to be more developed,
and in trying to achieve that aim they have turned to
national development projects, huge business ventures
that call for the expertise of the managers and not the
emotions of large numbers of people elected to play roles
in the national stockholders' meetings—the legislative
bodies.

Within the Socialist bloc the managers—technocrats—
are supreme, and the legislative bodies are rubber stamps.
One of the main traits of members of this bloc is economic

planning, which requires the services of professionals, technically trained people, the managers. These countries are run by the equivalents of presidents, executive vice-presidents of large corporations, and by the board of directors too.

The democratic countries are bound to cling to their system of free elections. Also, they are bound to attribute increasingly expanded power to the executives—the business-minded managers, members of the cabinet. The underdeveloped world is likely to continue with the one-party system, while going through the ritual of parliamentary elections. As to the Communist countries, it is not likely that their present managerial system will be changed. Recent events in Czechoslovakia furnish an incontrovertible proof.

In the socialist bloc the "board of directors" is called by diverse names, usually "Politbureau" or "Presidium." It is the supreme planning body. It forms interlocking directorates with the chief executive organ, the Council of Ministers, the administrative superagency. Both bodies have to have at least the tacit acceptance, if not the backing, of the major "stockholders" (in reality, of the "opinionholders") everywhere and always a minority of the people, an elite, forming the substratum from which members of the highest echelons are recruited.

Then there is the rank and file of the "voters." Elections in the bloc are, of course, prefabricated, but what they lack in impact, they make up in frequency—elections of all kinds, at all levels. They mean something, too: they manifest the uneasy conscience of autocracy laboring in the awareness of a more popularly desirable system.

It would be a fatal mistake for the governmental managers within the bloc to ignore public opinion. No regime could afford to be delinquent in that respect. Even Nero had to provide *panem et circensem* for the mob. The reversion to nationalism in these countries has been in response to the elemental force of nationalist sentiment. The paroxysm of patriotism displayed by the Kremlin had never been known under the Czarist regime.

The more robust a nation feels, the more it flexes its muscles. The Czars' Russia was considered a "Great Power," one among ten, and this was not on account of her intrinsic strength (often tested and often found wanting), but because of her bicontinental size. Today the Soviet Union is one of two major powers, its nationalism commensurate with its new status. It is further fueled by the peoples' mystic attachment to "Mother Russia," the sanctified soil.

If the soviets were to become "Mother Russia" again, under a noncommunist board of directors, would she undertake a major realignment of her foreign policy? Would she take her place in a new "concert of the world," somewhat on the pattern of the "concert of Europe" of the past? It is most unlikely that the new Kremlin masters would abandon the posts established under the Communist regime. They would consider the area of the bloc countries their extended defense region. The "Brezhnev doctrine," the right of the Kremlin to keep the arc of Eastern European small countries in line, would be maintained under another new name. Two invasions in one generation from that direction have invested that area with special significance for Moscow.

Nor would there be a basic change in the domestic field. The word "communism" is used very loosely and inappropriately in our part of the world. Not one of the countries we call "communist" calls itself by that name. "People's Republic," "Democratic Republic," or, at most, "Socialist Republic," yes, but not "Communist Republic." The most aggressive of these countries calls itself the "People's Republic of China."

By one of those miracles that seem to be the hallmark of our age, let us suppose that the regimes of all of them are crushed. Would they return to capitalism, "free enter-prise," laissez-faire? It would be a grave miscalculation on our part to assume such a course. The majorities in all of these countries have adjusted themselves to these regimes. The rank and file have received too many social benefits that the previous regimes failed to provide, and they could no longer do without the governmental services that have become integrated into their lives. Previous property rights have been lost through desuetude. To restore scrambled eggs is beyond man's ken. Instruments of large-scale production would not—because they could not—cease to be public property.

Withal, a compromise with the market system cannot be halted in the socialist bloc. "Libermanism," "New Method," or whatever the national idiosyncratic terms, the process will gather momentum—up to a point. The rejection of private property as a dogma, an article of quasi-religious faith, is going by the board. Small traders, small handicraftsmen, small farmers have been accepted in an increasing number of countries, China included. Eventually, Soviet Russia will have to fall into line. That it has not done so is owed to the religious aura which the Utopian impracticality of the early apostles, the "found-ing fathers," had acquired and which keeps on shining above the Kremlin, the seat of the "Fourth Rome."

What about the "freedom of speech" in the countries of the "Communist" world? The noted Soviet physicist Pyotr L. Kapitsa expressed the thought of many in the late spring of 1969, when he criticized the ideological stagnation in his own country. People need the stimula-tion of beliefs, creeds, ideologies, to fill their lives with content. Instead of that, the regime fills them with clichés, tired, old, uninspiring, boring. Unbending dogma-tism has stripped the Kremlin of the ideological initiative which it sought at one time to thrust upon the world. The "Fourth Rome" looks more like the "First Rome" in the days of its incipient decay, lacking faith, élan, and verve. Can it offer a revived creed, or must it drown in the tidal wave of its own clichés? If it cannot renew itself, it may fall prey to what Professor Toynbee calls the "nemesis of creativity," which turns the radicals into reactionaries, stripped of their élan and yielding to the obsessive desire to stay in power at any price—even at the price of relinquishing their dogmas—and turns the formerly guiding minority into an uncreative dominant ruling class.

The "battle of giants"—the awesome feud between the Soviets and China—was bound to happen as soon as the people of Han were goaded into action by the frenzied nationalism of their Communist masters. The philosophical ideology, evidently, has made little difference. Because of their size, historic tradition, and ideological structuring, both countries were bound to revert to their historic pattern: imperialism. Lenin said that imperialism was the last stage of capitalism. It may become one of the factors of the last stage of communism.

While the satellite countries are fretting under the Kremlin's reign, they pursue their own miniature policies of imperialism within the sphere allotted them by Moscow. Hungary, for instance, lost two-thirds of her population to her neighbors after the first World War. With the exception of Austria, all those neighbors are either "fraternal" countries or fellow-Socialist, such as Yugoslavia. In the redistribution following World War I, millions of Hungarians were assigned to the neighbors' alien rules. No realignment of the frontiers has been proposed by the fraternal countries in order to remedy the injustice, the work of "Western imperialists." Here is a textbook illustration of nationalism within the sphere of the Kremlin. In this instance, too, the so-called communism is another manifestation of an exaggerated type of nationalism.

Index